DATA HANDLING IN SCIENCE AND TECHNOLOGY — VOLUME 1

Microprocessor programming and applications for scientists and engineers

RICHARD R. SMARDZEWSKI

*Chemistry Division, Naval Research Laboratory,
Washington, DC 20375, U.S.A.*

ELSEVIER

Amsterdam — Oxford — New York — Tokyo   1984

ELSEVIER SCIENCE PUBLISHERS B.V.
Molenwerf 1
P.O. Box 211, 1000 AE Amsterdam, The Netherlands

Distributors for the United States and Canada:

ELSEVIER SCIENCE PUBLISHING COMPANY INC.
52, Vanderbilt Avenue
New York, NY 10017

First edition 1984
Second impression 1985

Library of Congress Cataloging in Publication Data

Smardzewski, R. R. (Richard R.), 1942–
    Microprocessor programming and applications for
scientists and engineers.

    (Data handling in science and technology ; v. 1)
    Bibliography: p.
    Includes index.
    1. Microprocessors--Programming. 2. 6502 (Microproces‑
sor)--Programming. I. Title. II. Series.
QA76.6.S6153 1984   001.64'2   84-13759
ISBN 0-444-42407-5 (U.S.)

ISBN 0-444-42407-5 (Vol. 1)
ISBN 0-444-42408-3 (Series)

Printed in The Netherlands

CONTENTS

CONTENTS

CONTENTS

CONTENTS

EXPERIMENTS

EXPERIMENTS

To Marguerita, whose encouragement and
assistance made this work possible

"The introduction of the microprocessor in 1971
immediately pointed to the implementation of an entire
computer system on a single silicon chip, which by 1981
has become the most perfect symbol of the integrated
circuit. Today, one can buy a computer that possesses
32 I/O lines, two internal timer/counters, serial
communication facilities, 128 flags that can be set,
reset, and tested for control branching, 128 bytes of
RAM, 4000 bytes of ROM code storage, a complex
interrupt structure, and extensions of RAM and ROM to
64 Kbytes each in external memory additions, with
submicrosecond instruction executions and power
dissipation of less than one watt. And all this may be
had in a 40-pin package costing less than $30 in
quantity. Such power is formidable and, to the newly
initiated, almost incomprehensible".

E. E. Klingman
IEEE Micro Vol.1, No.1
February, 1981

PREFACE

During the past ten years the growth of the microprocessor could be appropriately described as volcanic. Today it impacts nearly all aspects of our daily lives to one extent or another. Likewise, the research applications of this marvelous device have proliferated. It is used to measure and control laboratory analog signals in instruments ranging from simple single-pan balances to complex particle-beam accelerators.

Before a microprocessor can be of any use in a laboratory situation, it must be properly programmed and interfaced to the system of interest, many of which are becoming increasingly sophisticated. As new and varied situations evolve, there is an ever increasing time gap between instrumental development and deployment. For those researchers and students wanting to automate their laboratories, the choice is simple, i.e. either wait for a particular device/instrument to be designed and developed or directly design and automate a particular experiment. It is for this last reason that this manuscript has been written. Its purpose is to provide the researcher and student with specific guidelines on how to accomplish this task.

Throughout the text, emphasis is placed on the fundamental concepts and applications of machine language programming and microcomputing. A series of programmed instructional experiments is used to reinforce these principles. No prior

background in microprocessors or computer science is assumed.
The particular microprocessor chosen for examination is the
popular 6502 (500 million in use as of 1984). It was selected
primarily because of its popularity and its widespread use in a
variety of microcomputing systems (Apple, Acorn, Atari, BBC,
Commodore, Rockwell and others). The programming examples
throughout the text were generated and tested on a Rockwell
AIM 65 Microcomputing System. The principles and ideas
demonstrated, however, are applicable to any 6502-based system.

As with any new endeavor, proficiency is a direct result of
the frequency of practice and the researcher is strongly
encouraged to apply this knowledge to his/her particular
situation.

Before finishing this preface, I would like to thank my
many colleagues, past and present, whose help and guidance made
this book possible. I should also like to acknowledge Mrs. Jean
Fino for typing the earlier versions of this manuscript and
Rockwell International for their timely assistance in providing
helpful documentation. Finally, and most importantly, I would
like to thank my wife, Marguerita, for her continual support and
assistance during the preparation of this manuscript.

Richard R. Smardzewski

May, 1984

Washington, DC

CHAPTER 1

```
┌─────────────────────────────────┐
│      COMPUTER ORGANIZATION       │
└─────────────────────────────────┘
```

A computer can be organizationally broken down into four functions: SENSE, RESOLVE, STORE, and ACT.

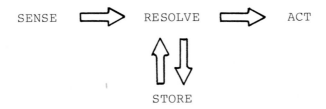

SENSE ⟹ RESOLVE ⟹ ACT

⇧⇩

STORE

The SENSE function receives information from outside the system and transmits it to the machine for interpretation. The RESOLVE function performs all the logical and operational functions. The STORE function must <u>remember</u> the correct instructions and sequence of operations. Finally, the ACT function executes the decision. A <u>human</u> analogy to this system is a Builder. In order for a Builder (Resolve) to make a House (Act), he/she must use Materials (Sense) according to a set of Plans (Store).

MATERIALS ⟹ BUILDER ⟹ HOUSE

⇧⇩

PLANS

In a computer, the SENSE function is described by Inputs, the RESOLVE function by Processor, the STORE function by Memory, and the ACT function by Outputs.

INPUTS ⟹ PROCESSOR ⟹ OUTPUTS

MEMORY

The processor or central controlling element of a computer, when available in integrated circuit (IC) form is called a microprocessor. Connecting memory and input/output (I/O) circuits to a microprocessor produces a computer. When such a completed digital system is in the smallest size range and slowest speed range when compared to all other digital systems, it is called a microcomputer.

1.1 BITS, BYTES, AND NIBBLES

A "bit" is defined as a binary digit equal to either 0 or 1, i.e. either off or on. In the 6502 and most microprocessors, logic "1" is defined as a voltage level of +2.4 to +5VDc, and logic "0" as 0 (ground) to +0.8VDc.

N bits can be arranged into 2^N different patterns.

$\quad$ 2 bits $-->$ 2^2 = 4 patterns $\quad$ 00, 01, 10, 11

$\quad$ 4 bits $-->$ 2^4 = 16 patterns
$\quad$ "Nibble"

$\quad$ 8 bits $-->$ 2^8 = 256 patterns
$\quad$ "Byte"

$\quad$ 16 bits $-->$ 2^{16} = 65,536 patterns

The 6502 is an 8-bit microprocessor which means that the primary informational unit is the byte (8-bits). All transfers to and from the 6502 are done 8-bits at a time on an 8-line data bus. A complete byte of information is shuttled to and from memory locations, registers, I/O circuits (another memory location) and every external device. The data bus is bidirectional in nature.

Every memory location accessed by the 6502 microprocessing unit (MPU) is capable of containing 8-bits (one byte) and is specified by a unique address. Sixteen lines which are designated the address bus are used to identify the 16-bit (two byte) address of every location. Since there are 2^{16} unique 16-bit binary numbers, the 6502 can address 65,536 or 64K (1K=1024) memory locations. The amount of actual memory depends upon how many external memory chips are available to the 6502.

Since one byte = 8 bits and one memory location can contain one byte, the information in one location can represent any one of 2^8 or 256 different things. It can be:

(a) a number.
(b) a character.
(c) a pattern.
.
.

An example illustrating the 3-bit case is depicted in Fig. 1-1. Here, the 3 binary (on/off) switches are used to generate $2^3 = 8$ different light patterns.

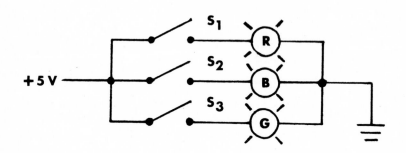

Switches   Lights

S_1	S_2	S_3		R	B	G	
0	0	0		0	0	0	
0	0	1		0	0	1	
0	1	0		0	1	0	
0	1	1		0	1	1	"1" = ON
1	0	0		1	0	0	"0" = OFF
1	0	1		1	0	1	
1	1	0		1	1	0	
1	1	1		1	1	1	

$2^3 = 8$ different patterns

Fig. 1-1. Light Patterns generated by Three Binary Switches.

In the 6502 Microprocessor, the standard unit of information acted on and transmitted to all the components is the digital code called the byte (8 bits). In all cases the pattern of 0's and 1's in this 8-bit number (or combinations thereof) mean certain things to certain subsystems. It can represent:

1. Instructions
2. Locations in Memory
3. Locations of I/O Devices
4. Data
5. Character Representations

1.2   INSTRUCTIONS

The microprocessor or microprocessing unit (MPU) acts on an instruction in the following manner as determined by the system clock (usually a crystal oscillator).

1. Locate (Address) instruction in memory
2. Read (Fetch) instruction from memory
3. Interpret (Decode) instruction
4. Execute instruction

1.3   LOCATIONS IN MEMORY

Memory locations (or cells containing 8-bit numbers) are indicated by Address Codes (16-bit numbers) which represent where in the computer that memory location can be found. The microprocessor can read a byte from or write a byte to a memory location.

Memory which can only be read from and <u>not</u> written to is called <u>ROM</u> (Read Only Memory). It is nonvolatile (remains on when the power is off) and usually contains such functions as instructions, initialization routines, I/O routines, etc. Memory which can be both read from and written to is called <u>RAM</u> (Random Access Memory). It should more appropriately be called R/W (Read-Write) Memory since ROM is also randomly accessible (viz., the speed of transfer to and from a memory location does not depend on its address).

The microprocessor reads from or writes to a particular memory location by sending out a specific 16-bit voltage pattern of 0´s and 1´s on the 16-line <u>address bus</u> which locates that specific memory location and an appropriate control signal on the READ/WRITE line (R/$\overline{W}$). Usually a binary "1" is sent for a READ operation and a "0" for a WRITE operation. $\overline{W}$ indicates that the WRITE operation is activated when this particular signal line is brought to a low voltage (i.e. ground). Reading an instruction from memory (ROM or RAM) is called "fetching" an instruction.

1.4 LOCATIONS OF I/O DEVICES

In the 6502 microprocessor, the instructions used to access memory are the same instructions used to perform <u>input</u> (read) and <u>output</u> (write) operations on peripheral devices. Unlike many other microprocessors, no distinction is made between

memory and I/O devices. Every external device is treated as
memory. This technique is called memory-mapped I/O. The
complexities of having to pass all data handling/manipulation
through a working register are eliminated.

1.5 DATA

     Data in the 6502 is an 8-bit number (byte) representing an
instruction, an alphanumeric character, a control signal, or the
on/off status of some subsystem of the computer. It is
transferred by the microprocessor to and from memory on an
8-line, bidirectional data bus. An input device transfers data
to the microprocessor and an output device receives data from
the microprocessor.

1.6 PROGRAMMING LANGUAGES

     In order for a computer to perform a useful function, it
must be instructed or programmed to do so. The language that
the computer understands is a series of binary voltages
represented by 0´s and 1´s in a digital code called the machine
code or machine language. Specific bit patterns mean specific
things to the computer (instructions, addresses, data, I/O
devices...). Unfortunately, machine language is not very
meaningful to humans and programs are usually written in
assembly language or higher-level languages. Instructions
written in assembly language usually correspond on a one-to-one

basis with machine language instructions. In a sense, assembly language is one step removed from machine language. Higher level languages, on the other hand, contain statements that may be comprised of many machine-language instructions. As a result, these languages are several steps removed from machine language.

The assembly language program (sometimes called a source code) is converted into a machine language program (sometimes called an object code) by a special program called an Assembler. The reverse process (machine--> assembly language) is executed by a program called a Disassembler.

Although assembly language is preferred to machine language programming, it does have one serious drawback. It is dependent upon the instruction set of the particular microprocessor in use at the time. Program exchange between different microprocessors is virtually nonexistent. In order to overcome this and other difficulties, higher level languages have been developed. Examples of these include BASIC, FORTRAN, COBOL as well as numerous others. Programming efficiency is much greater with higher level languages and program exchange is possible between different computer systems (within limits). The drawbacks are increased memory requirements and slower execution times although in many applications this does not present a problem. In some applications, however, slow execution speed is not only undesirable but unacceptable.

Higher level languages can generally be classified according to two types: <u>Compilers</u> and <u>Interpreters</u>.

Compilers are similar to assemblers in the fact that they take the higher-level language (source code) and convert (translate) it into an executable machine language program (object code). They are special programs that translate the <u>entire</u> high-level program into machine code for storage and later execution. Once the object (machine) code is generated, it can be executed <u>independently</u> from the source code or the compiler program. That is to say, it does not need to be co-resident in memory with the source code and/or Compiler.

Interpreters are programs that not only translate higher-level languages into machine code but also execute the code, usually on a line-by-line basis. Once a section of a higher level program is translated and executed, it is scrapped and the Interpreter goes on to another section. No object code is generated and all executing is done by machine code programs <u>within</u> the Interpreter. They are simply called upon as needed. As a result, the source code for the high-level program must be co-resident in memory with the Interpreter for proper execution.

Compilers and Interpreters have their advantages and disadvantages. While Compilers produce object code which can be executed at high speed, they tend to be less <u>interactive</u> than Interpreters. If an error (bug) is discovered in a compiled program, the source code must be edited and the entire program

re-compiled prior to execution. Interpreters, on the other
hand, allow such changes to be easily made. However, the price
paid for this capability is speed. Interpreters generally
execute programs 20-30 times slower than the machine language
programs generated by Compilers. This very fact is
experimentally demonstrated in the last Chapter.

FORTRAN and COBOL are typical examples of compiled
high-level languages while most microcomputers today employ
BASIC Interpreters (Usually in system ROM). BASIC Compilers do
exist, however, and are available for some computers where
demanding applications require shorter, faster programs.
Fig. 1-2 depicts the hierarchical order of compiled programming
languages.

Notwithstanding the utility and programming ease of
higher-level languages, they do possess the singular drawback of
removing the programmer increasingly further from the actual
operations of the computer. While this may not be much of a
concern in number-crunching or business (viz., word-processing)
applications using a limited number of conventional I/O devices
(keyboards, CRT´s, printers...), it is a problem in scientific
and/or industrial process control schemes where nonstandard
peripheral devices are used. Furthermore, assembly language
provides the opportunity to execute a program as fast as
possible, an important feature in high speed data acquisition
and control systems.

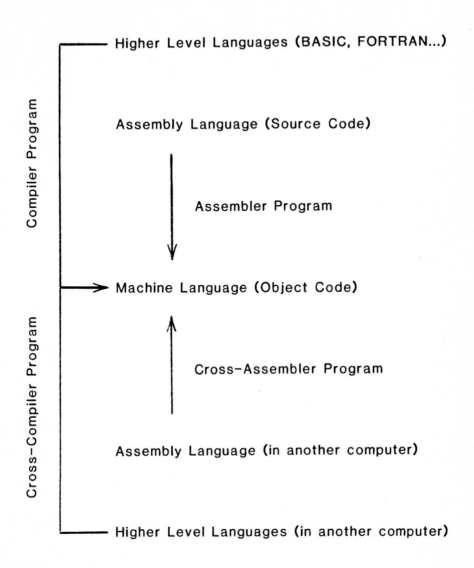

Fig. 1-2.   Hierarchy of Compiled Programming Languages.

1.7   AIM 65 MICROCOMPUTER

The preceding principles and concepts are most clearly
demonstrated in the AIM 65 Microcomputer manufactured by
Rockwell International Corporation. Like the Apple II/IIe
(Apple Computer, Inc.), the Commodore 64/VIC-20/Pet 2001
(Commodore Business Machines) and the Atari computers (Warner
Communications, Inc.), it is a machine based on a version of the
6502 microprocessor. The AIM 65 was primarily designed as an
instructional tool for individuals interested in learning about
microcomputers and their interfacing possibilities. Its
advanced features also make it attractive as a low cost
development system for laboratory/industrial applications.

In the AIM 65 Microcomputing System, the 6502 MPU,
operating at 1 MHz is capable of accessing 20K bytes of on-board
ROM and 4K bytes of on-board RAM. An Expansion Connector
extends the system busses (address, data and control) out to
additional memory. The Advanced Interactive Monitor is
allocated to 8K of ROM with the remainder (12K) available for
various on-board PROM/ROM options (8K BASIC Interpreter, 4K
two-pass Assembler, 8K FORTH Interpreter, 8K PL/65 ...).

Two 6522 Versatile Interface Adapters (VIA´s) provide I/O
capability to the 6502. One device supports the on-board
thermal printer and the TTY and dual audio cassette interfaces
while the General Purpose I/O Ports of the other VIA are
available to the user for a variety of interfacing

configurations. Each VIA has two parallel and one serial 8-bit,
bidirectional I/O ports, two 2-bit peripheral handshake control
lines (useful for interfacing displays, printers, A/D & D/A
Converters...) and two fully programmable 16-bit interval
timer/event counters (used in timing and frequency measurement
applications). A 6532 RAM-Input/Output-Timer (RIOT) chip is
used by the AIM Monitor for scratchpad memory and keyboard
operations. Fig. 1-3 illustrates the overall system layout.

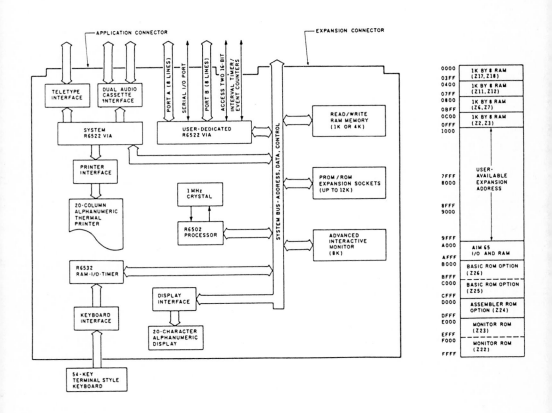

Fig. 1-3.   AIM 65 Block Diagram and Memory Map. (Courtesy of
Rockwell International Corporation).

CHAPTER 2

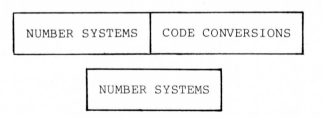

Just as a string of decimal digits can represent a decimal number greater than 9, so too can a group of binary digits (bits) be used to represent a number of any magnitude.

2.1 DECIMAL NUMBERS

In the decimal system, the number 41769 really represents $4x10^4 + 1x10^3 + 7x10^2 + 6x10^1 + 9x10^0$. Combinations of powers of base 10 multiplied by a <u>decimal</u> digit can represent a decimal number of any size.

2.2 BINARY NUMBERS

A binary number of any size is likewise generated by combinations of powers of base 2 multiplied by a <u>binary</u> digit (i.e. either 0 or 1).

$$1101 = 1x2^3 + 1x2^2 + 0x2^1 + 1x2^0 = 13_{10}.$$

In this example, binary 1101 represents decimal 13.

2.3 OCTAL AND HEXADECIMAL NUMBERS

Manipulating 8 and 16-bit long binary numbers can be tedious at best not to mention cumbersome. In order to overcome this drawback, various shorthand notations have been designated.

Two of these, <u>octal</u> and <u>hexadecimal</u>, are based on the grouping of binary digits into sets of three or four.

A set of three binary digits will generate 8 unique combinations (2^3). This is the basis of the <u>octal</u> system using the octal digits 0, 1, 2, 3, 4, 5, 6, and 7.

$$41769_{10} = 1010001100101001 \qquad \text{(in binary)}$$
$$= 001\ 010\ 001\ 100\ 101\ 001$$
$$= \ 1 \quad 2 \quad 1 \quad 4 \quad 5 \quad 1$$
$$= @121451 \qquad \text{(in octal)}$$

An octal number is usually preceded by the ampersand (@) symbol. The reverse process (octal--> decimal) is executed as follows:

$$@121451 = 121451_8$$
$$= 1x8^5 + 2x8^4 + 1x8^3 + 4x8^2 + 5x8^1 + 1x8^0$$
$$= 32,768 + 8192 + 512 + 256 + 40 + 1$$
$$= 41769_{10}$$

A set of four binary digits will generate 16 unique combinations (2^4). By grouping the binary digits into sets of four, the number is converted to a <u>hexadecimal</u> (10+6) base which includes the hexadecimal digits 0, 1, 2, 3, 4, 5, 6, 7, 8, 9, A, B, C, D, E, and F. So as not to confuse a hexadecimal digit with a decimal digit, a preceding dollar ($) sign is commonly used to designate a hex number.

$$41769_{10} = 1010001100101001 \quad \text{(in binary)}$$
$$= 1010 \quad 0011 \quad 0010 \quad 1001$$
$$= \quad A \quad\quad 3 \quad\quad 2 \quad\quad 9$$
$$= \$A329 \quad\quad \text{(in hexadecimal)}$$

The reverse process (hexadecimal--> decimal) is executed as follows:

$$\$A329 = A329_{16}$$
$$= A x 16^3 + 3 x 16^2 + 2 x 16^1 + 9 x 16^0$$
$$= 40,960 + 768 + 32 + 9$$
$$= 41769_{10}$$

2.4 FRACTIONAL NUMBERS

Fractional numbers can also be represented by binary digits. Similar rules of behavior are followed, except in this case the concept of negative exponents is employed.

$$0.1101 = 1 x 2^{-1} + 1 x 2^{-2} + 0 x 2^{-3} + 1 x 2^{-4}$$
$$= 0.5 + 0.25 + 0 + 0.0625$$
$$= 0.8125_{10}$$

In this example, the fractional binary number 0.1101 represents the fractional decimal number 0.8125.

2.5 BINARY-CODED-DECIMAL (BCD) NUMBERS

Decimal numbers can also be specifically coded using binary digits. In order to encode each of the ten decimal digits 0-9, four binary digits (bits) are necessary (3 will generate only 8 unique combinations). Four bits allow 16 unique combinations which are 6 more than is necessary. These 6 extra combinations are ignored and the resulting bits comprise the Binary-Coded-Decimal (BCD) System. This system is employed whenever binary digits are used to represent decimal numbers. The binary values of these 4-bit groups are from 0000 to 1001 which code the decimal digits 0 through 9. A binary number such as 1011 has no meaning in the BCD system.

The following listing summarizes the relationships among the various number systems.

Hexadecimal 0-F	Decimal 0-9	Octal 0-7	BCD		Binary	
$0	0	@0	0000	0000	0000	0000
1	1	1		0001		0001
2	2	2		0010		0010
3	3	3		0011		0011
4	4	4		0100		0100
5	5	5		0101		0101
6	6	6		0110		0110
7	7	7		0111		0111
8	8	10		1000		1000
9	9	11		1001		1001
A	10	12	0001	0000		1010
B	11	13		0001		1011
C	12	14		0010		1100
D	13	15		0011		1101
E	14	16		0100		1110
F	15	17		0101		1111
10	16	20		0110	0001	0000
11	17	21		0111		0001
12	18	22		1000		0010
13	19	23		1001		0011
14	20	24	0010	0000		0100
15	21	25		0001		0101
.	.	.		.		.
.	.	.		.		.
.	.	.		.		.

2.6   BINARY TO DECIMAL

To calculate the decimal value of a binary number, multiply each Nth order bit value (0 or 1) by its appropriate weighting factor (i.e. 2^N) and add the total.

Namely, binary 0010 0111

$$= 0x2^7+0x2^6+1x2^5+0x2^4+0x2^3+1x2^2+1x2^1+1x2^0$$

$$=\ 0\ +\ 0\ +\ 32\ +\ 0\ +\ 0\ +\ 4\ +\ 2\ +\ 1$$

$$= 39$$

2.7   DECIMAL TO BINARY

The reverse process, converting a decimal value into a binary number, is done by successively dividing the decimal number by 2 and recording the remaining value (0 or 1) until zero is reached.

Namely, decimal 39   Remaining Value

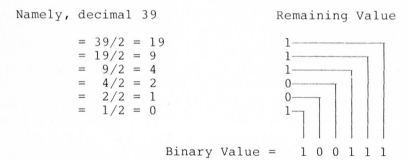

= 39/2 = 19	1
= 19/2 = 9	1
= 9/2 = 4	1
= 4/2 = 2	0
= 2/2 = 1	0
= 1/2 = 0	1

Binary Value =   1 0 0 1 1 1

2.8   BINARY ADDITION

An example of binary addition is the addition of two 16-bit numbers, each of which can be stored in two separate memory locations 8-bits wide (4 memory locations altogether).

```
                                       HEX
      10110001   10101101   =   $B1AD
  +   00010110   01110100   =   $1674
      11000111   00100001

  + 0          1             =   Carries
      11001000   00100001   =   $C821
```

The carry from each byte is added to the least significant
bit of the next byte and so on.

2.9   BINARY SUBTRACTION

Computers can't subtract binary numbers, they can only add.
The subtraction process, therefore, is really executed as a
modified addition. In the decimal system 9 - 5 is equivalent to
9 + (-5). A (-5) in the decimal system is defined in such a way
that 5 + (-5) = 0. An analogous definition exists in the binary
system; b + (-b) = 0 where b = a binary number. A (-b) is
sometimes written as $\overline{b}$ (the inverse of b). $\overline{b}$ is also called the
two's complement of b. It is derived by adding 1 to the one's
complement of b.

```
                                            HEX
      10011101   =  binary number (b)       $9D
      01100010   =  one's complement
         + 1
      01100011   =  two's complement (b̄)    $63
```

It is a simple matter to show from the above discussion
that b + $\overline{b}$ = 0 or, in HEX format, $9D + $63 = $00.

In binary multibyte subtraction, a similar process occurs.
However, a 1 is only added to the lower order byte of the
number.

```
                             HEX
01001000   10011101        $489D
10110111   01100010        one´s complement
               + 1
10110111   01100011        $B763
```

2.10   SIGNED BINARY NUMBERS

The common convention for defining the sign of a binary number is the status of the high order bit. If it is equal to 1, the number is negative. If it is equal to 0, the number is positive.

```
Obbbbbbb = a positive 7-bit number
1bbbbbbb = a negative 7-bit number
```

A positive binary number is converted to its negative by two´s complementing it and ignoring any carry out.

```
00000010  =  +2
11111101  =  one´s complement
     + 1
11111110  =  -2
```

The range of signed binary numbers using 8 binary digits is from -128 to +127.

```
10000000  =  -128  =  $80
    .          .
    .          .
11111110  =   -2
11111111  =   -1
00000000  =    0
00000001  =   +1
00000010  =   +2
    .          .
    .          .
01111111  =  +127  =  $7F
```

2.11   BINARY MULTIPLICATION

The process of multiplying two binary numbers is similar to that of multiplying two decimal numbers except that each partial product is either a 0 or a 1.

```
        1010                    10
      x 0011                  x  3
        1010                  ----
       1010
      0000
     0000
     -------
     0011110     = 16 + 8 + 4 + 2 = 30
```

2.12   BINARY DIVISION

Binary division is the reverse of multiplication.

```
            1010                  10
    0011/ 0011110               3/30
          0011
          ----
           0011
           0011
           ----
            000
            000
            ---
              0
```

2.13   REGISTER SHIFTS

Shifting a binary number one bit to the left has the overall effect of multiplying that number by 2.

```
                 shift
    0011110     ------->   0111100
                 left
```

```
    30   ----->    32 + 16 + 8 + 4 = 60
```

In a similar manner, shifting a binary number one bit to the right has the effect of dividing that number by 2.

```
                    shift
    0011110     ------->    0001111
                    right

     30   ----->   8 + 4 + 2 + 1 = 15
```

Register-shift operations are used extensively in routines involving multiplication, division, number-base conversion and servo-type analog--> digital conversion schemes.

CODE CONVERSIONS

If a computer is to be useful there must be some means of communication between the central processing unit (CPU) and external devices. Since computers are digital devices, they will only recognize digital information. On the other hand, humans (a type of external device) usually communicate (at least visually) in language forms containing characters and numeric symbols (i.e. alphanumerics). In order for humans to interact with computers and vice-versa, their languages (codes) must be translated (converted) into each other's format. This process of Code Conversion is used to both input data to the CPU (from a keyboard, for example) and output data from the CPU (to a printer, for example). Three such techniques of converting one code into another may be classified as using (a) lookup tables, (b) number base conversions and (c) hardware devices.

2.14 LOOKUP TABLES

Lookup tables are usually employed with a limited set of
data or when there is no simple relationship between codes.
They can hold such items as display codes, printer codes and
alphanumeric strings. One example of how such a lookup table is
used is the manner in which a microcomputer communicates with a
Seven Segment Display using the Seven Segment Codes. Fig. 2-1
illustrates the components of a 7-segment LED display in a
typical configuration followed by the codes that produce a
specific decimal display character (0-9). Each bit of the code
controls the "on" or "off" status of a particular display
segment. Other display characters (letters + special
characters) require additional coding (viz. "F" = $71).

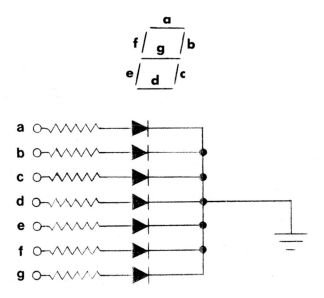

Fig. 2-1. Common Cathode 7-Segment Display.

BCD to 7-Segment Conversion

BCD Number	Decimal Eq.	g	f	e	d	c	b	a	HEX
0000	0	0	1	1	1	1	1	1	$3F
0001	1	0	0	0	0	1	1	0	$06
0010	2	1	0	1	1	0	1	1	$5B
0011	3	1	0	0	1	1	1	1	$4F
0100	4	1	1	0	0	1	1	0	$66
0101	5	1	1	0	1	1	0	1	$6D
0110	6	1	1	1	1	1	0	0	$7C
0111	7	0	0	0	0	1	1	1	$07
1000	8	1	1	1	1	1	1	1	$7F
1001	9	1	1	0	0	1	1	1	$67

2.15 NUMBER BASE CONVERSION

An example of a code which can be converted by using various number base conversion routines is the American Standard Code for Information Interchange, ASCII for short. It represents the most commonly used data type for peripheral devices in addition to BCD and binary numbers. It is a standardized 7-bit code for data communication on public networks. Besides numerics it contains upper and lower case letters and a large number of device and transmission control characters. In serial data transmissions, start, stop and parity bits are also included. Parity implies that the number of "on" bits should add up to an even number for even parity and an odd number for odd parity. One reason for this is to check for a loss of bits during transmission. The example below is the word A-I-M in even parity transmission. Bit one of the ASCII code is transmitted first.

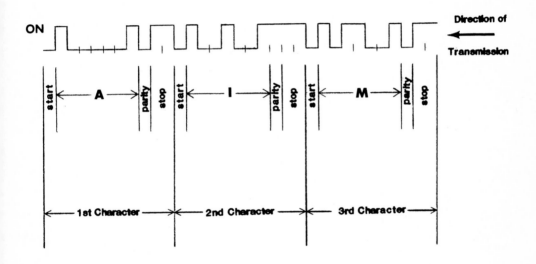

Fig. 2-2. Serial ASCII Transmission.

Note that in even parity transmission each character contains an even number of "on" bits. In a data communications network using even parity ASCII, one way of checking to see if the data has been transferred correctly is to add up the total number of bits. The result should be an even number. The bit strings and Hex/Decimal numbers for the various ASCII characters and functions are contained in Figs. 2-3 and 2-4.

Hex. No.	Binary No.	0 0000	1 0001	2 0010	3 0011	4 0100	5 0101	6 0110	7 0111
0	0000	NUL 0	DEL 16	SP 32	0 48	@ 64	P 80	96	p 112
1	0001	SOH 1	DC1 17	! 33	49	A 65	.Q 81	a 97	q 113
2	0010	STX 2	DC2 18	'' 34	2 50	B 66	R 82	b 98	r 114
3	0011	ETX 3	DC3 19	# 35	3 51	C 67	S 83	C 99	s 115
4	0100	EOT 4	DC4 20	$ 36	4 52	D 68	T 84	d 100	t 116
5	0101	ENQ 5	NAK 21	% 37	5 53	E 69	U 85	e 101	u 117
6	0110	ACK 6	SYN 22	& 38	6 54	F 70	V 86	f 102	v 118
7	0111	BEL 7	ETB 23	' 39	7 55	G 71	W 87	g 103	w 119
8	1000	BS 8	CAN 24	(40	8 56	H 72	X 88	h 104	x 120
9	1001	HT 9	EM 25	) 41	9 57	I 73	Y 89	i 105	y 121
A	1010	LF 10	SUB 26	* 42	: 58	J 74	Z 90	j 106	z 122
B	1011	VT 11	ESC 27	+ 43	; 59	K 75	[91	k 107	{ 123
C	1100	FF 12	FS 28	, 44	< 60	L 76	\ 92	l 108		124
D	1101	CR 13	GS 29	− 45	= 61	M 77	] 93	m 109	} 125
E	1110	SO 14	RS 30	. 46	> 62	N 78	^ 94	n 110	~ 126
F	1111	SI 15	US 31	/ 47	? 63	O 79	− 95	o 111	DEL 127

Fig. 2-3.   The 7-Bit ASCII Code.

NUL - Null, or all zeros

SOH - Start of Heading

STX - Start of Text

ETX - End of Text

EOT - End of Transmission

ENQ - Enquiry

ACK - Affirmative Acknowledge

BEL - Bell or audible signal

BS - Backspace

HT - Horizontal Tabulation

LF - Line Feed

VT - Vertical Tabulation

FF - Form Feed

CR - Carriage Return

SO - Shift Out

SI - Shift In

DLE - Data link escape

DC1 - Device Control 1

DC2 - Device Control 2

DC3 - Device Control 3

DC4 - Device Control 4

NAK - Negative Acknowledge

SYN - Synchronous Idle

ETB - End of Trans. Block

CAN - Cancel

EM - End of Medium

SUB - Substitute

ESC - Escape

FS - File Separator

GS - Group Separator

RS - Record Separator

US - Unit Separator

SP - Space

DEL - Delete

Fig. 2-4. Function Abbreviations of ASCII Control Codes.

An illustration of a number-based conversion is the ASCII-based Hexadecimal to Binary conversion routine.

Hex -->	Binary -->	ASCII Hex
$0	0000	$30
1	0001	31
2	0010	32
3	0011	33
4	0100	34
5	0101	35
6	0110	36
7	0111	37
8	1000	38
9	1001	39
A	1010	41
B	1011	42
C	1100	43
D	1101	44
E	1110	45
F	1111	46

First, for the values 0-9, it is immediately obvious that ASCII Hex can be converted to "normal" Binary Hex by masking out (to zero) the high order hex digit (3) of the ASCII code. For example,

$$\text{ASCII "5"} = \$35 = 35_{16}$$
$$35_{16} \longrightarrow 05_{16} = \$05$$

Secondly, the remaining ASCII values (A-F) can be converted to Binary Hex by masking out the high order hex digit (4) and adding 9 to the result.

$$\text{ASCII "A"} = \$41 = 41_{16}$$
$$41_{16} \longrightarrow 01_{16}$$
$$01_{16} + 9_{16} = 0A_{16} = \$0A$$

In both of these processes, a specific arithmetic/logical algorithm is used to effect the conversion. Further examples of this approach include such code conversion routines as: ASCII Hex <--> Binary, Binary <--> BCD, Binary <--> ASCII Decimal and BCD <--> ASCII Decimal.

2.16 HARDWARE DEVICES

Hardware devices comprise the third code conversion technique and are readily available for some specific code conversion tasks. Typical devices include BCD --> Seven Segment Decoders, Universal Asynchronous Receiver/Transmitters (UART´s) and ACIA´s (Asynchronous Communications Interface Adapters). These last two devices are used for parallel <--> serial bit conversions in various data transmission schemes. In many applications, however, the preferred choice is to do the code conversion in software. The slight increase in execution time is more than offset by the savings in external components and their associated complexity/reliability problems.

CHAPTER 3

LOGIC GATES

A logic <u>gate</u> is a device or circuit that passes or prevents
a signal from passing according to well defined rules. Since
the signals we are talking about are digital in nature, they can
have only two values which are commonly represented by logical
"1" and logical "0". Logical 1 and 0 are also referred to as
either on/off or high/low and all three expressions are used
interchangeably. The basic types of logic gates are the
INVERTER (NOT gate), AND, OR, NAND, NOR and XOR (Exclusive-OR)
gates.

In the following pages, examples of the various 2-input
gates are illustrated using simple analog switching circuits.
The symbols for the various logic gates are illustrated along
with their Boolean expressions and Truth Tables. Interspersed
throughout the diagrams are examples of solid state devices and
components which emulate the various gates. All of these
systems share the common feature of being decision elements.
They make certain logical decisions based on their input
signals. By interconnecting enough combinations of such basic
logic gates, any complex digital system can be constructed.

3.1   INVERTER (NOT) GATE

The inverter gate is just what its name implies.   It
inverts the input signal to produce an opposite output signal.
A 0/1 on the input produces a 1/0 at the output.

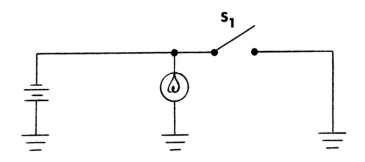

Fig. 3-1.   Inverter (Not) Gate.

Input	Output	Symbol	Boolean Eq.
S_1	light		
0	1		$C = \overline{A}$
1	0		

(0=off, 1=on)

Truth Table   Example

A	C
0	1
1	0

1011 0110

NOT --> 0100 1001

3.2 AND GATE

For two inputs, an AND gate's operation is defined as
producing a 1 if both inputs are 1, otherwise the result is 0.
For three or more inputs, a logic 1 is output only if all inputs
are 1.

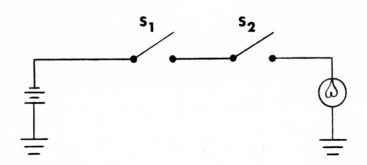

Fig. 3-2. AND Gate.

Input		Output
S_1	S_2	light
1	1	1
0	1	0
1	0	0
0	0	0

(0=off, 1=on)

Symbol

A ─┐
   ┤ ──── C
B ─┘

Boolean Eq.

C = A x B

Truth Table		
A	B	C
1	1	1
0	1	0
1	0	0
0	0	0

Example

```
        1011 0110
AND     0111 0000
        0011 0000
```

3.3 OR GATE

For two inputs, an OR gate's operation is defined as producing a 1 if either or both inputs are 1, otherwise the result is 0. For three or more inputs, a logic 0 is output only if all inputs are 0.

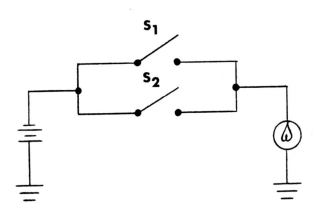

Fig. 3-3. OR Gate.

Input		Output	Symbol	Boolean Eq.
S_1	S_2	light		
1	1	1		$C = A + B$
1	0	1		
0	1	1		
0	0	0		

(0=off, 1=on)

Truth Table

A	B	C
1	1	1
1	0	1
0	1	1
0	0	0

Example

```
      1011 0110
OR    0111 0000
      1111 0110
```

3.4 NAND GATE

The NAND gate is simply an inverted AND gate. A logic 0 is output only if all inputs are 1, otherwise the result is 1.

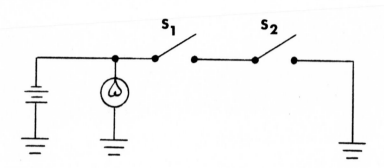

Fig. 3-4.   NAND Gate.

Input		Output
S_1	S_2	light
0	0	1
0	1	1
1	0	1
1	1	0

(0=off, 1=on)

Symbol

$$C = A \uparrow B$$

Boolean Eq.

A ─┐
    │ ─o─ C
B ─┘

Truth Table

A	B	C
0	0	1
0	1	1
1	0	0
1	1	0

Example

```
   1011 0110
NAND 0111 0000
   1100 1111
```

3.5 NOR GATE

In like fashion, the NOR gate is an inverted OR gate. A logic 1 is output only if all inputs are 0, otherwise the result is 0.

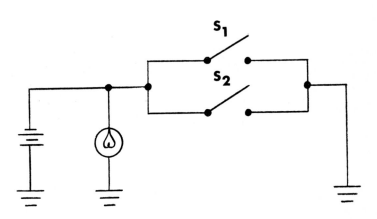

Fig. 3-5. NOR Gate.

Input		Output	Symbol	Boolean Eq.
S_1	S_2	light		
0	0	1		$C = A \downarrow B$
0	1	0		
1	0	0		
1	1	0		

(0=off, 1=on)

Truth Table

A	B	C
0	0	1
0	1	0
1	0	0
1	1	0

Example

1011 0110

NOR 0111 0000
     0000 1001

3.6 XOR GATE

For any number of inputs, an XOR gate´s operation is defined as producing a <u>0 when all inputs are the same</u>, otherwise the result is 1.

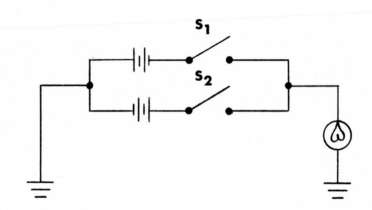

Fig. 3-6. XOR Gate.

Input		Output		Symbol	Boolean Eq.
S_1	S_2	light			
0	0	0			$C = A \oplus B$
0	1	1			
1	0	1			
1	1	0			

(0=off, 1=on)

Truth Table			Example
A	B	C	1011 0110
1	1	0	XOR 0111 0000
1	0	1	1100 0110
0	1	1	
0	0	0	

3.7   DIODE AND FUNCTION

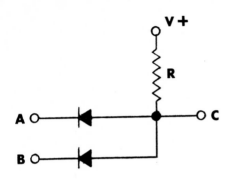

Input		Output
A	B	C
0	0	0
0	1	0
1	0	0
1	1	1

3.8   DIODE OR FUNCTION

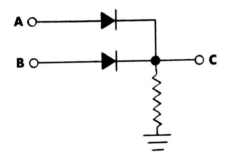

Input		Output
A	B	C
0	0	0
0	1	1
1	0	1
1	1	1

3.9   TRANSISTOR INVERTER

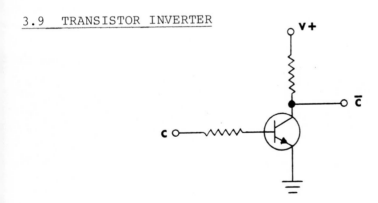

Fig. 3-7.   Examples of Diode and Transistor Gates.

3.10 EQUIVALENT GATES

Multiple Input OR Gate

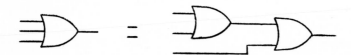

Multiple Input NOR Gate

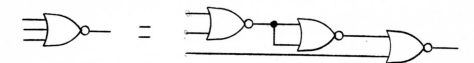

NOR Gate as Inverter

Multiple Input NAND Gate

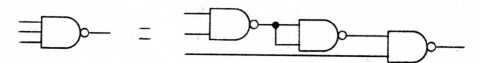

NAND Gate as Inverter

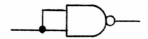

Fig. 3-8. Examples of Equivalent Gates.

3.11 INVERTED INPUTS, OUTPUTS

3.12 SUMMARY TABLE

A	B	AND	OR	NAND	NOR	XOR
1	1	1	1	0	0	0
1	0	0	1	1	0	1
0	1	0	1	1	0	1
0	0	0	0	1	1	0

3.13   FLIP-FLOPS

A flip-flop is a circuit that is capable of storing a
single bit.   It remembers an input and holds the output after
the data passes.   All common flip-flops are made from
combinations of the various gates; the NAND, NOR, and Inverter
(NOT) gates being most often used.

R-S Latch

The simplest flip-flop is the Reset-Set (R-S) Latch.   It
can be made from two NAND gates or two NOR gates although the
operation of each version is slightly different from the other.
The complementary outputs of a flip-flop are commonly called Q
and $\overline{Q}$ (not Q).

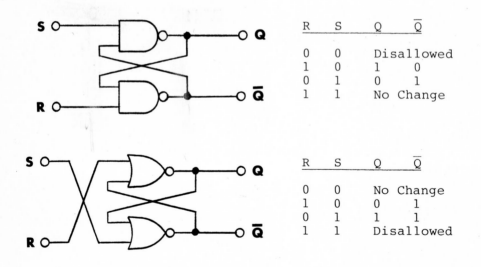

R	S	Q	$\overline{Q}$
0	0	Disallowed	
1	0	1	0
0	1	0	1
1	1	No Change	

R	S	Q	$\overline{Q}$
0	0	No Change	
1	0	0	1
0	1	1	1
1	1	Disallowed	

Fig. 3-9.   NAND and NOR Gate Flip-Flops.

Another more simple way of writing a flip-flop is:

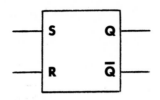

To make this a <u>clocked</u> flip-flop, a clock input must be added.

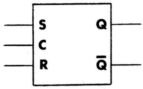

In a clocked flip-flop, the inputs (R & S) can only change the outputs (Q & $\overline{Q}$) during a high clock pulse. An example of a simple clocked flip-flop is:

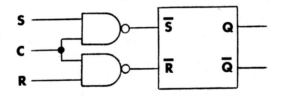

Data or D-Type Flip Flop

By adding an inverter to the inputs of a clocked flip-flop, we make a gated data latch.

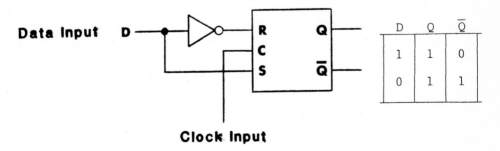

D	Q	$\overline{Q}$
1	1	0
0	1	1

A gated latch made from a NOR gate R-S latch is:

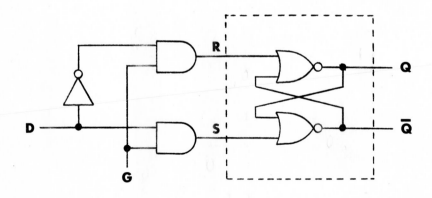

When the gating input G = 1, Q = D. When G then becomes 0
(latch), R or S then changes to 0 but the outputs are not
affected. A bit of information is thereby stored.

Master-Slave or J-K Flip-Flop

When data is to be trapped and latched at a specific point
in time, a "two-step" Master-Slave (J-K) flip-flop is used.

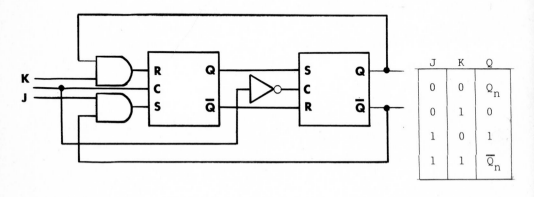

J	K	Q
0	0	Q_n
0	1	0
1	0	1
1	1	$\overline{Q}_n$

Q_n = value of Q during preceding clock cycle

Toggle or T-Type Flip-Flop

A T- or Toggle type flip-flop has no data inputs. It simply "toggles" or reverses outputs at every clock pulse. It can be constructed by providing feedback connections around an ordinary master-slave flip-flop.

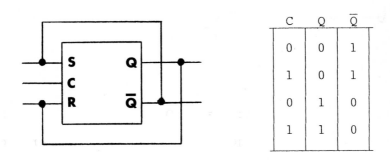

C	Q	$\overline{Q}$
0	0	1
1	0	1
0	1	0
1	1	0

This particular flip-flop is activated when the clock input goes from 1 --> 0 (‾↘_). It is an example of <u>edge triggering</u>. The outputs only change on the negative-going-transition of the clock pulse.

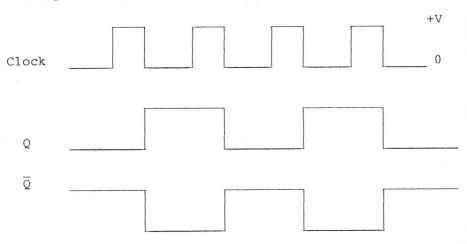

It is not difficult to see that the frequency of the Q (or $\bar{Q}$) output is 1/2 the clock frequency. T-Type flip-flops.and combinations/modifications thereof are used as binary dividers and digital counters (frequency dividers, e.g. digital watches).

3.14   DECODERS

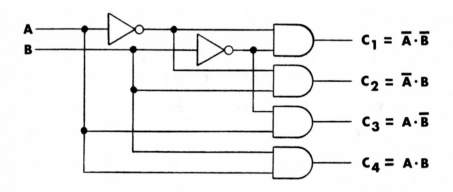

Fig. 3-10. Two-to-Four Line Decoder.

Inputs		Outputs			
A	B	C_1	C_2	C_3	C_4
0	0	1	0	0	0
1	0	0	0	1	0
0	1	0	1	0	0
1	1	0	0	0	1

In decoders there are more outputs than inputs. They are especially important in address decoding (memory expansion) and I/O port decoding. They are also useful in converting the binary or BCD output of a computer to a form that a human can understand. An example of this is a BCD/Seven Segment Decoder IC. General-purpose Decoders are commonly available in 2-->4, 3-->8, 4-->10 and 4-->16 line configurations.

3.15 MULTIPLEXERS

In multiplexers there are many inputs but only one output. Another name for a multiplexer is a Data Selector. It is equivalent to a manually operated multiple-throw switch.

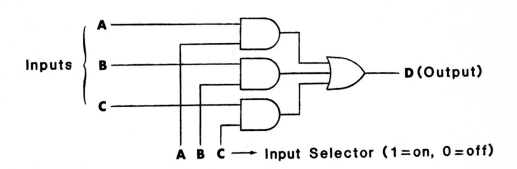

Fig. 3-11. Three-to-One Line Multiplexer.

Suppose we put the A-input selector switch on ("1"), then the following input/output table results.

| Inputs | | | Output |
A	B	C	D
1	0	0	1
0	1	0	0
0	0	1	0
1	1	0	1
1	1	1	1
0	1	1	0
1	0	1	1
0	0	0	0

Note that the output (D) "tracks" the A input regardless of the binary values present at the other inputs (B and C). By turning the A-input selector switch on we select only the A-channel. A popular device of this type is the 74150 16-channel multiplexer.

3.16   OPEN-COLLECTOR LOGIC

In several instances it is often desirable to connect the outputs of several gates together to create a single input into another gate. However, ordinary TTL logic gates do not allow for this possibility. If the outputs of two such gates were wired together and one output was high (+5V) while the other was low (ground), each gate would try to make its output prevail

until the output transistor of one of the gates burned out.
This problem is eliminated by the use of open-collector gates.
The internal differences between the output driving circuits of
both gates are shown below.

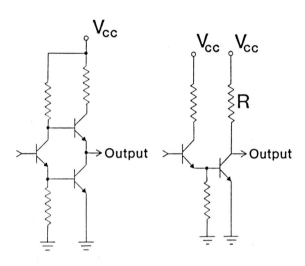

Fig. 3-12.   Standard (left) and Open Collector (right) Drivers.

The standard TTL output driver is often referred to as a
"totem-pole" structure because of the stacked transistor
configuration. Pullup resistor R serves the dual function of
establishing (pulling) a high output level when the driving
transistor is not conducting and limiting the current through
the same transistor when it is conducting. The outputs of
several gates can be safely wired together with a single pullup
resistor provided that the maximum current sinking capability of
any one gate is not exceeded. Some open collector gates can

also be operated with voltages greater than +5V thereby driving
such devices as lamps, relays and CMOS switches. The MOS analog
of the open-collector output is the open_drain output which is
often employed in a "wired-OR'ed" configuration in the design of
microprocessor Interrupt Request (IRQ) lines. The chief
drawback of the open collector configuration is the slow
switching time for the low--> high transition. The
current-limiting pullup resistor R cannot drive the output
terminal voltage as fast as the totem-pole output can. To a
great extent however, this problem is obviated in the
three-state or tri-state output configuration.

3.17   TRI-STATE_LOGIC

In a microcomputer, data (bytes) are shuttled to and from
different parts of the system on the data bus. In an 8-bit
microcomputer the data bus is comprised of an 8-line conductor.
If a large number of devices are attached to this conductor, the
load driving capabilities of the microprocessor or other devices
that are connected to it may be exceeded. To overcome this
difficulty, various sections of the system are buffered from the
data bus. This simply means that each system can be selectively
connected/disconnected to the data bus at appropriate times
thereby allowing the microprocessor to communicate with one (and
only one) device while all others are disabled. Most logic
gates, however, have only two output states (1/0 or high/low).

As a result, there is a need for a special type of output that has three states (high, low and off). This is referred to as three-state or tri-state logic. A tri-state logic gate, when enabled via a separate enable line, will function like the standard gates that we have already examined. However, when they are disabled, their outputs will remain in a high-impedance or off-state. Consequently, a large number of tri-state devices can be connected to a common conductor without interference as long as one and only one device is enabled to output to that conductor at any given time.

A typical example of a tri-state device is the 74126 Quad Bus Buffer/Driver depicted below.

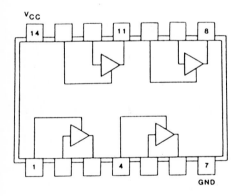

Fig. 3-13. 74126 Quad Bus Driver.

This is a positive logic device which means that the outputs are equal to the inputs (logical 0 or 1) when the corresponding enable lines are high (i.e. = logic 1). When the enable lines are low (=0), the outputs are in the high-impedance (disabled)

state. The analogous 74125 device operates in an identical
fashion except that the enabling lines are active low. Other
popular tri-state devices are the 8216/8226 Quad, 74LS367 Hex
and the 74LS244/5 Octal Bus Buffer/Drivers.

3.18 MOS AND CMOS DEVICES

In the previous sections, analog switches and simple,
discrete components (diodes, resistors, transistors) were used
to illustrate examples of several logic elements. In the early
days of (solid state) computers, these devices were frequently
employed to obtain the various logic functions. Today however,
the large scale semiconductor integrated circuits (IC's) used in
nearly all computing systems are products of what is commonly
referred to as MOS (Metal Oxide Semiconductor) technology. The
extremely low power consumption and high packing density of MOS
devices (the latter being a result of the former) enable the
fabrication of low cost IC's with exceedingly complex logic
circuits. In order to acquaint the reader with an overview of
this important technology, the following descriptive outlines of
an MOS device and a CMOS (Complementary Metal Oxide
Semiconductor) structure are presented.

The elementary device based on MOS technology is the MOSFET
(MOS Field Effect Transistor). In the MOSFET, a metal gate
electrode is situated on a thin silicon dioxide insulator as
described in Fig. 3-14.

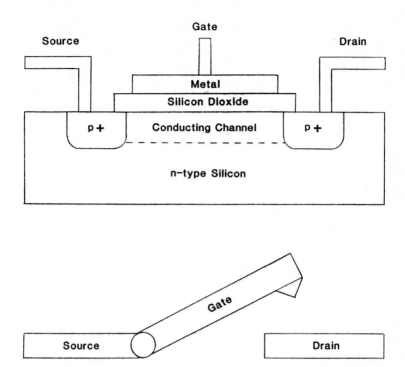

Fig. 3-14. Basic Construction of a P-Channel MOSFET.

The drain and source regions are carrier-doped p+ regions in an

n-type silicon substrate. The p and n designations refer

respectively to an excess of positive or negative charge

carriers in the substrate material (silicon). In the absence of

any negative gate voltages, the MOSFET acts like an open circuit

between the source and drain. When a negative voltage is

applied to the gate, the negative field effects (attracts) a conducting channel of positively charged holes between the source and drain regions. When this occurs, current flows between the source and the drain by virtue of the positive charges (holes) conducted through the opened channel (p-channel). As the gate voltage is made more negative, conduction (by holes) is enhanced. MOSFET´s with a p-channel are usually referred to as PMOS devices. The n-channel analog is the NMOS device where the current is conducted between the source and the drain through an n-channel by negative charges (electrons) when a positive gate voltage is applied. Fig. 3-15 contains the standard circuit symbol for a MOS transistor where the direction of the arrow indicates whether the device is n-channel (arrow in) or p-channel (arrow out).

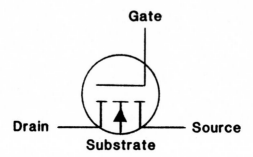

Fig. 3-15. Schematic Symbol for an NMOS Transistor.

The majority of currently existing computers utilize NMOS technology where positive gate voltages are employed to effect conducting electrons. An example of a logic element based on these principles is the inverter (NOT gate) depicted in Fig. 3-16.

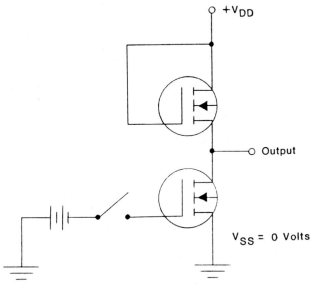

Fig. 3-16. NMOS Inverter.

In an effort to lower quiescent powers and increase packing densities, the benefits offered by CMOS technology are continuing to be realized in a number of devices, especially those used in portable, battery-based systems (i.e. portable computers). In a typical CMOS structure, both n-channel and p-channel MOSFET´s are fabricated on the same IC chip. A logic inverter based on this dual-MOSFET is described in Fig. 3-17.

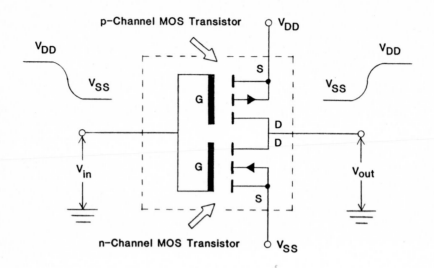

Fig 3-17.   CMOS Inverter.

When a voltage of given polarity is applied to the parallel-connected gates in this device, only one FET can conduct at any one time.   The substrate of the NMOS FET is at V_{SS} or ground potential while that of the PMOS FET is at V_{DD}.   When the gates are at a logic "1" (V_{DD}), the NMOS FET turns on while the PMOS FET turns off.   The output is thereby inverted and is a logic "0" (V_{SS}).   Similarly, when the gates are at a logic "0" (V_{SS}), the PMOS FET turns on while the NMOS FET turns off and the output is a logic "1" (V_{DD}).   Observe that in either stable logic state only one device is turned on.   Consequently, a minimal amount of current can flow from the supply (V_{DD}) to ground (V_{SS}) and the power consumed by the CMOS inverter is extremely low (usually measured in nanowatts, i.e. 10^{-9}W).   In actual practice however, the device does draw significant current during the logical switching transitions and the power consumed is proportional to the frequency of switching. Nevertheless, the low total average currents drawn by CMOS devices continue to drive their development and application in a variety of evolving semiconductor circuits.

CHAPTER 4

THE 6502 MPU

* Architecture

* Execution

* Mnemonics

* Registers

* Paging

* Instructions

* Addressing Modes

4.1 ARCHITECTURE

The architecture of a microcomputer system is depicted schematically in Fig. 4-1 for a "typical" 6502 system. The microprocessor (MPU) communicates with external devices, chips via three busses. The data bus is 8-bits wide and carries data (bytes) from the MPU to external devices and vice-versa. It is bidirectional in nature. The address bus is 16-bits wide and carries addresses generated in the MPU to the various external devices. These 16-bit addresses specify where (in memory) the data will go to or come from (on the data bus). A control bus carries the various synchronization signals such as $R/\overline{W}$ (i.e. is this a read or write operation?). ROM is Read Only Memory and contains such information as the operating program or Monitor for the system. It is non-volatile and remains on when the power is removed. RAM (Random Access Memory) is the Read/Write Memory which, as its name implies, is really a scratchpad (for bytes) which can be written into, written over or read from. It is volatile in nature and its contents are lost upon removal of power. Finally, the Input/Output (I/O) devices are those chips which enable the MPU to communicate with the outside world (i.e. keyboards, CRT's, switches, voltages, currents ....). They are also connected to the MPU via the three busses. Other additional chips such as buffers, decoders, drivers, etc. are necessary to construct a real system. For more information on the design and interfacing of an actual system, the reader is referred to the many available hardware texts on the subject.

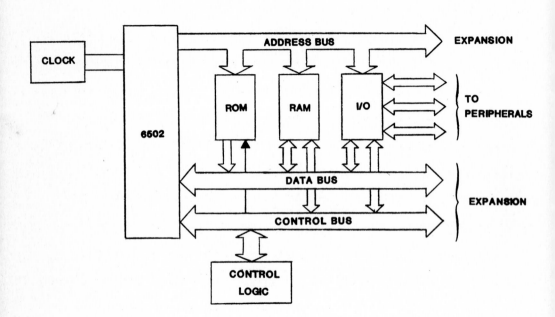

Fig. 4-1. A "Typical" 6502 System.

4.2 EXECUTION

The 6502 MPU executes programs by <u>fetching</u> an instruction
from memory, executing it, and then fetching the next
instruction. Instructions are 1-3 bytes long with the first
byte representing the <u>Operation Code (op-code)</u> of the
instruction, usually expressed in hexadecimal notation. For
example, $AA = TAX = <u>T</u>ransfer <u>A</u>ccumulator to <u>X</u> Index. The
remaining 1-2 bytes following the instruction can represent
either data or an address. The 6502 distinguishes instruction
bytes from address bytes or data bytes by noting their <u>relative</u>
<u>sequence</u> in a program. In a typical 6502 MPU operating at 1MHz,
instruction times vary between 2-7 microseconds depending upon
the particular type of instruction.

4.3 MNEMONICS

Mnemonics represent a shorthand notation or <u>Assembly</u>
<u>Language</u> which describes the instructions of the MPU in a more
understandable way (to humans) than hexadecimal op-codes or
8-bit groups of 0´s and 1´s. It is much easier to remember that
the TAX instruction means <u>T</u>ransfer <u>A</u>ccumulator to <u>X</u> Index than
the hex op-code $AA or the 8-bit number 1010 1010.
Microprocessors, on the other hand, operate only on binary
voltages represented by logical 0´s and 1´s (Machine Language).
Consequently, Mnemonics must be translated into such 0´s and 1´s
before the MPU can proceed. This is accomplished by a program

called an <u>Assembler</u> which is usually (but not always) available in most microcomputing systems. For instruction purposes, the Mnemonic format will be used to illustrate sample programs throughout the text. Keep in mind however, that this is <u>only</u> for the sake of human understanding.

4.4   REGISTERS

The 6502 Microprocessor uses seven Registers (6 Internal, 1 Temporary) in data manipulation/handling.

PC Register

The Program Counter (PC) Register is a 16-bit wide register which determines which memory location will be accessed next. It is automatically incremented after each memory access and contains the address of the next instruction to be executed. Being 16-bits wide, it can address any one of $2^{16} = 65,536$ locations. It is physically implemented in the 6502 as two 8-bit registers, PCL and PCH. L and H respectively refer to the lower (L) and higher (H) order bytes of the Program Counter. If the PC Register is loaded with a specific 16-bit number (2 bytes) during the execution of a program, control will be transferred to that particular address in memory and execution will resume from that point forward.

A, X, Y Registers

The Accumulator (A), X-Register (X) and Y-Register (Y) are three 8-bit wide general purpose registers which are used for a variety of operations. Arithmetic/Logical operations are performed in the Accumulator while the X and Y registers are employed as index registers or counters and are capable of being incremented/decremented in a controlled fashion.

<u>P Register - N, V, B, D, I, Z, C</u>

The Processor Status (P) Register contains seven usable bits called <u>Status Flags</u>. Five of these are affected by the outcome of a preceding instruction. During program execution these particular bits are constantly changing to reflect the <u>status</u> of the previous operation. The two remaining bits are <u>control bits</u> and can be set (=1) or cleared (=0) under program control.

N is the <u>Negative Flag</u> which is set (=1) whenever the result of the previous operation produces a negative value. Otherwise it is cleared (=0).

V is the <u>Overflow Flag</u> which is set (=1) if the result of a signed arithmetic operation produces a result greater than +127 or less than -128.

B is the <u>Break Command Flag</u> and is set (=1) by a "break" instruction.

D is the <u>Decimal Mode</u> bit which when set (=1) enables the 6502 to treat data as binary-coded-decimal (BCD) numbers.

I is the <u>IRQ Disable</u> bit which when set (=1) <u>prevents</u> the 6502 from being externally interrupted (by the IRQ line).

Z is the Zero Flag which is set (=1) if the result of the preceding operation is zero.

C is the Carry Flag and is used extensively during arithmetic operations. It can be viewed as a ninth bit which is set (=1) whenever the addition of two 8-bit numbers produces a result which exceeds 8-bits.

Stack

The Stack is an 8-bit wide temporary working register which is primarily used for transitory storage of program variables. It is implemented in the 256 locations at addresses $0100-01FF of the 6502´s address space and characterized as a push-down Stack. This simply means that it is loaded byte-wise from the top memory location ($01FF) downwards in memory and unloaded in reverse fashion. It can be thought of as a first-in last-out (FILO) memory.

Stack Pointer

The Stack Pointer (S) is an 8-bit wide internal register which is an abbreviated address register for the Stack. It represents the low order address byte of the next available location in the Stack. As such, it points to the next empty Stack location.

4.5   PAGING

The concept of paging is introduced as a helpful way of organizing memory in a microcomputer. The 6502 microprocessor is capable of accessing 2^{16} = 65,536 or 64K (1K = 1024) locations in memory. In hexadecimal notation this includes all 16-bit addresses from $0000 to $FFFF. If we define a Page as a block of 256 memory locations, then 64K locations can be represented as 256 Pages, each containing 256 locations. The higher order bits (nos. 8-15) of the 16-bit address represent the Page Number while the lower order bits (nos. 0-7) represent the location within a Page. For example, Page 3 represents all addresses in the range $0300-$03FF, Page 0 contains locations $0000-$00FF, while Page FF contains the addresses $FF00-$FFFF. Using this notation, Page 1 is normally reserved for the Stack area.

4.6 INSTRUCTIONS AND ADDRESSING MODES

The 6502 Microprocessor has 56 different instructions and can operate in 13 addressing modes. The various allowed combinations of instruction types and addressing modes permit a total of 151 different executable instructions. Each of these instructions is examined by way of discussion and example in the following pages. Mnemonic and hexadecimal ($) notations are used throughout the programming examples unless otherwise stated. The reader is encouraged to work through each programming example since each demonstrates the application of a particular instruction and/or addressing mode.

```
┌─────────────────────────────┐
│    6502 INSTRUCTION SET      │
└─────────────────────────────┘
```

Operation	Mnemonic
Load and Store Instructions	LDA,STA,LDX,LDY,STX,STY
Register Transfer Instructions	TAX,TAY,TXA,TYA
Break Instruction	BRK
No Operation Instruction	NOP
Jump Instruction	JMP
Increment/Decrement Instructions	INC,INX,INY,DEC,DEX,DEY
Logical Instructions	AND,ORA,EOR
Flag Instructions	CLC,SEC,CLD,SED,CLV
Arithmetic Instructions	ADC,SBC
Branch Instructions	BCC,BCS,BEQ,BNE,BMI,BPL, BVC,BVS
Compare Instructions	CMP,CPX,CPY
Bit Test Instruction	BIT
Shift and Rotate Instructions	ASL,LSR,ROL,ROR
Subroutine Instructions	JSR, RTS
Stack Instructions	PHA,PLA,PHP,PLP,TXS,TSX
Interrupt Instructions	RTI,SEI,CLI

Fig. 4-2. The 56 Instructions of the 6502 MPU.

```
┌─────────────────────────────┐
│   6502 ADDRESSING MODES      │
└─────────────────────────────┘
```

Absolute

Zero Page   *Non Indexed*

Immediate

Implied

Relative

Accumulator

Absolute Indexed, X

Absolute Indexed. Y

Zero Page Indexed, X

Zero Page Indexed. Y

Indirect Absolute

Indirect Indexed (Post-Indexed Indirect)

Indexed Indirect (Pre-Indexed Indirect)

Fig. 4-3.   The 13 Addressing Modes of the 6502 MPU.

MONITOR COMMANDS

In every microcomputing system or programming language there exists a prescribed set of functional commands which are input to the computer from a particular device (keyboard, tape, disk,...). Such commands are specific to that computer's operating system (Monitor Program) or programming language. For example, in the BASIC language (a type of program), the RUN command, when entered, begins program execution from the lowest numbered statement.

In the AIM 65 Microcomputing System, those Monitor Commands which are most useful and necessary are the <M>, </>, <*>, <G>, <K> and <R> Commands. They are entered from the keyboard and perform the following functions:

<M> = Displays the contents (in Hex) of the various memory locations in groups of four.

</> = Changes the contents of the various memory locations to the entered Hex values.

<*> = Sets/Re-Sets the Program Counter (PC) to the entered Hex value.

<G> = Begins program execution from that address currently contained in the Program Counter (PC).

<K> = Disassembles (i.e. converts machine--> assembly language) the contents (valid instruction op codes) of specified memory locations for display/printout.

<R> = Displays the contents (in Hex) of the six internal
      registers of the 6502.

```
**** = Program Counter (PC)
 PS  = Processor Status Register (P)
 AA  = Accumulator (A)
 XX  = X-Register (X)
 YY  = Y-Register (Y)
 SS  = Stack Pointer (S)
```

These Monitor Commands will be used from this
point forward to enter, alter and display machine/
assembly language programs in the instructional
experiments that follow. With few exceptions,
these machine-language programs can be used with
any 6502-based system with the single proviso that
they reside in or access those user-available
portions of the system's RAM.

```
┌─────────────────────────────────────────────┐
│  LDA - Load Accumulator with Memory          │
│                                              │
│  STA - Store Accumulator in Memory           │
└─────────────────────────────────────────────┘
```

The LDA and STA instructions can operate in three non-indexed addressing modes. They are the Absolute, Zero Page and Immediate Addressing Modes.

ABSOLUTE ADDRESSING

In the Absolute Addressing Mode, the second and third bytes of the instruction are the address of the location where the data is.

Exp.1 - Absolute Addressing

1. Store $AA in location $0211 using the Monitor <M> and
    </> Commands. Use the same commands to store $FF in
    location $0300.

2. Key in the following program in Hex format beginning
    at location $0100.

                              Comments

    $0100 AD LDA@   Load the Accumulator with the
        1 11   contents of $0211
        2 02
        3 8D STA@   Store the Accumulator at
        4 00   location $0300
        5 03
        6 00 BRK   Return to Monitor
    $0107 EA NOP   No Operation

3. After keying in the program, examine the contents of
    location $0300.

4. Next, run the program by keying in <*> = 0100 followed by RETURN then <G>/ and RETURN. The display should read <0107 EA NOP.

5. Examine the contents of location $0300. Has it changed? Answer: Yes, $FF to $AA.

6. AIM Printout:

```
<M>=0211 AA 3D 40 35
<M>=0300 FF 41 2C C3
<*>=0100
<G>/
 0107 EA NOP

<M>=0300 AA 41 2C C3

<K>*=0100
/04
 0100 AD LDA 0211
 0103 8D STA 0300
 0106 00 BRK
 0107 EA NOP
```

ZERO PAGE ADDRESSING

In the Zero Page addressing mode the second byte of the instruction is the low order address of the Zero Page memory location containing the data.

Exp. 2 - Zero Page Addressing

1. Store $EE in location $0020 using the Monitor <M> and </> Commands.

2. Store $FF in locations $0030 and 0350.

3. Key in the following program:

			Comments
$0100	A5	LDA$_z$	Load the accumulator with the
1	20		contents of $0020
2	8D	STA@	Store the accumulator at
3	50		location $0350
4	03		
5	AD	LDA@	Load the accumulator with the
6	50		contents of $0350
7	03		
8	85	STA$_z$	Store the accumulator at
9	30		location $0030
A	00	BRK	Return to Monitor
$010B	EA	NOP	No Operation

4. After keying in the program, examine the contents of locations $0030 and 0350.

5. Next, run the program by keying in <*> = 0100, RETURN, <G>/, RETURN. The display should read <010B EA NOP.

6. What are the current contents of locations $0030 and $0350? Answer: $EE, EE.

7. AIM Printout:

Zero Page Addressing

```
<M>=0020 45 9D F4 21
</> 0020 EE 00 00 00
<M>=0030 87 E9 B1 45
</> 0030 FF 00 00 00
<M>=0350 07 39 0D B5
</> 0350 FF 00 00 00

<M>=0020 EE 00 00 00
<M>=0030 FF 00 00 00
<M>=0350 FF 00 00 00

<*>=0100
<G>/
 010B EA NOP

<M>=0030 EE 00 00 00
<M>=0350 EE 00 00 00

<K>*=0100
/06
 0100 A5 LDA 20
 0102 8D STA 0350
 0105 AD LDA 0350
 0108 85 STA 30
 010A 00 BRK
 010B EA NOP
```

IMMEDIATE ADDRESSING

In the Immediate Addressing Mode the second byte of the instruction is the data.

Exp. 3 - Immediate Addressing

1. Store $EE in location $0021 and $FF in locations $0030 and $0350.

2. Key in the following program:

<u>Comments</u>

```
$0100 A9 LDA#      Load the accumulator with $BC
    1 BC
    2 85 STA       Store the contents of the
    3 20    z        accumulator at location $0020
    4 8D STA@      Store also at location $0350
    5 50
    6 03
    7 85 STA       And at $0030
    8 30    z
    9 00 BRK       Return to Monitor
$010A EA NOP       No Operation
```


3. Run the program.

4. What is now contained in locations $0020, 0030 and 0350? Answer: $BC

5. What is contained in the accumulator? Answer: $BC

6. Can you use the STA instruction in the Immediate Mode? Answer: NO. You can´t store Data into Data only into Memory locations.

7.   AIM Printout.

Immediate Addressing

```
<M>=0020 37 CC 36 C2
</> 0020 EE 00 00 00
<M>=0030 D8 C7 F9 C3
</> 0030 FF 00 00 00
<M>=0350 34 E8 3D CC
</> 0350 FF 00 00 00

<*>=0100
<G>/
 010A EA NOP

<M>=0020 BC 00 00 00
<M>=0030 BC 00 00 00
<M>=0350 BC 00 00 00

<K>*=0100
/06
 0100 A9 LDA #BC
 0102 85 STA 20
 0104 8D STA 0350
 0107 85 STA 30
 0109 00 BRK
 010A EA NOP
```

```
┌─────────────────────────────────────────────┐
│ LDX - Load X Register with Memory            │
│ LDY - Load Y Register with Memory            │
│ STX - Store X Register in Memory             │
│ STY - Store Y Register in Memory             │
└─────────────────────────────────────────────┘
```

As with the LDA and STA instructions, the LDX, LDY, STX, and STY instructions can also be used in the Absolute, Zero Page and (for LDX, LDY) the Immediate Addressing Modes.

Exp. 4 - LDX, LDY, STX, STY Operations

1. Store $44 in locations $0066, 0067 and 0068.

2. Key in the following program:

Comments

```
$0100 A0 LDY#     Load the Y Register with $55
    1 55
    2 A6 LDX_z    Load the X Register with the
    3 66            contents of $0066
    4 84 STY_z    Store the Y Register at Zero
    5 67            Page Location $0067
    6 86 STX_z    Store the X Register at Zero
    7 68            Page Location $0068
    8 AC LDY@     Load the Y Register with the
    9 10            contents of $0110
    A 01
    B 8C STY@     Store the Y Register at Zero
    C 66            Page Location $0066
    D 00
    E 00 BRK      Return to Monitor
    F EA NOP      No Operation
$0110 66
```

3. Run the program

4. What are the contents of locations $0066, 0067 and
    0068? Answer: $66, 55, 44.

5. What is unusual about the instruction at
    location $010B?

6. Do not alter the program or the contents of $0066,
    0067 or 0068. They are used in Exp. 5.

7. AIM Printout.

LDX, LDY, STX, STY Operations

```
<M>=0066 33 C8 1A C7
</> 0066 44 44 44 00

<*>=0100
<G>/
 010F EA NOP

<M>=0066 66 55 44 00

<K>*=0100
/09
 0100 A0 LDY #55
 0102 A6 LDX 66
 0104 84 STY 67
 0106 86 STX 68
 0108 AC LDY 0110
 010B 8C STY 0066
 010E 00 BRK
 010F EA NOP
 0110 66 ROR 00
```

```
TAX - Transfer Contents of Accumulator to X Register
TAY - Transfer Contents of Accumulator to Y Register
TXA - Transfer Contents of X Register to Accumulator
TYA - Transfer Contents of Y Register to Accumulator
```

The Transfer instructions (TAX, TAY, TXA, TYA) are single byte instructions which use a special mode of addressing called Implied Addressing. Data is transferred to or from the accumulator and the X or Y Registers. No R/W Memory locations are accessed.

Exp. 5 - TAX, TAY, TXA, TYA Operations

1. Modify the program in Exp. 4 by keying in the following instructions beginning at location $0108.

                                    Comments

    $0108 98 TYA   Transfer contents of Y to A
          9 AA TAX   Transfer contents of X to A
          A 86 STX$_z$ Store contents of X at
          B 66   location $0066
          C 00 BRK   Return to Monitor
    $010D EA NOP   No Operation

2. Run the program starting at $0100.

3. What are the contents of $0066, 0067 and 0068?
   Answer: $55, 55, 66.

4. Run the program again starting at $0100. What are the contents of $0066, 0067 and 0068?
   Answer: $55, 55, 55.

5. Explanation:

$0100 A0 LDY#   Load the Y Register with $55
   1 55
   2 A6 LDX$_z$ Load the X Register with the
   3 66   contents of $0066[$66]
   4 84 STY$_z$ Store the contents of Y[$55] at
   5 67 $0067 --> $0067[$55]
   6 86 STX$_z$ Store the contents of X[$66] at
   7 68 $0068 --> $0068[$66]
   8 98 TYA   Transfer contents of Y[$55] to A
   9 AA TAX   Transfer contents of A[$55] to X
   A 86 STX$_z$ Store contents of X[$55] at
   B 66 $0066 --> $0066[$55]
   C 00 BRK   Return to Monitor
$010D EA NOP   No Operation

6. AIM Printout.

<u>TAX, TAY, TXA, TYA Operations</u>

```
<M>=0066 66 55 44 00

<*>=0100
<G>/
 010D EA NOP

<M>=0066 55 55 66 00

<*>=0100
<G>/
 010D EA NOP

<M>=0066 55 55 55 00

<K>*=0100
/09
 0100 A0 LDY #55
 0102 A6 LDX 66
 0104 84 STY 67
 0106 86 STX 68
 0108 98 TYA
 0109 AA TAX
 010A 86 STX 66
 010C 00 BRK
 010D EA NOP
```

```
┌─────────────────────────────────────────┐
│  BRK - Jump to Interrupt Routine         │
└─────────────────────────────────────────┘
```

The BRK instruction forces a halt to the program execution sequence and returns control to an Interrupt Routine whose starting address is contained in two consecutive memory locations designated IRQL and IRQH. Upon power-up or hitting the RESET button, IRQL and IRQH are loaded with the starting address of the Monitor Routine (or Master Control Program). All of the important registers in the 6502 are <u>saved</u> during execution of a BRK instruction. This makes it a very useful tool in program debugging since specific sections of a large program, separated by BRK instructions, can be run and sequentially stopped for Register (A, X, Y, S, P, PC) examination and checking. The specific interrupt sequences of the BRK instruction (which is really a software-forced interrupt) are discussed in greater detail in that Section dealing with <u>Interrupts</u>.

```
┌──────────────────────────────┐
│  NOP - No Operation          │
└──────────────────────────────┘
```

The NOP instruction is really a one-byte pseudo-instruction which does nothing but occupy time and memory. As such, it is especially useful in developing programs since a group of NOP´s can be used to reserve program space for later addition of instructions. It can also be used in those routines involving the generation of programmed time delays.

```
┌─────────────────────────────────────────┐
│                                         │
│    JMP - Jump to New Location           │
│                                         │
└─────────────────────────────────────────┘
```

When a JMP instruction is encountered during program execution, program control is transferred to that location specified by the JMP instruction and the program sequence continues from that point on. It, in effect, puts a new 2-byte value into the Program Counter (PCH-PCL) where PCH = higher order byte of PC and PCL = lower order byte of PC. The JMP instruction is a 3-byte long instruction with 2 Addressing Modes: Absolute and Indirect Absolute.

In the Absolute Mode the two bytes following the instruction are the low and high order bytes of the address in memory (PCL, PCH) where program control is transferred.

In the Indirect Absolute Mode, the two bytes following the instruction are the lower and higher order bytes of the address in memory (ADL, ADH) which contains the PCL byte of the memory address where program control is transferred. The PCH byte of the destination address is contained in the next memory location (i.e. ADH,ADL + 1). This process is depicted in Fig. 4-4.

Jump Absolute

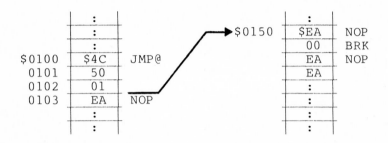

Jump Indirect Absolute

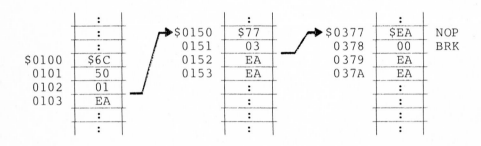

Fig. 4-4.   Absolute and Indirect Absolute JMP Operations.

Exp. 6 - JMP Operations

AIM printout:

Jump Absolute

```
<K>*=0100
/04
 0100 4C JMP 0150
 0103 00 BRK
 0104 EA NOP
 0105 EA NOP
<K>*=0150
/04
 0150 EA NOP
 0151 00 BRK
 0152 EA NOP
 0153 EA NOP

<*>=0100
<R>
 **** PS AA XX YY SS
 0100 00 00 00 00 FF
<G>/
 0152 EA NOP
<R>
 **** PS AA XX YY SS
 0152 30 00 00 00 FF
```

Jump Indirect Absolute

```
<K>*=0100
/04
 0100 6C JMP (0150)
 0103 00 BRK
 0104 EA NOP
 0105 EA NOP
<K>*=0150
/04
 0150 77 ???
 0151 03 ???
 0152 EA NOP
 0153 EA NOP
<K>*=0377
/04
 0377 EA NOP
 0378 00 BRK
 0379 EA NOP
 037A EA NOP

<*>=0100
<R>
 **** PS AA XX YY SS
 0100 00 00 00 00 FF
<G>/
 0379 EA NOP
<R>
 **** PS AA XX YY SS
 0379 30 00 00 00 FF
```

```
INC - Increment Memory by One
INX - Increment X Register by One
INY - Increment Y Register by One
DEC - Decrement Memory by One
DEX - Decrement X Register by One
DEY - Decrement Y Register by One
```

The INC and DEC instructions modify the contents of locations in memory and operate in either the Absolute or Zero Page Addressing Mode. They are either 2 or 3 bytes long. The INX, INY, DEX, and DEY instructions modify the X and Y Registers only, are 1 byte long, and operate in the Implied Addressing Mode.

Exp. 7 - INC and DEC Operations

1. Load $AF and $D0 in locations $0200 and $0201 respectively.

2. Key in the following program and run it.

                                    Comments

        $0100 EE INC@   Increment the contents of
            1 00   location $0200
            2 02
            3 CE DEC@   Decrement the contents of
            4 01   location $0201
            5 02
            6 00   Return to Monitor
        $0107 EA   No Operation

3. What are the contents of locations $0200 and $0201?
    Answer: $B0, CF

4. Run the program again starting from location $0100. What are the new contents of locations $0200 and $0201? Answer: $B1, CE

5. Binary Solution:

   INC

	Hex
1010 1111	$AF
+ 0000 0001	+ 01
1011 0000	B0

   DEC

	Hex		
1101 0000	$D0	0000 0001 = 1	
+ 1111 1111	- 01	1111 1110 = $\overline{1}$ (one's	
1100 1111	CF	+ 1	complement)
		1111 1111 = -1	

5. AIM Printout:

```
<K>*=0100
/04
 0100 EE INC 0200
 0103 CE DEC 0201
 0106 00 BRK
 0107 EA NOP

<M>=0200 AF D0 00 00
<*>=0100
<G>/
 0107 EA NOP
<M>=0200 B0 CF 00 00
<*>=0100
<G>/
 0107 EA NOP
<M>=0200 B1 CE 00 00
```

INSTRUCTION MNEMONIC ENTRY MODE

In the AIM 65, there are two primary ways of entering a machine language program into memory. The first uses the Monitor <M> and </> Commands to enter the various hexadecimal op-codes into specified memory locations. The second method involves the Instruction Mnemonic Entry Mode and employs the <I> Command. This is by far the preferred choice since it is much easier to remember and correlate instruction mnemonics than hexadecimal op-codes. Furthermore, the relative address offsets (used in Branch instructions) are computed by the Mnemonic Assembler from a simple entry of the destination location in the branch instruction (still 2-bytes long). Before program execution, however, the assembler must be exited by using the ESC key whereby the Monitor is automatically re-entered.

Two other Monitor Commands which are very useful in program development are the <R> and <K> Commands. The <R> Command is used to display the current contents of the six Internal Registers of the 6502 while the <K> Command is used to disassemble op-codes in memory for display/printout in Mnemonic format. For these tutorial reasons, instruction mnemonics rather than hexadecimal op-codes will be used from this point forward to demonstrate the various machine-language programs.

```
┌─────────────────────────────────────────┐
│ AND - AND Memory with Accumulator        │
│ ORA - OR Memory with Accumulator         │
│ EOR - Exclusive-OR Memory with           │
│             Accumulator                  │
└─────────────────────────────────────────┘
```

The AND, ORA, and EOR instructions perform logical operations on the current contents of the accumulator and the contents of the memory location accessed. The result is stored in the accumulator. Put another way, they modify the contents of the accumulator by using the contents of a memory location. They operate in the Immediate, Zero Page, Absolute, and Indirect Addressing Modes. The outcome of their individual operations is as follows:

The result of an AND operation = 1 only if both bits = 1.

The result of an ORA operation = 0 only if both bits = 0.

The result of an EOR operation = 0 only if both bits = SAME

[Contents]			Result [in Accumulator]		
Memory	Accumulator		AND	ORA	EOR
1	1		1	1	0
1	0	⟹	0	1	1
0	1		0	1	1
0	0		0	0	0

Using the AND, ORA, and EOR instructions with a suitable
bit MASK, one or more bits can be cleared, set or complemented.

1. Clearing a Bit to 0 with AND

```
          1100 1010
      AND 0111 1111    <-- MASK
          0100 1010
```

2. Setting a Bit to 1 with ORA

```
          1001 1010
      ORA 0100 0000    <-- MASK
          1101 1010
```

3. Complementing (Toggling) a Bit with EOR

```
          1010 0011
      EOR 0010 0000    <-- MASK
          1000 0011
      EOR 0010 0000    <-- MASK
          1010 0011
      EOR 0010 0000    <-- MASK
          1000 0011
```


AND - clears bits

ORA - sets bits

EOR - complements (toggles) bits

Exp. 8 - AND, ORA, EOR Operations

1. Store $AA, BB, CC and 44 in locations $0200-0203.

2. Key in the following program.

Comments

$0300	LDA	$0200	Load A with the contents of $0200
3	AND	$0203	AND A with contents of $0203
6	STA	$0200	Store the result in $0200
9	LDA	$0201	Load A with contents of $0201
C	ORA	$0203	OR A with contents of $0203
F	STA	$0201	Store result in $0201
$0312	LDA	$0202	Load A with contents of $0202
5	EOR	$0203	XOR A with contents of $0203
8	STA	$0202	Store result in $0202
B	BRK		Return to Monitor
$031C	NOP		No Operation

3. Run the program beginning from location $0300.

4. What are the new contents of $0200-0203?
   Answer: $00, FF, 88, 44.

5. Run the program again beginning at $0300.   What are
   the contents of locations $0200-0203 now?
   Answer: $00, FF, CC, 44.

6. AIM Printout.

```
<M>=0200 AA BB CC 44        <K>*=0300
<*>=0300                    /11
<G>/                         0300 AD LDA 0200
 031C EA NOP                 0303 2D AND 0203
<M>=0200 00 FF 88 44         0306 8D STA 0200
<*>=0300                     0309 AD LDA 0201
<G>/                         030C 0D ORA 0203
 031C EA NOP                 030F 8D STA 0201
<M>=0200 00 FF CC 44         0312 AD LDA 0202
                             0315 4D EOR 0203
                             0318 8D STA 0202
                             031B 00 BRK
                             031C EA NOP
```

```
CLC - Clear Carry Flag
SEC - Set Carry Flag
```

The CLC and SEC instructions respectively clear (=0) and set (=1) the Carry Flag (C) in the Processor Status (P) Register. The clearing and setting of this flag is an important step when doing binary or decimal (BCD) addition and subtraction. It can be thought of as a flag bit distinct from the accumulator itself but directly affected by accumulator operations as though it were a Ninth Bit in the accumulator. CLC and SEC are both one-byte instructions operating in the Implied Addressing Mode.

```
CLD - Clear Decimal Mode
SED - Set Decimal Mode
```

CLD and SED are one-byte instructions which also operate in the Implied Addressing Mode and respectively clear (=0) and set (=1) the Decimal Flag (D) in the Processor Status Register. Setting the Decimal Mode (SED) allows the 6502 to carry out arithmetic operations on binary-coded-decimal (BCD) data and store/display the results in BCD format. Otherwise, all operations are carried out in straight binary format. For example, in the Binary Mode (D=0), 15_{10} = 0000 1111 whereas in the Decimal Mode (D=1), 15_{10} = 0001 0101.

```
┌─────────────────────────────────────────┐
│   ADC - Add to Accumulator with Carry    │
│   SBC - Subtract from Accumulator        │
│                with Borrow               │
└─────────────────────────────────────────┘
```

The ADC instruction adds the value of memory and the carry flag from the previous operation to the contents of the accumulator and stores the result in the accumulator. If the result of a binary add exceeds 255 or a decimal add exceeds 99, the carry flag is set (=1) otherwise it is cleared (=0). If the result contains a 1 in the Bit #7 position, the negative flag (N) is set (=1) otherwise it is cleared (=0). If the result is zero, the zero flag (Z) is set otherwise it is not. If the result exceeds +127 or -128, the overflow flag (V) is set.

SBC subtracts the value of memory and borrow from the value of the accumulator using two's complement arithmetic and stores the result in the accumulator. Borrow is defined as carry complemented (C). The carry flag is set (borrow cleared) if the result $\geq$ 0. The carry flag is cleared (borrow set) if the result < 0. The N, Z, and V flags operate in the same manner as with ADC.

Prior to first using an ADC instruction, the carry flag should be cleared (CLC) to indicate a no-carry condition. Similarly, before using the SBC instruction, the carry flag should be set (SEC) to indicate a <u>no-borrow condition</u>.

* Clear the carry flag (CLC) prior to add (ADC)
* Set the carry flag (SEC) prior to subtract (SBC)

CLV - Clear Overflow Flag

The Overflow Flag (V) is set (=1) if the addition (ADC) or subtraction (SBC) of two <u>signed</u> binary numbers produces a result (in the Accumulator) which is > +127 or < -128. It can be reset (=0) by the one-byte long CLV instruction. It is also automatically reset (=0) at the beginning of the next ADC or SBC instruction.

<u>Exp. 9</u> - Addition of two Binary Numbers

GOAL: Add the contents of location $0203 to locations $0200-0202 and store the results in $0100-0102.

1. Load $05, 06, 07, and 04 into locations $0200-0203.

$0200	0201	0202	0203
$05	06	07	04

2. Key in the following program beginning at $0300.

Comments

```
$0300  CLC           Clear the carry flag
    1  CLD           Clear the decimal mode
    2  LDA $0200     Load A with the contents of $0200
    5  ADC $0203     Add the contents of $0203
    8  STA $0100     Store the result in $0100
```

```
      B  LDA $0201    Load A with the contents of $0201
      E  ADC $0203    Add the contents of $0203
$0311  STA $0101    Store the result in $0101
      4  LDA $0202    Load A with the contents of $0202
      7  ADC $0203    Add the contents of $0203
      A  STA $0102    Store the result in $0102
      D  BRK          Return to Monitor
$031E  NOP          No operation
```

3. Run the program.

4. Examine the contents of locations $0100, 0101, 0102. What are they? Answer: $09, 0A, 0B.

5. Replace the CLD instruction in location $0301 with the SED instruction.

6. Repeat steps 1 and 3 again and examine the contents of $0100-0102. What are they? Answer: $09, 10, 11.

7. Why is the CLC instruction included in both programs? Answer: To indicate an initial <u>no-carry</u> condition.

8. AIM Printout.

<u>Binary Addition</u>   <u>Decimal Addition</u>

```
<M>=0200 05 06 07 04        <M>=0200 05 06 07 04
<*>=0300                    <*>=0300
<G>/                        <G>/
 031E EA NOP                 031E EA NOP
<M>=0100 09 0A 0B 00        <M>=0100 09 10 11 00

<K>*=0300                   <K>*=0300
/13                         /13
 0300 18 CLC                 0300 18 CLC
 0301 D8 CLD                 0301 F8 SED
 0302 AD LDA 0200            0302 AD LDA 0200
 0305 6D ADC 0203            0305 6D ADC 0203
 0308 8D STA 0100            0308 8D STA 0100
 030B AD LDA 0201            030B AD LDA 0201
 030E 6D ADC 0203            030E 6D ADC 0203
 0311 8D STA 0101            0311 8D STA 0101
 0314 AD LDA 0202            0314 AD LDA 0202
 0317 6D ADC 0203            0317 6D ADC 0203
 031A 8D STA 0102            031A 8D STA 0102
 031D 00 BRK                 031D 00 BRK
 031E EA NOP                 031E EA NOP
```

Exp. 10 - Subtraction of 2 Binary Numbers

GOAL: Subtract $81 from $E9 twice. $E9 is stored in
     location $0300, $81 in location $0301 and the
     results in locations $0302, 0303.

1. Load $E9 and $81 into locations $0300 and $0301.

    (XX = doesn't matter) $0300 0301 0302 0303
                                   $E9   81   XX   XX

2. Key in the following program beginning at $0200.

                                    Comments

    $0200 CLD   Clear the decimal mode
       1   SEC   Set the carry flag
       2   LDA $0300   Load A with the contents of $0300
       5   SBC $0301   Subtract the contents of $0301
       8   STA $0302   Store the result in $0302
       B   SBC $0301   Subtract contents of $0301 again
       E   STA $0303   Store the result in $0303
    $0211 BRK   Return to Monitor
    $0212 NOP   No operation

3. Run the program from $0200.

4. What are the contents of $0302, 0303?
    Answer: $68, E7.

5. What is the value of the carry flag? Answer: 0.

6. Binary Solution.

                          Hex
            1110 1001 $E9   81 = 1000 0001
    [C]   + 0111 1111   - 81
     →1   0110 1000   68 $\overline{81}$ = 0111 1110
          + 0111 1111   - 81   + 1
     →0   1110 0111   E7 $\overline{81}$ + 1 = -81 = $\overline{0111\ 1111}$

          ──── Carry Flag = set (borrow flag = cleared), result = +

         ──── Carry flag = cleared (borrow flag = set), result = -

Exp. 11 - Subtraction of 2 Numbers in the Decimal Mode

GOAL: Subtract 81 from 89 twice. 89 and 81 are stored in
      locations $0030, 0301 and the first and second
      results of the successive subtractions are stored
      in locations $0302, 0303.

1. Load 89 and 81 into locations $0300 and $0301.

    (XX) = doesn't matter $0300   0301   0302   0303
                                 89   81   XX   XX

2. Key in the following program beginning at $0200.

                              Comments

    $0200   SED   Set the decimal mode
        1   SEC   Set the carry flag (Clear borrow)
        2   LDA $0300   Load A with the contents of $0300
        5   SBC $0301   Subtract the contents of $0301
        8   STA $0302   Store the result in $0302
        B   SBC $0301   Subtract contents of $0301 again
        E   STA $0303   Store the result in $0303
    $0211   BRK   Return to Monitor
    $0212   NOP   No operation

3. Run the program starting from location $0200.

4. What are the contents of locations $0302, 0303?
    Answer: 08, 27.

5. What is the state of the Carry Flag? Answer: 0.

6. When performing BCD subtraction, a negative result is
    indicated by a cleared (=0) Carry Flag (set Borrow
    Flag). This is similar to Binary subtraction except
    that the answer is in ten's complement form not in
    two's complement form. In order to convert the result
    of the second subtraction (27) into a meaningful
    (positive) number with a (separate) negative sign, it
    must be ten's complemented.

$$\overline{27}_{10} = 27-100 = -73$$

7. AIM Printout.

Binary Subtraction

```
<M>=0300 E9 81 00 00
<*>=0200
<G>/
 0212 EA NOP
<M>=0300 E9 81 68 E7

<K>*=0200
/09
 0200 D8 CLD
 0201 38 SEC
 0202 AD LDA 0300
 0205 ED SBC 0301
 0208 8D STA 0302
 020B ED SBC 0301
 020E 8D STA 0303
 0211 00 BRK
 0212 EA NOP
```

Decimal Subtraction

```
<M>=0300 89 81 00 00
<*>=0200
<G>/
 0212 EA NOP
<M>=0300 89 81 08 27

<K>*=0200
/09
 0200 F8 SED
 0201 38 SEC
 0202 AD LDA 0300
 0205 ED SBC 0301
 0208 8D STA 0302
 020B ED SBC 0301
 020E 8D STA 0303
 0211 00 BRK
 0212 EA NOP
```

```
BCC - Branch on Carry Clear (C = 0)
BCS - Branch on Carry Set (C = 1)
BEQ - Branch on Result Zero (Z = 1)
BNE - Branch on Result not Zero (Z = 1)
BMI - Branch on Negative Result (N = 1)
BPL - Branch on Positive Result (N = 0)
BVC - Branch on Overflow Clear (V = 0)
BVS - Branch on Overflow Set (V = 1)
```

Each branch instruction (BCC...) interrogates (tests) a specific bit (C, Z, N, V) in the Processor Status (P) Register. Depending upon the state (0 or 1) of the bit, a branch to another instruction may occur. If no branch occurs, the program continues along as if the branch instruction weren´t there. Branch instructions employ the Relative Addressing Mode which means that the destination location of the branch is relative to the location following the branch instruction. It can be forwards or backwards from that point by a maximum of +127 ($7F) or -128 ($80) locations and may cross a page boundary (Ex. --> going from location $02FF to location $0300 crosses the Page 2->3 boundary). All branch instructions are two bytes long; the first byte representing the instruction and the second byte the relative displacement. In most assemblers, including the primitive AIM instruction mnemonic entry mode, this relative displacement is computed from the 16-bit destination address entry following the branch instruction.

```
CMP - Compare Memory and Accumulator
CPX - Compare Memory and X Register
CPY - Compare Memory and Y Register
```

The CMP, CPX, and CPY instructions compare the contents of memory locations to the current contents of the Accumulator (A), X-Register (X) and Y-Register (Y), respectively to determine if the difference between the two is positive, negative or zero. The specified contents of a particular memory location are subtracted from the current contents of A, X, or Y. No memory locations are altered and only the Processor Status (P) Register is changed. The Z flag (of the P register) is set (=1) by an equality, otherwise it is reset (=0). The N flag is set (=1) and reset (=0) by the status of the sign bit (Bit No. 7) while the Carry flag is set/reset if the contents of the accessed memory location are less/greater than the current contents of the register (A, X, Y) under examination. These comparison instructions are almost always used in conjunction with branch instructions and operate in the Absolute, Zero Page and Immediate Addressing Modes. Depending upon the results of the comparison, a branch to another part of the program can be taken.

Exp. 12 - Branch and Comparison Operations

GOAL: Branch to different routines depending upon the
      value of the number written to location $0200 being
      equal to, greater, or less than $75. If = $75,
      store in location $0201. If > $75, store in $0202.
      If < $75, store in location $0203.

1. Load $75 in location $0200 and $00 in $0201-0203.

                          $0200   0201   0202   0203
                           $75   00   00   00

2. Key in the following program.

                              Comments

        $0300 CLC   Clear the carry flag
            1 LDA $0200   Load A with the contents of $0200
            4 CMP #75   Compare $75 with the contents of A
            6 BEQ $030C   If equal (i.e. Z=1) go to $030C
            8 BCS $0311   If greater (i.e. C=1) go to $0311
            A BCC $0316   If less (i.e. C=0) go to $0316
            C STA $0201   Store equal result in $0201
            F BRK   Return to Monitor
        $0310 NOP
            1 STA $0202   Store greater result in $0202
            4 BRK   Return to Monitor
            5 NOP
            6 STA $0203   Store lesser result in $0203
            9 BRK   Return to Monitor
        $031A NOP   No operation

3. Run the program. What does the display read?
    Answer: < 0310 EA NOP.

4. What are the contents of locations $0200-0203?
    Answer: $75, 75, 00, 00.

5. Run the program again after loading $74, 00, 00, 00
    in locations $0200-0203.

6. What are the new contents of $0200-0203?
   Answer: $74, 00, 00, 74.

7. Run program again <u>after</u> loading $76, 00, 00, 00 in
   locations $0200-02<u>03.</u>

8. What are the new contents of $0200-0203?
   Answer: $76, 00, 76, 00.

9. AIM Printout.

```
<M>=0200 75 00 00 00
<*>=0300
<G>/
 0310 EA NOP
<M>=0200 75 75 00 00
</> 0200 74 00 00 00
<*>=0300
<G>/
 031A EA NOP
<M>=0200 74 00 00 74
</> 0200 76 00 00 00
<*>=0300
<G>/
 0315 EA NOP
<M>=0200 76 00 76 00

<K>*=0300
/15
 0300 18 CLC
 0301 AD LDA 0200
 0304 C9 CMP #75
 0306 F0 BEQ 030C
 0308 B0 BCS 0311
 030A 90 BCC 0316
 030C 8D STA 0201
 030F 00 BRK
 0310 EA NOP
 0311 8D STA 0202
 0314 00 BRK
 0315 EA NOP
 0316 8D STA 0203
 0319 00 BRK
 031A EA NOP
```

> PROGRAMMED TIME DELAYS

One very important use of Branch instructions is the generation of time delays. These routines are important in those cases where a very fast computer has to communicate with a relatively slow I/O device (keyboards, printers, plotters...). Branch instructions are also useful in generating infinite time-delays more commonly known as idling loops. These are employed in those cases where the microprocessor/microcomputer is waiting for a specific interrupt. Since every instruction in a microprocessor takes a known number of clock cycles (a clock cycle being equal to 1 microsecond in the AIM 65), repeating these instructions a specified number of times will produce a specific programmed time-delay. This is illustrated in the sample program below which contains three nested time-delaying counting loops.

Exp. 13 - Programmed Time Delay

GOAL: This short program illustrates the use of timing loops for outputting an ASCII "A" ($41) to the printer of the AIM 65. The number of printouts is contained in location $0000. The Accumulator-Printout routine is located at $E97A while location $0001 is used for temporary storage.

1. Load $07 into location $0000.

2. Key in the following program.

Comments

```
$0200   LDY #04      Initialize Y-counter to $04
    2   STY $01      Store in location $0000
$0204   LDX #FF      Initialize X-counter to $FF
$0206   DEX          Decrement X-counter
    7   BNE $0206    If not = 0, go to $0206
    9   DEC $01      Decrement contents of $0001
    B   BNE $0204    If not = 0, go to $0204
    D   DEY          Decrement Y-counter
    E   BNE $0204    If not = 0, go to $0204
$0210   LDA #41      Load A with ASCII code for "A"
    2   JSR $E97A    Jump to Monitor printout routine
    5   DEC $00      Decrement print counter
    7   BNE $0200    Repeat entire process
    9   BRK          Return to Monitor
$021A   NOP          No operation
```

3. Run the program and note the rate of display and printout

4. Change the contents of location $0201 to $02 and note the display rate. (Don´t forget to reload location $0000 with $07.

5. Change the contents of $0201 to $0A and the contents of $0000 to $14, run program, and note display rate.

6. AIM Printout.

```
<M>=0000 14 00 00 00
<*>=0200
<G>/
AAAAAAAAAAAAAAAAAAAA
 021A EA NOP
```

```
<K>*=0200
/15
0200 A0 LDY #0A
0202 84 STY 01
0204 A2 LDX #FF
0206 CA DEX
0207 D0 BNE 0206
0209 C6 DEC 01
020B D0 BNE 0204
020D 88 DEY
020E D0 BNE 0204
0210 A9 LDA #41
0212 20 JSR E97A
0215 C6 DEC 00
0217 D0 BNE 0200
0219 00 BRK
021A EA NOP
```

BIT - Test Bits in Memory with Accumulator

The BIT instruction performs a logical AND between the contents of the accumulator and a memory location but does not store the result into the accumulator. Only the Processor Status (P) Register is affected. Bits #7 and #6 of the memory location tested are transferred to the corresponding locations in the P register. If the AND operation produces a zero, the Z flag is set (=1) otherwise it is cleared (=0). When used with a MASK, it is a very useful tool for testing the condition (0 or 1) of a particular bit in a memory location.

Exp. 14 - Bit Test

GOAL: Test Bit #2 in memory location $0000. If it is set (=1), store the contents in location $0001, otherwise store $00 in location $0001.

1. Load $AB into location $0000.

2. Key in the following program.

```
                              Comments                    #2 Bit
                                                             ↓
$0200   LDA #04      Load the bit mask, $04 = 0000 0100
    2   BIT $00      Test location $0000
    4   BNE $020C    If #2 bit is set (=1), go to $020C
    6   LDA #00      If #2 bit is not set, store $00 in
    8   STA $01       location $0001
    A   BRK          Return to Monitor
    B   NOP
    C   LDA $00      Store contents of $0000
    E   STA $01       into $0001
$0210   BRK          Return to Monitor
$0211   NOP          No operation
```

3. Run the program.

4. What are the contents of $0000 and $0001?
   Answer: $AB, 00.

5. Store $AC into $0000 and run the program again

6. What are the contents of $0000 and $0001?
   Answer: $AC, AC.

7. AIM Printout.

```
<M>=0000 AB FF FF FF
<*>=0200
<G>/
 020B EA NOP
<M>=0000 AB 00 FF FF
</> 0000 AC FF FF FF
<*>=0200
<G>/
 0211 EA NOP
<M>=0000 AC AC FF FF

<K>*=0200
/11
 0200 A9 LDA #04
 0202 24 BIT 00
 0204 D0 BNE 020C
 0206 A9 LDA #00
 0208 85 STA 01
 020A 00 BRK
 020B EA NOP
 020C A5 LDA 00
 020E 85 STA 01
 0210 00 BRK
 0211 EA NOP
```

```
ASL - Arithmetic Shift Left
LSR - Logical Shift Right
ROL - Rotate Left
ROR - Rotate Right
```

ASL: Arithmetic Shift Left

Here every bit in either the Accumulator (A) or the memory location accessed is shifted 1 bit to the left with Bit #7 shifted into the Carry Flag (C) and a 0 shifted into Bit #0.

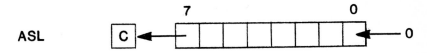

LSR: Logical Shift Right

Every bit in either the Accumulator (A) or the memory location accessed is shifted 1 bit to the right with Bit #0 shifted into the Carry Flag (C) and a 0 shifted into Bit #7.

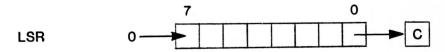

ROL: Rotate Left

Every bit in either the Accumulator (A) or the memory location accessed is shifted 1 bit to the left (as with ASL) with Bit #7 shifted into the Carry Flag (C) and the Carry Flag (C) shifted into Bit #0.

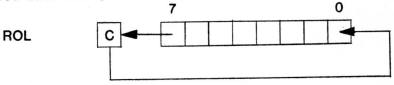

ROR: Rotate Right

Every bit in either the Accumulator (A) or the memory location accessed is shifted 1 bit to the right (as with LSR) with Bit #0 shifted into the Carry Flag (C) and the Carry Flag (C) shifted into Bit #7.

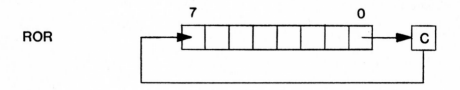

The Register-Shift instructions (ASL, LSR, ROL, ROR) operate in the Absolute, Zero Page and Accumulator Addressing Modes. Since they change the contents of the Accumulator or a specified memory location without affecting any internal registers, they are called read-modify-write instructions. They are also the only instructions which operate in the Accumulator Addressing Mode, a mode of addressing which affects only one register - the Accumulator. They are particularly useful in Multiplication/Division schemes as well as in Number Conversion Routines (viz. ASCII Hex-> Binary, Binary-> ASCII Decimal, serial-> parallel, parallel-> serial..). This is demonstrated in Exp. 15 where a 2-digit decimal number is converted into its hexadecimal equivalent.

Exp. 15 - Decimal to Hexadecimal Conversion

GOAL: A two-digit decimal (base 10) number entered in
location $0000 is converted to a hexadecimal (base
16) number stored in location $0001.

Comments

```
$0200   CLD          Clear decimal mode
   1    LDA $00      Get decimal number from location $0000
   3    TAY          Save A temporarily in Y-register
   4    AND #0F      Mask out higher-order-nibble (HON) and
   6    STA $01      Store lower-order-nibble (LON) in $0001
   8    TYA          Restore decimal number from Y-register
   9    AND #F0      Mask out LON and
   B    LSR A        Divide HON by 2
   C    STA $02      Store result temporarily in $0002
   E    LSR A        Divide HON by 4
   F    LSR A        Divide HON by 8
$0210   CLC          Clear the carry flag for addition
   1    ADC $02      Add HON/8 to HON/2 and
   3    ADC $01      Add result to LON in location $0001
   5    STA $01      Then store overall result in $0001
   7    BRK          Return to Monitor
$0218   NOP          No operation
```

Example

If 42_{10} is input to the computer, it is read as
$\$42 = 42_{16} \cong 4 \bullet 16 + 2 \bullet 1$. What is needed is to divide
the higher order nibble ($4) by 16 and multiply by $A(10).
The result is then added to the lower order nibble ($2) to
complete the conversion.

$$
\begin{aligned}
42_{10} &= 4 \bullet 10 + 2 \bullet 1 \\
&= 4 \bullet \$A + 2 \bullet \$1 \\
&= (4 \bullet 16)\$A/16 + 2 \bullet \$1 \\
&= (4 \bullet 16)(\$8 + \$2)/16 + 2 \bullet \$1 \\
&= (4 \bullet 16)(1/2 + 1/8) + 2 \bullet \$1 \\
&= 2 \bullet 16 + 4 \bullet 2 + 2 \bullet 1 \\
&= \$20 + \$08 + \$02 \\
&= \$2A
\end{aligned}
$$

Note: Multiplication by $A/16 or 10/16 is equivalent to
multiplication by (1/2 + 1/8).

INDEXED ADDRESSING

ABSOLUTE INDEXED ADDRESSING

This is a form of addressing whereby the effective address is computed (or indexed) by adding the contents of the X (or Y) Registers to the absolute address. It may be used with either the X (Absolute, X) or Y (Absolute, Y) Registers. If a page boundary is crossed, the Carry Flag is set (viz. going from location $02FF to $0300 will set the Carry Flag). The contents of the X or Y Registers are not affected by the use of this mode of addressing.

ZERO PAGE INDEXED ADDRESSING

This form of addressing is analogous to Absolute Indexed Addressing in that the contents of the X Register are added to a Zero Page address to determine the effective address (also in Zero Page). Except for the LDX and STX instructions, it can only be used with the X Register. No page crossing is allowed and no carry is generated. If the indexed address exceeds the Page 0 -> 1 boundary, a wrap-around will occur within Page Zero. The Hex value $00 is always forced into the higher order byte (ADH) of the effective address.

Exp. 16 - Absolute Indexed Addressing

GOAL: Fill the entire contents of Page 3 with the value
      contained in location $0000.

1. Load $65 into location $0000.

2. Key in the following program.

                                    Comments

    $0200   LDA $00   Load A with contents of $0000
       2   LDX #00   Initialize X Index to $00
       4   STA $0300,X   Store contents of A in Page 3
       7   INX   Increment X Index
       8   BNE $0204   Branch to $0204 if Page 3 is
                              not filled
       A   BRK   Return to Monitor when done
    $020B   NOP   No operation

3. Run the program and verify that $65 is contained in
    locations $0300-03FF.

4. Load any byte (other than $65) in location $0000 and
    repeat the program. Is it written into Page 3?
    Answer: Yes.

5. Change the instruction in location $0202 to LDX #FF
    and the instruction in $0207 to DEX and repeat steps
    1 and 3 above.

6. Is $65 written into all locations of Page 3?
    Answer: No, location $0300 does not contain $65
    because the loop is exited precisely when X = $00
    and before location $0300 can be written into.

7. AIM Printout.

Absolute Indexed Addressing

①

②

③

```
<M>=0000 65 00 00 00
<*>=0200
<G>/
 020B EA NOP

<M>=0300 65 65 65 65
< > 0304 65 65 65 65
< > 0308 65 65 65 65
< > 030C 65 65 65 65
< > 0310 65 65 65 65
< > 0314 65 65 65 65
< > 0318 65 65 65 65
< > 031C 65 65 65 65
       .  .  .  .  .
<M>=03E0 65 65 65 65
< > 03E4 65 65 65 65
< > 03E8 65 65 65 65
< > 03EC 65 65 65 65
< > 03F0 65 65 65 65
< > 03F4 65 65 65 65
< > 03F8 65 65 65 65
< > 03FC 65 65 65 65

<K>*=0200
/07
 0200 A5 LDA 00
 0202 A2 LDX #00
 0204 9D STA 0300,X
 0207 E8 INX
 0208 D0 BNE 0204
 020A 00 BRK
 020B EA NOP
```

```
<M>=0000 65 00 00 00
</> 0000 A4 00 00 00
<*>=0200
<G>/
 020B EA NOP

<M>=0300 A4 A4 A4 A4
< > 0304 A4 A4 A4 A4
< > 0308 A4 A4 A4 A4
< > 030C A4 A4 A4 A4
< > 0310 A4 A4 A4 A4
< > 0314 A4 A4 A4 A4
< > 0318 A4 A4 A4 A4
< > 031C A4 A4 A4 A4
       .  .  .  .  .
<M>=03E0 A4 A4 A4 A4
< > 03E4 A4 A4 A4 A4
< > 03E8 A4 A4 A4 A4
< > 03EC A4 A4 A4 A4
< > 03F0 A4 A4 A4 A4
< > 03F4 A4 A4 A4 A4
< > 03F8 A4 A4 A4 A4
< > 03FC A4 A4 A4 A4

<K>*=0200
/07
 0200 A5 LDA 00
 0202 A2 LDX #00
 0204 9D STA 0300,X
 0207 E8 INX
 0208 D0 BNE 0204
 020A 00 BRK
 020B EA NOP
```

```
<M>=0000 A4 00 00 00
</> 0000 65 00 00 00
<*>=0200
<G>/
 020B EA NOP

<M>=0300 A4 65 65 65
< > 0304 65 65 65 65
< > 0308 65 65 65 65
< > 030C 65 65 65 65
< > 0310 65 65 65 65
< > 0314 65 65 65 65
< > 0318 65 65 65 65
< > 031C 65 65 65 65
       .  .  .  .  .
<M>=03E0 65 65 65 65
< > 03E4 65 65 65 65
< > 03E8 65 65 65 65
< > 03EC 65 65 65 65
< > 03F0 65 65 65 65
< > 03F4 65 65 65 65
< > 03F8 65 65 65 65
< > 03FC 65 65 65 65

<K>*=0200
/07
 0200 A5 LDA 00
 0202 A2 LDX #FF
 0204 9D STA 0300,X
 0207 CA DEX
 0208 D0 BNE 0204
 020A 00 BRK
 020B EA NOP
```

Exp. 17 - Zero Page Indexed Addressing

GOAL: Load Page Zero with $00, 01, 02, 03 . . . . $FF.

1. Key in the following program.

                                    Comments

```
$0300   LDY #00        Initialize Y Index to $00
    2   LDX #00        Initialize X Index to $00
    4   STX $00,Y      Store X value in Page Zero
    6   INX            Increment X Index
    7   INY            Increment Y Index
    8   BNE $0304      Branch to $0304 for next X value
    A   BRK            Return to Monitor when finished
$030B   NOP            No operation
```

2. Run the program and verify the results.

3. AIM Printout.

```
            <*>=0300
            <G>/
             030B EA NOP

            <M>=0000 00 01 02 03
            < > 0004 04 05 06 07
            < > 0008 08 09 0A 0B
            < > 000C 0C 0D 0E 0F
            < > 0010 10 11 12 13
                   •  •  •  •  •
                   •  •  •  •  •
                   •  •  •  •  •
            <M>=00EC EC ED EE EF
            < > 00F0 F0 F1 F2 F3
            < > 00F4 F4 F5 F6 F7
            < > 00F8 F8 F9 FA FB
            < > 00FC FC FD FE FF

            <K>*=0300
            /08
             0300 A0 LDY #00
             0302 A2 LDX #00
             0304 96 STX 00,Y
             0306 E8 INX
             0307 C8 INY
             0308 D0 BNE 0304
             030A 00 BRK
             030B EA NOP
```

SORTING

Indexed addressing is a particularly valuable technique for sorting data into organized lists. The elements of such lists can be arranged sequentially in memory where each element occupies one (or several) adjacent memory locations. They can be further arranged in either ascending or descending order in memory according to (among other things) their values.

In the assembly language program of Exp. 18, the algorithm used for the sorting routine compares the first element of an 8-element table in locations $0300-$0307 with each successive element. If its value is greater than any of these, the addresses of each are switched (in the SWITCH routine). The new element is then compared to the remaining 7 elements and this process of comparing and switching addresses is repeated until the element having the smallest value occupies the first position. In subsequent passes the remaining elements are likewise examined and arranged until the entire table of values is arranged in ascending order.

Figuratively speaking, the smallest element "bubbles" to the top of the array- hence the name bubble-sort for this popular routine. Simple modifications allow its extension to an N-element array of values arranged in either ascending or descending order. As described in Fig. 4-5, 7-passes are needed to sort this particular 8-element array.   On average, N/2 passes

are needed to sort an N-element array.

```
$FF FA 89 45 78 01 09 12    ⎫
 FA FF 89 45 78 01 09 12    ⎪
 89 FF FA 45 78 01 09 12    ⎬  Pass 1
 45 FF FA 89 78 01 09 12    ⎪
 01 FF FA 89 78 45 09 12    ⎭

$01 FA FF 89 78 45 09 12    ⎫
 01 89 FF FA 78 45 09 12    ⎪
 01 78 FF FA 89 45 09 12    ⎬  Pass 2
 01 45 FF FA 89 78 09 12    ⎪
 01 09 FF FA 89 78 45 12    ⎭

$01 09 FA FF 89 78 45 12    ⎫
 01 09 89 FF FA 78 45 12    ⎪
 01 09 78 FF FA 89 45 12    ⎬  Pass 3
 01 09 45 FF FA 89 78 12    ⎪
 01 09 12 FF FA 89 78 45    ⎭

$01 09 12 FA FF 89 78 45    ⎫
 01 09 12 89 FF FA 78 45    ⎬  Pass 4
 01 09 12 78 FF FA 89 45    ⎪
 01 09 12 45 FF FA 89 78    ⎭

$01 09 12 45 FA FF 89 78    ⎫
 01 09 12 45 89 FF FA 78    ⎬  Pass 5
 01 09 12 45 78 FF FA 89    ⎭

$01 09 12 45 78 FA FF 89    ⎫  Pass 6
 01 09 12 45 78 89 FF FA    ⎭

$01 09 12 45 78 89 FA FF    ─  Pass 7
```

Fig. 4-5.   Bubble-Sort of 8-Elements into Ascending Order.

Exp. 18 - Use of Indexed Addressing in Sorting Elements

GOAL: Sort a random array of 8 unsigned binary numbers in
memory locations $0300-0307 into ascending order.
Location $0000 is used for temporary storage.

1. Load the eight binary numbers $FF, FA, 89, 45, 78, 01,
09 and $12 into locations $0300-0307.

2. Key in the following program.

			Comments
START	$0200	CLD	Clear the decimal mode
	1	CLC	Clear the carry flag
	2	LDY #00	Initialize Y counter to $00
	4	TYA	
	5	TAX	Initialize X counter to $00
TABLE	$0206	LDA $0300,Y	Load A with first element
	9	CMP $0301,X	Compare to second element
	C	BCS $0216	If greater, go to SWITCH
	E	INX	Increment X counter
	F	CPX #07	Finished with 8 comparisons?
	$0211	BEQ $022A	If yes, go to NXTEL
	3	JMP $0206	If no, go to TABLE
SWITCH	$0216	LDA $0301,X	Load A with second element
	9	STA $00	Store temporarily in $0000
	B	LDA $0300,Y	Move first element --->
	E	STA $0301,X	---> to second position
	$0221	LDA $00	Load A with second element
	3	STA $0300,Y	and store in first position
	6	CLC	Reset carry flag (=0)
	7	JMP $020E	Go to next element in table
NXTEL	$022A	INY	Increment Y counter
	B	CPY #07	Finished with 8 elements?
	D	BEQ $0232	If yes, return to Monitor
	F	JMP $0204	If no, resume comparisons
	$0232	BRK	Return to Monitor
END	$0233	NOP	No operation

3. Run the program.

4. Verify that the contents of locations $0300-0307 are arranged in ascending order.

5. Change the CLC instructions in $0201 and $0226 to SEC and the instruction in $020C to BCC $0216.

6. Run the program again.

7. How are the contents of $0300-0307 changed?
    Answer: They are now arranged in <u>descending</u> order.

8. Change the instructions in $020F and $022B to CPX #FF and CPY #FF respectively.

9. Run the program again and verify that the <u>entire</u> contents of Page 3 (256 bytes) are arranged in descending order in memory.

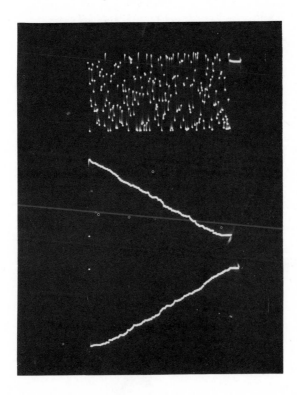

Fig. 4-6. Oscilloscope Traces of the Initially Random (top) Contents of Page 3 Arranged into Descending (middle) and Ascending (bottom) Order in Memory.

114

10. AIM Printout.

Ascending Order

Descending Order

```
<M>=0300 FF FA 89 45
< > 0304 78 01 09 12
<*>=0200
<G>/
 0233 EA NOP
<M>=0300 01 09 12 45
< > 0304 78 89 FA FF

<K>*=0200
/26
 0200 D8 CLD
 0201 18 CLC
 0202 A0 LDY #00
 0204 98 TYA
 0205 AA TAX
 0206 B9 LDA 0300,Y
 0209 DD CMP 0301,X
 020C B0 BCS 0216
 020E E8 INX
 020F E0 CPX #07
 0211 F0 BEQ 022A
 0213 4C JMP 0206
 0216 BD LDA 0301,X
 0219 85 STA 00
 021B B9 LDA 0300,Y
 021E 9D STA 0301,X
 0221 A5 LDA 00
 0223 99 STA 0300,Y
 0226 18 CLC
 0227 4C JMP 020E
 022A C8 INY
 022B C0 CPY #07
 022D F0 BEQ 0232
 022F 4C JMP 0204
 0232 00 BRK
 0233 EA NOP
```

```
<M>=0300 01 09 12 45
< > 0304 78 89 FA FF
<*>=0200
<G>/
 0233 EA NOP
<M>=0300 FF FA 89 78
< > 0304 45 12 09 01

<K>*=0200
/26
 0200 D8 CLD
 0201 38 SEC
 0202 A0 LDY #00
 0204 98 TYA
 0205 AA TAX
 0206 B9 LDA 0300,Y
 0209 DD CMP 0301,X
 020C 90 BCC 0216
 020E E8 INX
 020F E0 CPX #07
 0211 F0 BEQ 022A
 0213 4C JMP 0206
 0216 BD LDA 0301,X
 0219 85 STA 00
 021B B9 LDA 0300,Y
 021E 9D STA 0301,X
 0221 A5 LDA 00
 0223 99 STA 0300,Y
 0226 38 SEC
 0227 4C JMP 020E
 022A C8 INY
 022B C0 CPY #07
 022D F0 BEQ 0232
 022F 4C JMP 0204
 0232 00 BRK
 0233 EA NOP
```

INDIRECT ABSOLUTE ADDRESSING

In this form of addressing, the second and third bytes of an instruction refer to a memory location which contains the low address byte (ADL) of the data. The high address byte (ADH) of the data is contained in the next memory location. Thus, in Indirect Absolute Addressing, the data is not directly accessed but rather the location of the data. The data is indirectly accessed. The only instruction in the 6502 microprocessor which uses this mode of addressing in the JMP instruction.

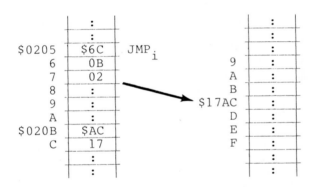

Fig. 4-7.   Jump Indirect Absolute Instruction.

In the short program sequence above, the JMP-(Indirect) instruction, when encountered (as op-code $6C), transfers program control to the address contained in locations $020B and $020C. From that point on program execution proceeds from location $17AC.

INDIRECT INDEXED ADDRESSING

As the name implies, this mode of addressing combines the concepts of indirect addressing and indexed addressing. To obtain the effective address (containing the data), the contents of the Y-Register are added to the two-byte address contained in two consecutive Page Zero locations. It is sometimes referred to as Post-Indexed Indirect Addressing. As an example, the instruction

STA ($9C),Y

stores the current contents of the Accumulator (A) in the memory location contained in Page Zero locations $009C (ADL) and $009D (ADH) indexed by the current contents of the Y-Register (Y). The contents of A would subsequently reside in memory location ADH, ADL+Y. This is a particularly useful mode of addressing for accessing similar elements in different data tables (viz. very useful in background subtraction, ratioing, signal-averaging schemes, moving data tables in memory, ----). It uses the Y-Index Register only. The indexing is performed after the indirect addressing hence the name Post-Indexed Indirect Addressing.

Exp. 19 - Indirect Indexed Addressing

GOAL: Write any 8-bit binary number contained in location
$0000 into two, 256-element data tables starting at
the addresses written into Zero Page locations $01,
$02 and $03, $04.

1. Store $55 into Zero Page location (ZPL) $00.

2. Store $00 into ZPL's $01 and $03.

3. Store $02 and $03 into ZPL's $02 and $04.

4. Key in the following program and run it.

Comments

```
$0100   LDA $00        Load A with the contents of $0000
    2   LDY #00        Initialize Y Index to $00
$0014   STA ($01),Y    Store A indirectly in Page 2
    6   STA ($03),Y    And also in Page 3
    8   INY            Increment Y Index
    9   BEQ $001E      Finished loading Pages 2 and 3?
    B   JMP $0014      If no, repeat for next locations
    E   BRK            If yes, return to Monitor
$001F   NOP            No operation
```

5. Verify that $55 is written into the entire contents
of Pages 2 and 3 of memory.

6. AIM Printout.

```
<M>=0000 55 00 02 00        <K>*=0010
<  > 0004 03 00 00 00       /09
<+>=0010                     0010 A5 LDA 00
<G>/                         0012 A0 LDY #00
 001F EA NOP                 0014 91 STA (01),Y
                             0016 91 STA (03),Y
<M>=0200 55 55 55 55         0018 C8 INY
      .  .  .  .  .          0019 F0 BEQ 001E
      .  .  .  .  .          001B 4C JMP 0014
      .  .  .  .  .          001E 00 BRK
<M>=02FC 55 55 55 55         001F EA NOP
<  > 0300 55 55 55 55
      .  .  .  .  .
      .  .  .  .  .
<M>=03FC 55 55 55 55
```

INDEXED INDIRECT ADDRESSING

In this mode of addressing, the contents of the X-Register (X) are added to a Zero Page address to produce another Zero Page location which containes the ADL of the data. The ADH of the data is contained in the next (X+1) Zero Page location. As an example, the instruction

STA ($9C,X)

stores the current contents of the Accumulator (A) at that address (ADH-ADL) contained in the indexed Page Zero locations $009C+X (ADL) and $009C+X+1 (ADH). It is sometimes called Pre-Indexed Indirect Addressing and uses the X-Index Register only. It is useful in selecting a specific address from an array of addresses located in Page Zero. The indexing is performed before the indirect addressing hence the name Pre-Indexed Indirect Addressing.

Exp. 20 - Indexed Indirect Addressing

GOAL: Write the binary value contained in location $0000 into the entire contents of the (nonzero) page contained in location $0001.

1. Load $66 into location $0000 and $03 into location $0001

2. Key in the following program and run it.

<u>Comments</u>

```
$0200   LDA $01       Load A with contents of $0001
    2   STA $11       Store value[$03] into $0011
    4   LDX #00       Initialize X Index to $00
    6   TXA
    7   TAY           Initialize Y Index to $00
$0028   STY $10       Store contents of Y at $0010
    A   LDA $00       Load A with contents of $0000
    C   STA ($10,X)   Store indirectly into Page 3
    E   INY           Increment Y Index
    F   BNE $0028     Repeat process to fill page
$0031   BRK           Return to Monitor when done
$0032   NOP           No operation
```

3. Verify that Page 3 contains <u>only</u> $66.

4. AIM Printout.

```
<M>=0000 66 03 00 00
<*>=0020
<G>/
 0032 EA NOP

<M>=0300 66 66 66 66
    :    :  :  :  :
<M>=03FC 66 66 66 66
```

```
<K>*=0020
/12
 0020 A5 LDA 01
 0022 85 STA 11
 0024 A2 LDX #00
 0026 8A TXA
 0027 A8 TAY
 0028 84 STY 10
 002A A5 LDA 00
 002C 81 STA (10,X)
 002E C8 INY
 002F D0 BNE 0028
 0031 00 BRK
 0032 EA NOP
```

SUBROUTINES

A subroutine is simply a routine (sub-program) that is part of another routine (main program) and can be called from more than one location (in the main program). The provision for returning control to the main program is included in the subroutine.

JSR - Jump to Subroutine
RTS - Return from Subroutine

The JSR instruction is a 3-byte instruction which transfers program control to a subroutine which begins at the address (ADH, ADL) contained in the second (ADL) and third (ADH) bytes of the instruction. Before the transfer of program control, however, the address of the third byte of the JSR instruction is stored in a special working register called the Stack.

The RTS instruction is a 1-byte instruction which when encountered (usually as the last instruction of a subroutine) transfers program control back to the main program at the instruction following the JSR instruction. It does so by fetching the address of the third byte of JSR from the Stack and loading it into the Program Counter (PC) which is then automatically incremented by one to point at the next instruction following JSR in the main program.

THE STACK

The Stack is a temporary working register comprised of a series of 256, 8-bit wide, volatile R/W memory locations in Page One of memory ($0100-$01FF). It is a push-down Stack which means that it is loaded by starting with the highest Page One location ($01FF) first then extending downward in memory to location $0100. It is unloaded in reverse fashion.

Besides the JSR and RTS instructions (and excepting the TXS and TSX instructions), the following self-evident 1-byte instructions load (push on) and unload (pull from) the Stack and operate in the Implied Addressing Mode.

```
PHA - Push Accumulator on Stack
PLA - Pull Accumulator from Stack
PHP - Push P Register on Stack
PLP - Pull P Register from Stack
TXS - Transfer X Register to Stack Pointer
TSX - Transfer Stack Pointer to X Register
```

The last two instructions (TXS, TSX) do not operate on the Stack but rather on the Stack Pointer (S) which is an 8-bit wide internal register of the 6502 microprocessor. It contains the low-order address byte (ADL) of the next available location in the Stack. As such, it points to the next available Stack location. For an empty Stack its contents are $FF and it is always initialized to this value by a RESET operation.

One important use of the Stack involves the storage of various registers <u>before</u> a subroutine call for use <u>after</u> subroutine execution. For example, if the Accumulator (A) and X-Registers are used in both the main program and a subroutine, they can be easily saved by the following sequences <u>in the main program</u>,

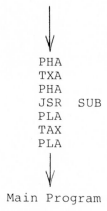

```
        PHA
        TXA
        PHA
        JSR    SUB
        PLA
        TAX
        PLA
```

Main Program

or <u>in the subroutine</u>.

```
SUB    PHA      Start of Subroutine
       TXA
       PHA
        .
        .       } Subroutine Instructions
        .
       PLA
       TAX
       PLA
       RTS      End of Subroutine
```

One useful rule: In most circumstances, every PHA instruction should have a corresponding PLA instruction.

```
┌─────────────────────┐
│     INTERRUPTS      │
└─────────────────────┘
```

Interrupts are <u>external</u> processes which effect an <u>immediate</u>
branch from a programmed routine to another routine (interrupt
routine). When they occur, the 6502 microprocessor completes
the instruction that it was currently executing, saves the
contents of certain important registers (usually on the Stack)
and jumps to the starting address of the interrupt routine.
After the interrupt routine is completed (serviced), the various
registers are restored and a return to the main program is
effected whereupon execution resumes at the first address
following the point of interrupt. In one sense an interrupt
routine can be regarded as an <u>externally generated subroutine</u>.

```
┌──────────────────────────────────────┐
│  IRQ - Interrupt Request             │
│  NMI - Non-Maskable Interrupt        │
│  BRK - Jump to Interrupt Routine     │
│  RES - Reset                         │
└──────────────────────────────────────┘
```

Other than turning the power off, there are four primary
ways of interrupting the 6502 <u>during</u> a program execution. Three
of these (IRQ, NMI, RES) are hardware-type interrupts which are
provided by 3 external pins on the 6502 chip. They allow
external devices (keyboards, timers, switches ...) to exercise
control over the program flow. The third (BRK) is a
software-forced interrupt request.

Interrupt Request (IRQ)

As the name implies, an interrupt is requested of the 6502 when the voltage level on this pin changes from logic 1 to logic 0. When this happens, the following events occur:

(1) If Bit #2 in the P Register (the Interrupt Disable Flag) equals 1, the interrupt request is ignored.

(2) If the Interrupt Disable Flag (I) equals 0, then it is set equal to 1 to prevent further interrupts from occurring until the present one is processed.

(3) The current instruction being executed by the 6502 is completed.

(4) The current value of the Program Counter (PC) is stored (pushed) onto the Stack for later retrieval.

(5) The Processor Status (P) Register is stored (pushed) onto the Stack for later retrieval.

(6) The microprocessor reads the contents of memory locations $FFFE and $FFFF which become the new program counter (PCH-PCL). PCL is contained in $FFFE and PCH is contained in $FFFF and are collectively known as the IRQ Vector.

(7) Program execution continues from PCH-PCL (start of Interrupt Service Routine).

Non Maskable Interrupt (NMI)

A series of similar events occur when an NMI interrupt is encountered. However, there are distinct differences. First, the NMI pin will cause an interrupt on a 1-> 0 voltage transition (⎴⎳). This is commonly called "negative-edge triggering". When this transition occurs, the 6502 is interrupted regardless of the value of the Interrupt Disable

Flag (I) in the P Register. Hence the name Non-Maskable.
Program control is transferred to the NMI Vector contained in
memory locations $FFFA and $FFFB immediately after completion of
the current instruction. An NMI can interrupt an IRQ routine
but not vice-versa.

In the AIM 65 computer, various indirect jumps are used to
relocate the IRQ and NMI Vectors to R/W memory locations

$$\begin{array}{l} \$A402 - PCL \\ \$A403 - PCH \end{array} \Big\} \text{ NMI}$$

$$\begin{array}{l} \$A404 - PCL \\ \$A405 - PCH \end{array} \Big\} \text{ IRQ}$$

Jump to Interrupt Routine (BRK)

A BRK type interrupt is really a software-forced IRQ. In
the absence of external interrupts, an interrupt request routine
can be entered by using the BRK instruction. In the programs
used thus far in the text, it has been used primarily to enter
the Monitor Program whose starting address is pre-loaded into
the IRQ Vector upon power-up or reset. However, it can be used
to enter any IRQ routine provided that the starting address of
the interrupt routine is first written into the IRQ Vector.
Unlike an IRQ-type interrupt however, the main program is
re-entered at the second address following the point of
interrupt (i.e. the second location following the address of the
BRK instruction). This is a consequence of the use of BRK in

merging existing programs where BRK replaces a 2-byte instruction. For this reason, the No Operation instruction (NOP = $EA) is commonly placed after a BRK instruction.

Reset (RES)

A special type of hardware interrupt on the 6502 microprocessor chip is the RES pin which will effect an interrupt when pulled low (i.e. logic 0). It is usually used to initialize the 6502 and certain memory locations upon power-up as well as to re-initialize certain registers during program execution. The RES Vector is contained in memory locations $FFFC and $FFFD which is the starting address of the Reset/Initialization routines. In the AIM 65, the Hex values $BF and $E0 are pre-loaded into these locations which indicate that the Reset routines begin at address $E0BF in ROM space.

```
RTI - Return from Interrupt
```

The RTI instruction, which is usually the last instruction in an IRQ or NMI interrupt routine, enables control to be transferred back to the main program. It does this by pulling the Program Counter (PC) and the Processor Status (P) Registers from the Stack, both of which were placed there when the interrupt occurred. In addition, it clears the Interrupt

Disable (I) Flag (which was set (=1) by the IRQ or NMI
interrupts) in the P Register to allow further interrupts.

```
SEI - Set Interrupt Disable Flag
CLI - Clear Interrupt Disable Flag
```

Besides being set by an IRQ (or NMI) and cleared by an RTI,
the Interrupt Disable Flag (I) can be set by the SEI instruction
and cleared by the CLI instruction. These instructions are
useful in preventing (SEI) certain program segments (or
subroutines) from being interrupted while other routines are
permitted (CLI) to be interrupted.

One important point --> Since many of the same
Registers (A, X, Y, ...) are often used in the Interrupt
Service Routine (really a type of subroutine) as well as in
the Main Program, all the Register-Save instructions (Stack
instructions) must be included in the interrupt routine.
Obviously, it would be pointless to include them in the
main program (as can be done for a subroutine call) since
there would be no way of knowing beforehand when an
interrupt occurs and when to save the Registers.

CHAPTER 5

```
┌─────────────────┐
│  THE 6522 VIA   │
└─────────────────┘
```

* Input/Output

* Timing

* Shifting

* Function Control

* Interrupt Control

Next to the 6502 MPU, the 6522 Versatile Interface Adaptor (VIA) chip is one of the most complex IC´s available. As its name implies, it is truly versatile and can be adapted to a large variety of interfacing situations. It is equipped with sixteen (16) internal, 8-bit wide registers which are located at addresses $A000-$A00F in the AIM 65 computer. In other 6502-based systems, these registers can be (and usually are) located at different sets of 16 locations in the address space of the particular system. For the sake of instruction, we will refer only to those on-board VIA locations in the AIM 65 computer system. Keep in mind, however, that these 16 VIA registers can, within limits, be configured anywhere in the memory of a particular operating system.

The sixteen registers are functionally broken down into five (5) specific operations:

1. Input/Output   — $A000-$A003, $A00F

2. Timing   — $A004-$A009

3. Shifting   — $A00A

4. Function Control   —. $A00B, $A00C

5. Interrupt Control   — $A00D, $A00E

Hardware interfacing to the outside world is accomplished by way of two (2) 8-bit I/O ports (Port A and Port B) and four (4) status/control lines (CA1, CB1, CA2, CB2). CA1 and CA2 are associated with Port A and CB1, CB2 with Port B for a sum total of twenty (20) I/O lines.

Location	Function	Abbreviation
$A000	I/O Port B (PB0 to PB7)	ORB
$A001	I/O Port A (PA0 to PA7)	ORA
$A002	Port B Data Direction Register	DDRB
$A003	Port A Data Direction Register	DDRA
$A004	Timer One Counter Low	T1C-L
$A005	Timer One Counter High	T1C-H
$A006	Timer One Latch Low	T1L-L
$A007	Timer One Latch High	T1L-H
$A008	Timer Two Low	T2-L
$A009	Timer Two High	T2-H
$A00A	Shift Register	SR
$A00B	Auxiliary Control Register	ACR
$A00C	Peripheral Control Register	PCR
$A00D	Interrupt Flag Register	IFR
$A00E	Interrupt Enable Register	IER
$A00F	I/O Port A (PA0 to PA7)	ORA

Fig. 5-1. 6522 VIA Memory Locations in the AIM 65 Computer.

5.1   INPUT/OUTPUT

Five (5) Registers of the 6522 VIA are concerned with input/output (I/O).

			Abbreviation
$A000	–	Port B	ORB
$A001	–	Port A	ORA
$A002	–	Data Direction Register-Port B	DDRB
$A003	–	Data Direction Register-Port A	DDRA
$A00F	–	Port A	ORA

Port A (ORA) and Port B (ORB) respectively represent pins PA0-PA7 and PB0-PB7 on the 6522 VIA and are brought out to the AIM 65 Application Connector. These Ports are bidirectional in nature and can represent an input or an output depending upon the corresponding bit values (0=input, 1=output) loaded into the Data Direction Registers DDRA and DDRB. For example, if pins PA5, PA3 and PA1 are to be configured as outputs with the remainder as inputs, then location $A003 (DDRA) must be loaded with $4A (0010 1010). Similarly, if pins PB0-PB7 are chosen as outputs, then $FF (1111 1111) must be loaded into location $A002 (DDRB). A RESET or power-up initializes all bit values in DDRA and DDRB to zero (a cautious practice since an output line should not be left uncontrolled).

5.2 TIMING

Six (6) Registers of the 6522 VIA are concerned with timing.

$A004	Timer One Counter Low	T1C-L
$A005	Timer One Counter High	T1C-H
$A006	Timer One Latch Low	T1L-L
$A007	Timer One Latch High	T1L-H
$A008	Timer Two Low	T2-L
$A009	Timer Two High	T2-H

The 6522 VIA has two internal timers (Timer 1 and Timer 2) which can be used as inputs (pulse counters) or outputs (pulse generators). Conceptually, the timers (T1 and T2) may be thought of as Counters, each equipped with a 16-bit register. The hex number placed into the register is decremented by one for every successive clock pulse. When $0000 is reached, the timer (T1,T2) is said to have timed out. Since both timers are 16-bits wide, two 1-byte locations are necessary to contain the value loaded (in two steps) into the timer. Timer T1 is comprised of two 8-bit latches and a 16-bit counter. Timer T2 consists of one 8-bit latch and a 16-bit counter. The latches can store data which is loaded into the counters. After loading, the counters are decremented at the system clock rate. Upon timing out, an interrupt flag in the Interrupt Flag

Register (IFR) is set (=1).

5.3 SHIFTING

Converting serial data to parallel data and vice-versa is accomplished by the Shift Register (SR) of the VIA.

$A00A   Shift Register   SR

As specified by appropriate bit values loaded into Bits ACR2, ACR3 and ACR4 of an Auxiliary Control Register (ACR, discussed on following pages), the Shift Register operates in eight (8) modes.

    One   -   Disables

    Three -   Enables Input (Serial--> Parallel)

    Four -   Enables Output (Parallel--> Serial)

The Shift Register (SR) is connected to control line CB2. All input/output pulses to and from the SR are sensed on this specific line and shifted according to the specific mode determined by the bit patterns of ACR2-4.

5.4   FUNCTION CONTROL

Function control is accomplished by two (2) Registers.   One is concerned with <u>where</u> signals are going to/coming from while the other decides <u>how</u> signals are sent/received.

$A00B	Auxiliary Control Register	ACR
$A00C	Peripheral Control Register	PCR

Auxiliary Control Register (ACR)

The Auxiliary Control Register (ACR) provides control over the Timers (T1, T2) and Shift Register (SR) of the VIA and enables/disables data latching on Port A (ORA) and Port B (ORB). Data latching simply means "capturing" that data (8-bits) present on a Port's I/O lines at the time of an active transition on control lines CA1 or CB1 for either input to the 6502 microprocessor or output to peripherals.   CA1 can latch Port A on input only.   CB1 can latch Port B on input and output. Whether or not latching is enabled or disabled depends upon the value of the bit (0 = disable, 1 = enable) written into ACR0 for Port A and ACR1 for Port B.

Shift Register Control is accomplished by ACR Bits 2, 3, and 4 and is described in more detail in Appendix B.

Timers T1 and T2 operate in several modes which are controlled by the bit values contained in ACR6, ACR7 (Timer T1) and ACR5 (Timer T2). The simpler T2 Timer operates in two (2) Modes: One-shot (ACR5=0) and Pulse-counting (ACR5=1) on PB7 and can only generate a single time interval. Timer T1 operates in four (4) Modes: One-shot (ACR6=0) or Free-running (ACR6=1) with an output signal on PB7 Enabled (ACR7=1) or Disabled (ACR7=0). In the free running mode, Timer T1 is re-loaded automatically after every time-out for a continuous countdown (viz. a clock that never stops).

Peripheral Control Register (PCR)

The Peripheral Control Register (PCR) specifies how the control lines should operate in the input (CA1, CA2, CB1, CB2) and output (CA2, CB2) modes. In the input mode, the control interrupt flags (IFR0, IFR1, IFR3, IFR4) are set (=1) by specified transitions on the control lines and cleared (=0) by specified Read/Write operations. In the output mode, various transitions and logic levels are generated on the CA2 and CB2 control lines as determined by the bit values loaded into PCR1-3 (for CA2) and PCR5-7 (for CB2). With this type of control, an output pulse of virtually any duration and polarity can be sent to a peripheral device.

AUXILIARY CONTROL REGISTER - (ACR)

ACR7	ACR6	ACR5	ACR4	ACR3	ACR2	ACR1	ACR0
T1 CONTROL		T2 CONTROL	SHIFT REGISTER CONTROL			ORB LATCH	ORA LATCH

SHIFT REGISTER CONTROL

ACR4	ACR3	ACR2	
0	0	0	Shift Register disabled
0	0	1	Shift in under control of T1
0	1	0	Shift in under control of ø2
0	1	1	Shift in under control of external clock
1	0	0	Free-running output at rate determined by T2
1	0	1	Shift out under control of T2
1	1	0	Shift out under control of ø2
1	1	1	Shift out under control of external clock

ORB LATCH

0= disable
1= enable

ORA LATCH

0= disable
1= enable

T2 Mode

0= generate single time-out at Clock Rate
1= generate single time-out at Rate determined by signal at PB6

T1 Mode

```
0 0  -  generate single time-out at Clock Rate, PB7 disabled    } One Shot Mode
1 0  -  generate single time-out at Clock Rate, PB7 enabled
0 1  -  generate continuous time-outs at Clock Rate, PB7 disabled } Free Running Mode
1 1  -  generate continuous time-outs at Clock Rate, PB7 enabled
```

PERIPHERAL CONTROL REGISTER - (PCR)

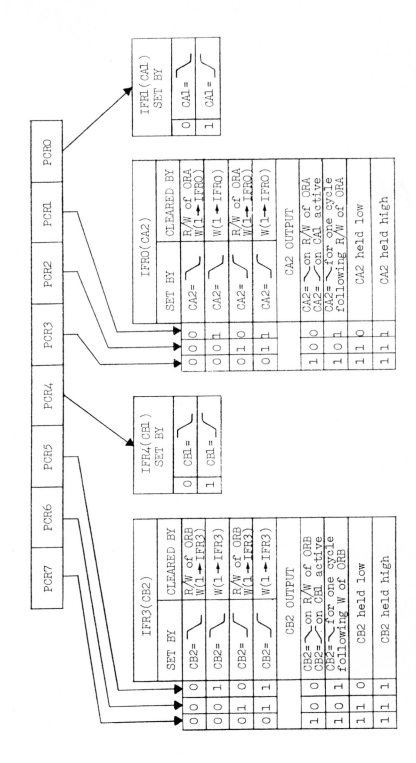

5.5 INTERRUPT CONTROL

The 6522 VIA has provisions for seven (7) different types of interrupts. The 6502, however, has only one (1) Interrupt Request Line (IRQ). How then does the 6522 prioritize its interrupts? Simple. It uses two (2) internal registers; (1) one to determine which interrupt(s) are active (flagged) and (2) another to determine which interrupt(s) are allowed (enabled). If a particular interrupt (1 of 7) is both active and allowed, an IRQ signal is generated and the 6502 is interrupted. These two registers are called the Interrupt Flag Register (IFR) and the Interrupt Enable Register (IER).

$A00D   -   Interrupt Flag Register   IFR

$A00E   -   Interrupt Enable Register   IER

Appropriate bits in the IFR are set (=1) by (a) active transitions on the control lines, (b) an 8-bit register shift, and (c) time-outs of Timers T1 and T2. They are cleared (=0) by Reading/Writing the I/O Ports, Shift Register and the Timers. Once an interrupt has set (=1) a particular bit in the IFR it can cause an IRQ (to the 6502) only if the corresponding bit in the IER is also set (=1). Otherwise, no IRQ is generated and the 6502 is not interrupted (from its main program).

INTERRUPT FLAG REGISTER - (IFR)

INTERRUPT ENABLE REGISTER - (IER)

BIT	SET(=1) BY	CLEARED(=0) BY
IFR0	Active transition on CA2	Reading/Writing ORA
IFR1	Active transition on CA1	Reading/Writing ORA
IFR2	Completion of eight shifts	Reading/Writing SR
IFR3	Active transition on CB2	Reading/Writing ORB
IFR4	Active transition on CB1	Reading/Writing ORB
IFR5	Time-out of Timer T2	Reading T2C-L / Writing T2C-H
IFR6	Time-out of Timer T1	Reading T1C-L / Writing T1C-H
IFR7	Any IFR Bit with corresponding IER Bit also set(=1)	Writing Logic 0 to appropriate Bit(s) in IFR and IER

IFR7	IFR6	IFR5	IFR4	IFR3	IFR2	IFR1	IFR0
IRQ	T1	T2	CB1	CB2	SR	CA1	CA2

SET / CLEAR	T1	T2	CB1	CB2	SR	CA1	CA2
IER7	IER6	IER5	IER4	IER3	IER2	IER1	IER0

(Enable specific interrupt(s) to the $\overline{IRQ}$ line)

If = 0 then Writing a 1 to an IER Bit clears(=0) that Bit
If = 1 then Writing a 1 to an IER Bit sets(=1) that Bit

TO 6502 $\overline{IRQ}$ LINE

Effects of Read/Write Operations on the 6522 VIA Registers

Loc.	WRITE	READ
$A000	Data Bus--> Port B (ORB) IFR3(CB2) and IFR4(CB1) Cleared (=0)	ORB--> Data Bus IFR3(CB2) and IFR4(CB1) Cleared (=0)
$A001	Data Bus--> Port A (ORA) IFR0(CA2) and IFR1(CA1) Cleared (=0)	ORA--> Data Bus IFR0(CA2) and IFR1(CA1) Cleared (=0)
$A002	Data Bus--> DDRB 0 = Input 1 = Output	DDRB--> Data Bus 0 = Input 1 = Output
$A003	Data Bus--> DDRA 0 = Input 1 = Output	DDRA--> Data Bus 0 = Input 1 = Output
$A004	Data Bus--> Timer One Latch Low (T1L-L)	T1C-L--> Data Bus IFR6(T1) Cleared (=0)
$A005	Data Bus--> Timer One Counter High (T1C-H) T1L-L --> T1C-L IFR6(T1) Cleared (=0) Timer T1 Started	T1C-H--> Data Bus
$A006	Data Bus--> Timer One Latch Low (T1L-L)	T1L-L--> Data Bus

Effects of Read/Write Operations on the 6522 VIA Registers

Loc.	WRITE	READ
$A007	Data Bus--> Timer One Latch High (T1L-H) IFR6(T1) Cleared (=0)	T1L-H--> Data Bus
$A008	Data Bus--> Timer Two Latch Low (T2L-L)	T2C-L--> Data Bus IFR5(T2) Cleared (=0)
$A009	Data Bus--> Timer Two Counter High (T2C-H) T2L-L --> T2C-L IFR5(T2) Cleared (=0) Timer T2 Started	T2C-H--> Data Bus
$A00A	Data Bus--> Shift Register (SR) IFR2(SR) Cleared (=0)	SR--> Data Bus IFR2(SR) Cleared (=0)
$A00B	Data Bus--> Auxiliary Control Register (ACR)	ACR--> Data Bus
$A00C	Data Bus--> Peripheral Control Register (PCR)	PCR--> Data Bus
$A00D	Data Bus--> Interrupt Flag Register (IFR)	IFR--> Data Bus
$A00E	Data Bus--> Interrupt Enable Register (IER)	IER--> Data Bus
$A00F	Data Bus--> Port A (ORA)	ORA--> Data Bus

Exp. 21 - Using VIA Timer T1 to Generate Precisely
            Timed Interrupts

GOAL: Increment and display the hexadecimal contents
      of location $0001 every 1/2 second. Locations
      $EA13 and $EA46 are the entry points for the AIM
      Monitor display routines.

Note: Toggle the printer off before running program.

Comments

```
$0200   SEI              Disable IRQ interrupts
    1   LDA #31          Load LSB of IRQ Vector
    3   STA $A404
    6   LDA #02          Load MSB of IRQ Vector
    8   STA $A405
    B   LDA #C0          Set T1 in free running mode
    D   STA $A00B         (ACR7 = ACR6 = 1)
$0210   LDA #C0          Enable T1 Interrupts
    2   STA $A00E         (IER7 = IER6 = 1)
    5   LDA #4E          Load T1L-L with $4E
    7   STA $A004
    A   LDA #C3          Load T1L-H with $C3
    C   STA $A005        Start Timer, Generate
                          0.05 sec. interrupts
    F   LDA #0A          Load interrupt counter
$0221   STA $00           with $0A = 10_{10}
    3   CLI              Enable IRQ interrupts
    4   BRK              Force first interrupt
    5   NOP              No operation
DISP $0226 JSR $EA13     Output carriage return
                          to Display routine
    9   LDA $01          Load A with contents of $0001
    B   JSR $EA46        Convert to ASCII and display
    E   JMP $0226        Refresh display in continuous
                          closed loop
IRQ $0231  PHA           Save Accumulator on Stack
    2   DEC $00          10 interrupts yet?
    4   BNE $023C        If no, go to DONE
    6   LDA #0A          If yes, reload interrupt
    8   STA $00           counter
    A   INC $01          Increment contents of $0001
DONE $023C LDA $A004     Clear T1 interrupt flag
                          (IFR6 --> 0)
    F   PLA              Restore accumulator
$0240   RTI              Return from Interrupt
```

Total Delay Interval = $0A x [$C34E x 1 µS + 2 µS(overhead)]
                     = 10 x [49,998 + 2] µS
                     = 500,000 µS
                     = 0.5 sec

Exp. 21 - AIM Printout.

```
<K>*=0200
/31
 0200 78 SEI
 0201 A9 LDA #31
 0203 8D STA A404
 0206 A9 LDA #02
 0208 8D STA A405
 020B A9 LDA #C0
 020D 8D STA A00B
 0210 A9 LDA #C0
 0212 8D STA A00E
 0215 A9 LDA #4E
 0217 8D STA A004
 021A A9 LDA #C3
 021C 8D STA A005
 021F A9 LDA #0A
 0221 85 STA 00
 0223 58 CLI
 0224 00 BRK
 0225 EA NOP
 0226 20 JSR EA13
 0229 A5 LDA 01
 022B 20 JSR EA46
 022E 4C JMP 0226
 0231 48 PHA
 0232 C6 DEC 00
 0234 D0 BNE 023C
 0236 A9 LDA #0A
 0238 85 STA 00
 023A E6 INC 01
 023C AD LDA A004
 023F 68 PLA
 0240 40 RTI
```

Exp. 22 - Using the VIA Timer T2 to Measure Elapsed Time
         Between Two Events

GOAL: Measure and display the elapsed time (in seconds)
      from the start of program execution until any key
      (other than ESC) is depressed.

Note: Toggle the printer off before running program.

                                        Comments

```
$0200   LDA $00          Initialize Y Index and Seconds
2       TAY               Counter at temporary location
3       STA $00           $0000.
5       STA $A00B        Set T2 in one-shot mode
8       LDA #00
A       STA A00E         Disable T2 interrupts
                          (IER7 = IER5 = 0)
$020D   LDA #50
F       STA $A008        Load T2L-L with $50
$0212   LDA #C3
4       STA $A009        Load T2L-H with $C3, start timer,
7       LDA #20           generate 0.05 sec intervals
$0219   BIT $A00D        Idle here until T2 flag (IFR5)
C       BEQ $0219         is set (=1)
E       INY              Increment Y Index
F       CPY #14          20_{10} ($14) intervals completed?
$0221   BNE $020D        If no, generate more intervals
3       INC $00          If yes, increment Seconds Counter
5       LDY #00          Re-initialize Y Index
7       LDA #FF ┐
9       STA $A481        Enter keyboard scanning routines
C       STA $A482
F       LDA #00      ──> Is a key depressed?
$0231   STA $A483
4       STA $A480
7       LDA $A482
A       CMP #FF ┘
C       BEQ $020D        If no, continue timing
E       JSR $EA13        If yes, display Seconds Counter
$0241   LDA $00           In Hex format (i.e. $0A = 10_{10})
3       JSR $EA46
6       JSR $E907        Escape from display routine by
                          hitting <ESC> key
$0249   JMP $023E        Refresh display
```

Exp. 22 - AIM Printout.

```
<K>*=0200
/32
 0200 A9 LDA #00
 0202 A8 TAY
 0203 85 STA 00
 0205 8D STA A00B
 0208 A9 LDA #00
 020A 8D STA A00E
 020D A9 LDA #50
 020F 8D STA A008
 0212 A9 LDA #C3
 0214 8D STA A009
 0217 A9 LDA #20
 0219 2C BIT A00D
 021C F0 BEQ 0219
 021E C8 INY
 021F C0 CPY #14
 0221 D0 BNE 020D
 0223 E6 INC 00
 0225 A0 LDY #00
 0227 A9 LDA #FF
 0229 8D STA A481
 022C 8D STA A482
 022F A9 LDA #00
 0231 8D STA A483
 0234 8D STA A480
 0237 AD LDA A482
 023A C9 CMP #FF
 023C F0 BEQ 020D
 023E 20 JSR EA13
 0241 A5 LDA 00
 0243 20 JSR EA46
 0246 20 JSR E907
 0249 4C JMP 023E
```

CHAPTER 6

```
┌─────────────────────────┐
│    MONITOR  ROUTINES     │
└─────────────────────────┘
```

A Monitor Routine is a software program usually (but not
always) located in ROM. It supervises (monitors) the operations
of a microcomputer and allows humans to communicate with it
(usually in hex code). Since it is in ROM it canot be written
into or altered. It handles the two important functions of
Initialization (loading memory locations with certain preset
values before execution of certain operations) and Linking
(establishing dialog between programs and humans, programs and
I/O-devices, humans and I/O-devices and programs and programs).
It usually consists of many subroutines (Monitor Subroutines)
which perform specific system functions (scanning a keyboard for
depression of a key, for example). Many of these routines can
be externally accessed and executed by simply loading the
Program Counter (PC) with the starting address of the routine
and commencing execution. Once loaded, program control is
transferred to that particular subroutine and a powerful
software tool becomes available for our disposal. Many of these
subroutines can be used repeatedly without ever having to code
them in the main program.

A note of caution, however! Quite often these routines will
use the various registers (A, X, Y ...) for storage (temporary

or otherwise) of variables. If the same registers are used in the main program, they must be either reset after exiting the subroutine or saved prior to entering the subroutine. Otherwise, nonsense will prevail. A partial listing of some of the Monitor Subroutines in the AIM 65 follows. They are listed according to Name, Location, Registers Affected and Function.

SOME AIM 65 MONITOR SUBROUTINES

Name	Location	Registers Affected	Function
CKER00	$E394	-	Prints "ERROR" message
CLR	$EB44	A	Clears display and printer pointers
CLRF	$E9F0	A	Outputs one Carriage Return (CR) and one Line Feed (LF) to the active output device or one NUL to a TTY
CRLOW	$EA13	-	Outputs one Carriage Return (CR) and one Line Feed (LF) to the display/printer
DEBK1	$ED2C	A	5 Millisecond Delay Routine
HEX	$EA7D	A	Converts a hex number (0-F) in A from ASCII to HEX format and stores result in least significant nibble of A. Most significant nibble of A contains zero
INALL	$E993	A	Inputs one ASCII character from active input device and stores in A. Input device code must be in INFLG ($A412) before calling

Name	Location	Registers Affected	Function
INLOW	$E8F8	A	Puts a Carriage Return (CR= $0D) in INFLG ($A412) to designate keyboard as input device
NOUT	$EA51	A	Converts least significant nibble (Bits 0-3) of A to an ASCII character for output to active device
NUMA	$EA46	A	Converts two hex numbers in A from HEX to ASCII format and outputs them to the active output device, the most significant nibble being first
OUTALL	$E9BC	-	Outputs one valid ASCII character in A to the active output device
OUTDIS	$EF05	-	Outputs a valid ASCII character in A to the display. After display of 20 characters as counted by CURPO2 ($A415), the display is left-scrolled until 60 characters have been displayed
OUTLOW	$E901	A	Stores a Carriage Return ($0D) in OUTFLG ($A413) to designate display/printer as active output device
OUTPRI	$F000	-	Outputs a valid ASCII character in A to printer buffer. A line is printed when buffer is full (20 characters) or a Carriage Return ($0D) is encountered

Name	Location	Registers Affected	Function
OUTPUT	$E97A	-	Outputs a valid ASCII character in A to display/printer or TTY. If Bit 7 of PRIFLG ($A411)=1, it is printed. If TTY is active and Bit 0 of PRIFLG=0, output goes to TTY
PHXY	$EB9E	-	PUSH X and Y without changing the registers
PLXY	$EBAC	X,Y	PULL X and Y without changing accumulator (A)
RCHECK	$E907	A,X,Y	The keyboard is scanned. If no key is depressed, control goes back to the calling routine. If <ESC> is depressed, control goes to the Monitor. If <SPACE> is depressed, the subroutine waits for another key to be depressed before continuing on
READ	$E93C	A	Reads an ASCII character from the keyboard and inputs the ASCII code to the accumulator (A)
REDOUT	$E973	A	Same as READ with input character echoed to display/printer if not a Carriage Return ($0D)

Exp. 23 - Using a Monitor Printout Routine

GOAL: Output the contents of location $0000, which is a
valid ASCII character, to the printer. Monitor
Routine OUTPRI ($F000) is used in the process.

1. Load the contents of location $0000 with $40.

2. Key in and run the following program.

                                                Comments

```
$0200    LDA #80      Enable printer by making
   2     STA $A411      Bit 7 = 1 of PRIFLG ($A411)
   5     LDA $00      Load A with the contents of $0000
   7     JSR $F000     Output to printer buffer
   A     LDA #0D      Load A with ASCII code for a
                        Carriage Return ($0D)
   C     JSR $F000     Output to printer buffer whereupon
                        contents of buffer are printed
   F     LDA #00      Disable printer by making
$0211    STA $A411      Bit 7 = 0 of PRIFLG ($A411)
   4     BRK          Return to Monitor
$0215    NOP          No operation
```

3. What character is printed? Answer: Ampersand (@).

4. AIM Printout.

```
<M>=0000 40 00 00 00
<*>=0200
<G>/
@

<K>*=0200
/10
 0200 A9 LDA #80
 0202 8D STA A411
 0205 A5 LDA 00
 0207 20 JSR F000
 020A A9 LDA #0D
 020C 20 JSR F000
 020F A9 LDA #00
 0211 8D STA A411
 0214 00 BRK
 0215 EA NOP
```

Exp. 24 - Using the Monitor Display Routines

GOAL: Take any valid ASCII character stored in location
$0000 and incrementally/decrementally flash it on
the 20-character AIM display.

1. Load the contents of location $0000 with $52 ("R").

2. Key in and run the following program.

			Comments
INC $0200	LDA $00		Load A with the valid ASCII code in location $0000
2	JSR $EF05		Output to display routine and increment character pointer in $A415
5	JSR $ED2C		Delay for 5mS
8	LDA $A415		Examine value of character pointer
B	CMP #14		Is position #20($14) reached?
D	BNE $0200		If no, continue incremental display routine-> INC
DEC $020F	DEC $A415		If yes, decrement character pointer
$0212	LDA $00		Load A with the contents[valid ASCII code] of location $0000
4	JSR $EF05		Output to display routine and increment character pointer in $A415
7	DEC $A415		Decrement value of character pointer
A	JSR $ED2C		Delay for 5mS
D	LDA $A415		Load A with character pointer
$0220	CMP #00		Character #0 displayed yet?
2	BEQ $0200		If yes, go to incremental display routine-> INC
4	JSR $ED2C		If no, delay for 5mS
$0227	JSR $E907		Escape to Monitor if <ESC> key is depressed
END $022A	JMP $020F		Jump to decremental display routine-> DEC

3.

Location	Monitor Routine	AIM Listing
$EF05	Display Routine	OUTDIS
$ED2C	5mS Delay Routine	DEBK1
$A415	Character Position (0-19 or $00-$13)	CURPO2
$E907	Escape Routine	RCHECK

4.   AIM Printout.

```
<K>*=0200
/17
 0200 A5 LDA 00
 0202 20 JSR EF05
 0205 20 JSR ED2C
 0208 AD LDA A415
 020B C9 CMP #14
 020D D0 BNE 0200
 020F CE DEC A415
 0212 A5 LDA 00
 0214 20 JSR EF05
 0217 CE DEC A415
 021A 20 JSR ED2C
 021D AD LDA A415
 0220 C9 CMP #00
 0222 F0 BEQ 0200
 0224 20 JSR ED2C
 0227 20 JSR E907
 022A 4C JMP 020F
```

CHAPTER 7

```
┌─────────────────────┐
│  DATA ACQUISITION   │
└─────────────────────┘
```

* Sensors

* Signal Conditioners

* Digital-> Analog Conversions

* Analog-> Digital Conversions

* Hardware A/D Converters

* Other A/D Converters

* Beyond 8-Bits

* Sample and Hold Circuits

The elements of data acquisition and control are seen in
two ways; either separately or together. Taken separately in a
digital context, a data acquisition system acquires data
(usually analog in nature) for storage/display in a
digital/analog format while a control system converts a digital
code to a controlling analog quantity (voltage, current, heat,
light---). Taken together, these two operations form a very
powerful combination, i.e. a measurement and control system.
This concept is outlined in Fig. 7-1.

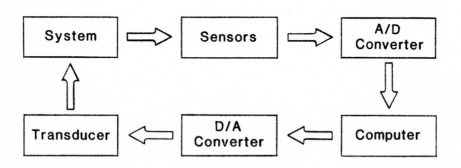

Fig. 7-1. Measurement and Control System.

A complete closed-loop design using sensors/transducers, A/D,
D/A-converters and a microcomputer provides appropriate outputs
to control the system processes as determined by the system's
physical variables (temp., press., strain ---). The examples
that follow will serve to introduce the various aspects of
data-acquisition and control, each taken separately.

DATA ACQUISITION

7.1 SENSORS

A sensor is used to detect a low-level laboratory analog signal. They are broadly defined as devices that are activated by various physical phenomena (heat, light ---) and provide electrical inputs to the front end of a measurement and control system. They fall into two classes, active and passive, depending upon the need for energy (electrical) input. For example, a thermocouple is a passive sensor as opposed to a photomultiplier (PM) tube which must have a voltage present to operate.

Sensors produce an analog voltage or current which is typically conditioned or amplified for input to an A/D converter or another similiar device which converts an analog input to an output suitable for interfacing to a microcomputer. These can include such devices as voltage-> frequency (V/F) converters, voltage-> pulse width converters, resistance-> frequency converters and so on.

7.2 SIGNAL CONDITIONERS

In most cases, the electrical output of a typical laboratory sensor, either active or passive, is too small for direct input into an Analog-to-Digital (A/D) converter or a

156

microcomputer. Thermocouples produce millivolts and photomultiplier tubes yield microamps while most A/D (and V/F)
converters require inputs of the order of 0-10V, -5V +5V, 0-5V,
---. As a result, the signals must be amplified/conditioned to
an appropriate level/quantity before input to an A/D converter.

Examples of some simple signal amplifiers and conditioners
are illustrated in the following diagrams. They are useful for
measuring analog signals at slow (<1kHz) data rates which is not
really a problem in many laboratory experiments. The selected
IC´s are popular, low cost, general purpose devices available at
most electronic suppliers. Used in conjunction with an A/D
converter, microcomputer and suitable output device (printer,
CRT, recorder...), many laboratory measurement problems can be
effectively and inexpensively solved.

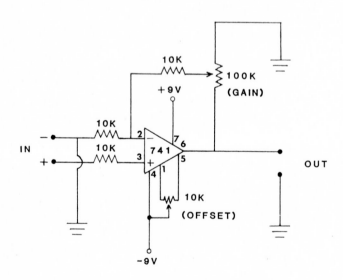

Fig. 7-2. Variable Gain Differential DC Amplifier.

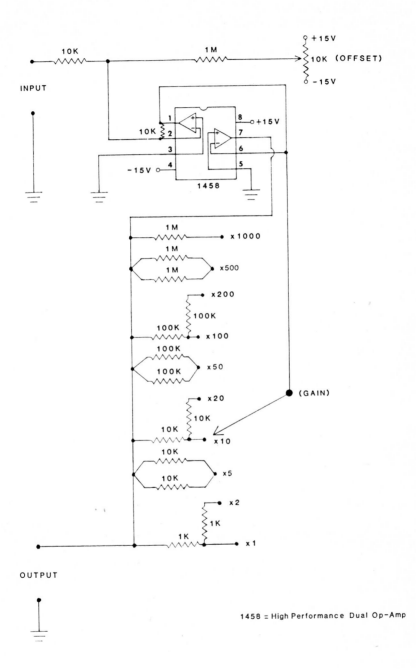

Fig. 7-3. Precision Voltage Amplifier.

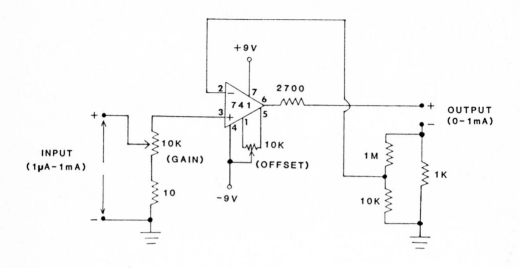

Fig. 7-4.   Current Amplifier.

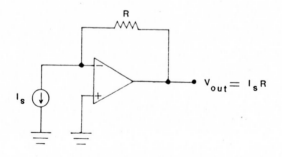

:for $I_s = 1\mu A$ and $R = 1K$, $V_{out} = 1mV$

Fig. 7-5.   Current to Voltage Converter.

Once a laboratory analog signal is amplified and/or
converted to an appropriate electrical quantity, it is then
input to the front-end of a data acquisition (DAQ) system which
is usually an A/D converter. If the analog sensor is situated
near the DAQ system, this poses no problem. However, in remote
applications and/or high noise environments, the signals must be
conditioned (or converted) to a quantity which is less prone to
noise. In most cases, this is accomplished by a
voltage-to-frequency (V/F) converter. They are especially
useful devices for accurately transmitting analog data through
high noise environments. Frequency output is directly
proportional to the input voltage over several decades peaking
out somewhere near 100kHz. An example of such a V/F circuit is
depicted in Fig. 7-6 for the Analog Devices´ 458 High Accuracy
Voltage-to-Frequency converter.

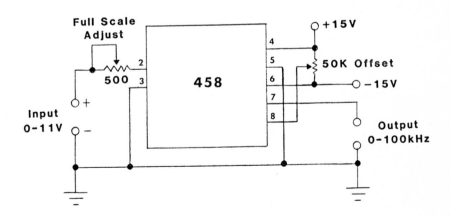

Fig. 7-6. Voltage-to-Frequency Converter.

At the front end of the DAQ system, the frequency generated by the V/F converter can be either input directly into the microcomputer (for frequency counting) or re-converted into an analog quantity for input to an A/D converter. The latter case is illustrated in Fig. 7-7 for a Raytheon 4151 V/F converter used in reverse fashion as a linear frequency-to-voltage (F/V) converter.

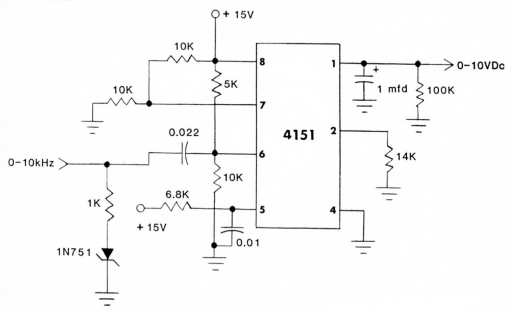

Fig. 7-7. Frequency-to-Voltage Converter.

The frequency output of many newer V/F converters is also TTL compatible. TTL is shorthand for transistor-transistor logic where a logic "0" level is any voltage from 0.0 to +0.8VDC and a logic "1" is any level from +2.4 to +5VDC.

Between a remote sensor and the front-end of a DAQ system, the conditioned analog signal can be transmitted by two general methods; one involving electrons, the other photons. A metallic conductor (wire) will transmit electrons and an optical fiber will conduct photons. In an especially noisy electrical (or radiofrequency) environment, transmission by optical fibers is the preferred route. In addition to their high information carrying capacity, they possess near total immunity to many of the interference sources which plague conducting transmission lines. A simple TTL-compatible optical transmitter is depicted in Fig. 7-8.

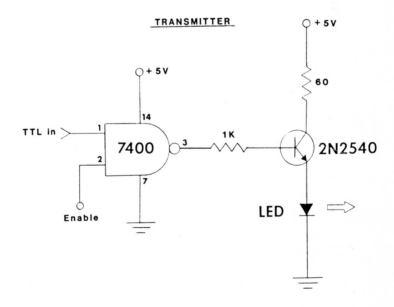

Fig. 7-8.   TTL-Compatible Optical Transmitter.

A light-emitting-diode (LED) produces the digital light pulses. The NAND gate is employed with a driving transistor to provide an <u>inverted</u> pulse pattern at the LED transmitter. When the TTL input is enabled, the LED will flash on for a logical "0" input and off for a logical "1" input. After transmission through an optical fiber waveguide, this train of inverted pulses is re-inverted by the phototransistor-detector circuit in Fig. 7-9 to produce a one-to-one TTL output versus input.

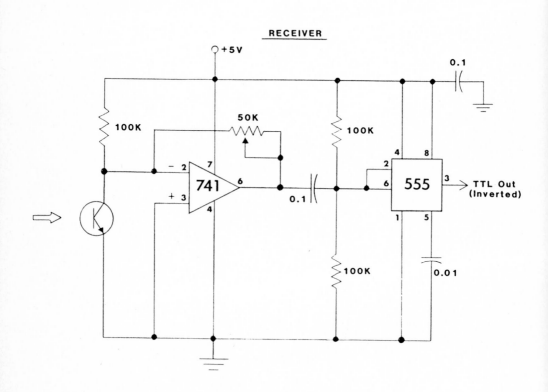

Fig. 7-9. TTL-Compatible Optical Fiber Receiver.

The rationale behind the inverted LED configuration in the transmitter is the on-line monitoring of fiber continuity. Namely, in the absence of any digital input, a steady "lights-on" condition prevails to indicate fiber continuity. If non-inverting logic were employed instead, this distinction could not be made.

7.3 DIGITAL-> ANALOG, ANALOG-> DIGITAL CONVERSIONS

Once a voltage signal from an analog sensor is amplified to an appropriate level (e.g. 0-10V), it can be input to an Analog-to-Digital (A/D) Converter. Once there, it is digitized and output to the microcomputer as a series of binary voltages or currents (i.e. 0´s and 1´s) for storage and manipulation. The reverse process, Digital-to-Analog (D/A) Conversion takes a series of logical 0´s and 1´s from a microcomputer and produces an analog voltage (or current) which is directly related to the digital input. In most D/A devices, this is accomplished by an op-amp/resistor network.

Many A/D converters employ a D/A converter to generate an analog signal for comparison with the signal to be digitized. The digital input is then changed in a manner specified by the results of the comparison until the input signal and the generated signal are equal (or nearly so). This is really an approximating technique and the two versions most often used in A/D conversion are the Ramp Approximation and the Successive

Approximation.

In the Ramp Approximation (sometimes called the Staircase Approximation) the generated voltage is increased or decreased in a linear fashion (i.e. ramped) until it equals the input voltage. One drawback of this technique is its speed. If a 10V signal is input to an 8-bit A/D converter using this approximation and the ramp begins at 0V, then 2^8-1 or 255 iterations are needed for a complete conversion.

The Successive Approximation routine is a more efficient method and is employed in many commercial A/D converters. Here the generated voltage is changed by successively dividing a range of voltages by two each time and comparing the result with the input voltage. This voltage variation is simply accomplished by a Shift Register. Recall that shifting a bit one position to the right is equivalent to division by 2. In this type of approximation, an n-bit converter will require n iterations for a complete conversion. A 12-bit converter with a 1MHz clock can complete a conversion every 12 microseconds.

The experiments that follow utilize the Analog Devices' AD558 8-bit Digital-to-Analog Converter (DAC) interfaced to the Ports (A and B) of a 6522 VIA chip in an AIM 65 computer to illustrate specific examples of the various D-> A routines. It is configured in a "transparent" latching mode which simply means that the process of converting a digital voltage pattern of 8-bits into an analog output (0-10V) is occurring

continually. The analog output thereby "tracks" the digital
input. The electrical circuit depicted in Fig. 7-9 also
illustrates how this particular DAC may be coupled with a fast
op-amp comparator to produce a software-driven Analog-to-Digital
(A/D) Converter. The digital inputs to the AD558 DAC (via Port
A) are varied in a specified manner until its analog voltage
output slightly exceeds that of the unknown analog voltage
input. This transition point is indicated by the status of the
NE531 comparator which is interrogated continually via PB7 of
Port B. Thereupon, the digitized voltage values are stored in
memory. Caution: Input and output voltages are restricted to
the 0-10V range!

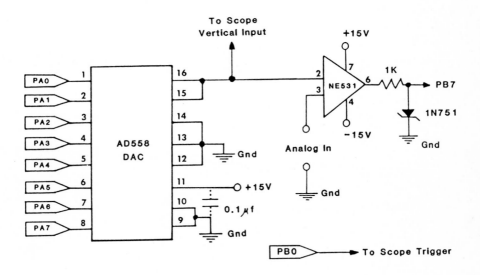

Fig. 7-9. Software-Driven A/D, D/A Converter.

166

Exp. 25 - Digital-> Analog Conversion

GOAL: Generation of High Frequency Square Waves.

```
START   $0300   LDA #FF                 Make Port A (ORA) Output
            2   STA $A003 (PADD)
LOOP    $0305   LDA #FF                 Load $FF into Accumulator
            7   STA $A001 (PAD)         Output to Port A
            A   LDA #00                 Load $00 into Accumulator
            C   STA $A001 (PAD)         Output to Port A
END     $030F   JMP $0305 (LOOP)        Repeat process
```

AIM Printout   Scope Trace

```
<K>*=0300
/07
 0300 A9 LDA #FF
 0302 8D STA A003
 0305 A9 LDA #FF
 0307 8D STA A001
 030A A9 LDA #00
 030C 8D STA A001
 030F 4C JMP 0305
```

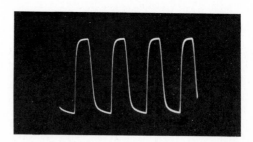

Note: Output frequency is ca. 67 kHz. Amplitude = 10V P-P.

Exp. 26 - Digital-> Analog Conversion

GOAL: Generation of Low Frequency Square Waves.


```
START   $0300   LDA #FF                      Make Port A Output
            2   STA $A003 (PADD)
LOOP    $0305   LDA #FF                      Load $FF into Accumulator
            7   STA $A001 (PAD)              Output to Port A
            A   JSR $ED2C (DEBK1)            5mS Delay Routine
            D   LDA #00                      Load $00 into Accumulator
            F   STA $A001 (PAD)              Output to Port A
        $0312   JSR $ED2C (DEBK1)            5mS Delay Routine
END     $0315   JMP $0305 (LOOP)             Repeat process
```


AIM Printout   Scope Trace

```
<K>*=0300
/09
 0300 A9 LDA #FF
 0302 8D STA A003
 0305 A9 LDA #FF
 0307 8D STA A001
 030A 20 JSR ED2C
 030D A9 LDA #00
 030F 8D STA A001
 0312 20 JSR ED2C
 0315 4C JMP 0305
```

Note: Output frequency is ca. 97 Hz. Amplitude = 10V P-P.

Exp. 27 - Digital-> Analog Conversion

GOAL: Generation of a Sawtooth (Ramp) Waveform.

```
START   $0300   LDA #FF            Make Port A (ORA) Output
            2   STA $A003 (PADD)
            5   LDX #00            Initialize X Index
RAMP    $0307   STX $A001 (PAD)    Output value to Port A
            A   INX               Increment value of X
END     $030B   JMP $0307 (RAMP)  Repeat process
```

AIM Printout   Scope Trace

```
<K>*=0300
/06
 0300 A9 LDA #FF
 0302 8D STA A003
 0305 A2 LDX #00
 0307 8E STX A001
 030A E8 INX
 030B 4C JMP 0307
```

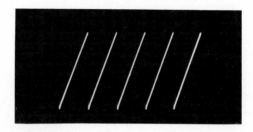

Note: Output frequency is ca. 420 Hz. Amplitude = 10V P-P.

Exp. 28 - Digital-> Analog Conversion

GOAL: Generation of a Triangular Waveform.

START	$0300	LDA #FF		Make Port A (ORA) Output
	2	STA $A003	(PADD)	
	5	LDX #FF		Load $FF into X Index
LOOP1	$0307	STX $A001	(PAD)	Store in Port A
	A	DEX		Decrement X Index
	B	BNE $0307	(LOOP1)	Stay in LOOP1 until X = 0
LOOP2	$030D	STX $A001	(PAD)	Otherwise store value of X in Port A
	$0310	INX		Increment X Index
	1	BNE $030D	(LOOP2)	Stay in LOOP2 until X = 0
END	$0313	JMP $0307	(LOOP1)	Otherwise go to LOOP1

AIM Printout

Scope Trace

```
<K>*=0300
/10
 0300 A9 LDA #FF
 0302 8D STA A003
 0305 A2 LDX #FF
 0307 8E STX A001
 030A CA DEX
 030B D0 BNE 0307
 030D 8E STX A001
 0310 E8 INX
 0311 D0 BNE 030D
 0313 4C JMP 0307
```

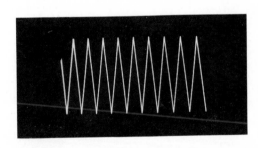

Note: Output frequency is ca. 220 Hz. Amplitude = 10V P-P.

Exp. 29 - Digital-> Analog Conversion

GOAL: Generation of a Delayed Triangular Waveform.

```
START   $0300   LDA #FF                  Make Port A (ORA) Output
          2     STA $A003 (PADD)
          5     LDX #FF                  Load $FF into X Index
LOOP1   $0307   STX $A001 (PAD)          Store in Port A
          A     DEX                      Decrement value of X
          B     BNE $0307 (LOOP1)        Stay in LOOP1 until X = 0
          D     JSR $ED2C (DEBK1)        Otherwise take 5mS Delay
                                           before
LOOP2   $0310   STX $A001 (PAD)          Storing X in Port A then
          3     INX                      Incrementing X Index and
          4     BNE $0310 (LOOP2)        Staying in LOOP2 until
                                           X = 0
END     $0316   JMP $0307 (LOOP1)        When X = 0 Repeat process
```

AIM Printout   Scope Trace

```
<K>*=0300
/11
 0300 A9 LDA #FF
 0302 8D STA A003
 0305 A2 LDX #FF
 0307 8E STX A001
 030A CA DEX
 030B D0 BNE 0307
 030D 20 JSR ED2C
 0310 8E STX A001
 0313 E8 INX
 0314 D0 BNE 0310
 0316 4C JMP 0307
```

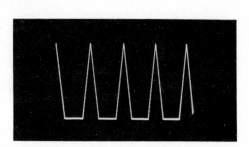

Note: Output frequency is ca. 100 Hz. Amplitude = 10V P-P.
      Delay Interval = 5mS.

Exp. 30 - Digital-> Analog Conversion

GOAL: Generation of a Trapezoidal Waveform.

```
START  $0300  LDA #FF              Make Port A (ORA) Output
          2  STA $A003 (PADD)
          5  LDX #FF              Load $FF into X Index
LOOP1  $0307  STX $A001 (PAD)      Store in Port A
          A  DEX                 Decrement value of X
          B  BNE $0307 (LOOP1)    Stay in LOOP1 until X = 0
          D  JSR $ED2C (DEBK1)    Otherwise take 5mS Delay
                                    before
LOOP2  $0310  STX $A001 (PAD)      Storing X in Port A then
          3  INX                 Incrementing X Index and
          4  BNE $0310 (LOOP2)    Staying in LOOP2 until
                                    X = 0
          6  JSR $ED2C (DEBK1)    Otherwise take 5mS Delay
END    $0319  JMP $0307 (LOOP1)    Before repeating process
```

AIM Printout

```
<K>*=0300
/12
 0300 A9 LDA #FF
 0302 8D STA A003
 0305 A2 LDX #FF
 0307 8E STX A001
 030A CA DEX
 030B D0 BNE 0307
 030D 20 JSR ED2C
 0310 8E STX A001
 0313 E8 INX
 0314 D0 BNE 0310
 0316 20 JSR ED2C
 0319 4C JMP 0307
```

Scope Trace

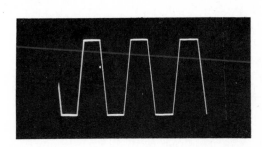

Note: Output frequency is ca. 67 Hz. Amplitude = 10V P-P.

Exp. 31 - Digital-> Analog Conversion

GOAL: Generation of Sharktooth Pulses.

```
START   $0300   LDA #FF              Make Port A (ORA) Output
          2     STA $A003 (PADD)
LOOP1   $0305   LDA #FF              Load $FF into Accumulator
LOOP2   $0307   STA $A001 (PAD)      Output to Port A
          A     LSR A               Divide contents of A by 2
          B     BNE $0307 (LOOP2)    Stay in LOOP2 until [A]=0
END     $030D   JMP $0305 (LOOP1)    Otherwise repeat process
```

AIM Printout   Scope Trace

```
<K>*=0300
/07
 0300 A9 LDA #FF
 0302 8D STA A003
 0305 A9 LDA.#FF
 0307 8D STA A001
 030A 4A LSR .A
 030B D0 BNE 0307
 030D 4C JMP 0305
```

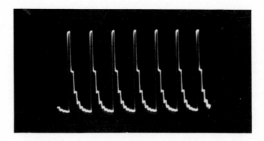

Exercise: Replace the LSR instruction in the preceding
          program with an ASL instruction and observe
          the effect on the shape of the pulses.

    Note: Output frequency is ca. 13 kHz.

The next four experiments (Nos. 32-35) illustrate (via software) the two most common approximating techniques involved in analog-> digital conversions; the Ramp Approximation (Exps. 32,33) and the Successive Approximation (Exps. 34,35). In Exp. 32, an unknown input voltage is digitized in real time via the Ramp Approximation for continuous output to the AIM 65 display (in Hex format). The Ramp Approximation is also employed in Exp. 33. Here however, the start of program execution enables 256 data points to be digitized and stored for later display on an oscilloscope. Repeated jumps to a 5mS Monitor subroutine produce the appropriate DELAY intervals (ca. 1 sec.) between data points. Exp. 34 is similar to Exp. 35 with the sole exception that the Successive Approximation routine is employed in Exp. 35. Exp. 36, besides using the Successive Approximation routine, demonstrates four additional programming features;

(1) the use of function keys (i.e. F1-F3) for selecting either conversion or display routines.

(2) automatic level-triggering of the start of the data-acquisition process.

(3) dynamic display during the entire acquisition process, and

(4) the generation of precise, program-independant, time delays using Timer T1 of the 6522 VIA in an interrupt-driven format.

Exp. 32 - Analog-> Digital Conversion - Ramp Approx.

GOAL: Analog-> Digital Conversion of Input Voltage and
      Output to the AIM 65 Display.

```
START   $0300   LDA #FF              Make Port A (ORA) Output
            3   STA $A003 (PADD)
CONVT   $0305   LDX #00              Initialize X Index
RAMP    $0307   STX $A001 (PAD)      Begin Ramp
            A   LDA $A000 (PBD)      Test PBD.  Branch to
            D   BPL $0313 (DISP)      DISP if PB7 = 0
            F   INX                  Increment value of X
        $0310   JMP $0307 (RAMP)     Ramp to next value
DISP    $0313   TXA                  Transfer X to Accumulator
            4   JSR $EA46 (NUMA)     Convert Hex value to
                                      ASCII value and output
                                      to AIM 65 display
            7   JSR $EB44 (CLR)      Clear display pointers
END     $031A   JMP $0305 (CONVT)    Go to CONVT for next data
                                      point
```

AIM Printout

```
<K>*=0300
/12
 0300 A9 LDA #FF
 0302 8D STA A003
 0305 A2 LDX #00
 0307 8E STX A001
 030A AD LDA A000
 030D 10 BPL 0313
 030F E8 INX
 0310 4C JMP 0307
 0313 8A TXA
 0314 20 JSR EA46
 0317 20 JSR EB44
 031A 4C JMP 0305
```

Note: Input voltages of 0-10V will register on the AIM
      display as the Hex values $00-$FF. This represents
      a precision of 1/256 or ca. 0.4%.

Exp. 33 - Analog-> Digital Conversion - Ramp Approx.

GOAL: Analog-> Digital Conversion (Ramp Approx.) and
Storage of 256 Data Points into Page 2 of RAM with
Readout on Laboratory Oscilloscope.

```
START   $0300   LDY #00                   Initialize Y Index
        $0302   LDA #FF
            4   STA $A003 (PADD)          Make Port A (ORA) Output
CONVT   $0307   LDX #00                   Initialize X Index
RAMP    $0309   STX $A001 (PAD)           Begin Ramp
            C   LDA $A000 (PBD)           Test PBD. Branch to
            F   BPL $0315 (TABLE)          TABLE if PB7 = 0
        $0311   INX                       Increment value of X
            2   JMP $0309 (RAMP)          Ramp to next value
TABLE   $0315   LDA $A001 (PAD)           Store Port A data in
            8   STA $0200,Y                Page 2 of RAM
            B   INY                       Increment value of Y
            C   BEQ $0332 (RDOUT)         Branch to RDOUT if done
            E   JSR $0329 (DELAY)         Delay between points
        $0321   LDA #00                   Initialize PB7 = 0 before
            3   STA $A000 (PBD)            starting new RAMP approx
            6   JMP $0307 (CONVT)         Go to CONVT for next data
                                           point
DELAY   $0329   LDX #C8                   Load Counter with $C8 for
                                           1 second delay
COUNT   $032B   JSR $ED2C (DEBK1)         Call 5mS Monitor Routine
            E   DEX                       Decrement Counter
            F   BNE $032B (COUNT)         Counter finished?
        $0331   RTS                       Return to Main Program
RDOUT   $0332   LDA #01
            4   STA $A002 (PBDD)          Make PB0 Output (Scope
                                           (Trigger)
            7   LDY #00                   Initialize Y Index of
                                           Table
TRIG    $0339   LDA $A000 (PBD)     ⎫
            C   EOR #01             ⎬     Toggle PB0(Scope Trigger)
            E   STA $A000 (PBD)     ⎭
DUMP    $0341   LDA $0200,Y         ⎫
            4   STA $A001 (PAD)     ⎪
            7   INY                 ⎬     Read out Table of Values
            8   BNE $0341 (DUMP)    ⎭
END     $034A   JMP $0339 (TRIG)          Re-trigger scope and
                                           Refresh Display
```

AIM Printout - Ramp Approximation

```
<K>*=0300
/33
 0300 A0 LDY #00
 0302 A9 LDA #FF
 0304 8D STA A003
 0307 A2 LDX #00
 0309 8E STX A001
 030C AD LDA A000
 030F 10 BPL 0315
 0311 E8 INX
 0312 4C JMP 0309
 0315 AD LDA A001
 0318 99 STA 0200,Y
 031B C8 INY
 031C F0 BEQ 0332
 031E 20 JSR 0329
 0321 A9 LDA #00
 0323 8D STA A000
 0326 4C JMP 0307
 0329 A2 LDX #C8
 032B 20 JSR ED2C
 032E CA DEX
 032F D0 BNE 032B
 0331 60 RTS
 0332 A9 LDA #01
 0334 8D STA A002
 0337 A0 LDY #00
 0339 AD LDA A000
 033C 49 EOR #01
 033E 8D STA A000
 0341 B9 LDA 0200,Y
 0344 8D STA A001
 0347 C8 INY
 0348 D0 BNE 0341
 034A 4C JMP 0339
```

Scope Trace

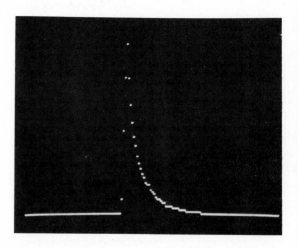

Digitized values of the amplified output of a thermocouple
momemtarily exposed to a flame.
Total scan time = 256 secs.

Exp. 34 - Analog-> Digital Conversion - Success. Approx.

GOAL: Analog-> Digital Conversion (Successive Approx.) and
Storage of 256 Data Points into Page 2 of RAM with
Readout on a Laboratory Oscilloscope. Location $0000
is used for temporary storage.

```
START   $0300   LDY #00                 Initialize Y Index
        $0302   LDA #FF
            4   STA $A003   (PADD)       Make Port A (ORA) Output
            7   LDA #00                  Initialize PB7 = 0 before
CONVT   $0309   STA $A000   (PBD)         starting Approximation
            C   LDA #80                  Load A with 1000 0000
            E   STA $00                  Store in temp. loc. $0000
TEST    $0310   STA $A001   (PAD)        Output value to Port A
            3   LDX $A000   (PBD)        Test PBD
            6   BMI $031B   (NEXT)       If PB7= 1, branch to next
                                            significant bit
            8   SEC                      If PB7= 0, subtract bit
            9   SBC $00                     from current value of A
NEXT    $031B   LSR $00                  Shift to next sig. bit
            D   BCS $0324   (TABLE)      Branch to TABLE if done
            F   ADC $00                  Add to A if not done
        $0321   JMP $0310   (TEST)       Test new apprximation
TABLE   $0324   LDA $A001   (PAD)        Store Port A data in
            7   STA $0200,Y               Page 2 of RAM
            A   INY                      Increment Y Index
            B   BEQ $033C   (RDOUT)      Branch to RDOUT if done
            D   JSR $0333   (DELAY)      Delay between points
        $0330   JMP $0309   (CONVT)      Go to CONVT for next data
DELAY   $0333   LDX #C8                  Load Counter with $C8 for
                                            1 second delay
COUNT   $0335   JSR $ED2C   (DEBK1)      Call 5mS Monitor Routine
            8   DEX                      Decrement Counter
            9   BNE $0335   (COUNT)      Counter finished?
            B   RTS                      Return to Main Program
RDOUT   $033C   LDA #01
            E   STA $A002   (PBDD)       Make PB0 Output (Scope
                                            Trigger)
        $0341   LDY #00                  Initialize Y Index
TRIG    $0343   LDA $A000   (PBD)     ⎫
            6   EOR #01                 ⎬  Toggle PB0(Scope Trigger)
            8   STA $A000   (PBD)     ⎭
DUMP    $034B   LDA $0200,Y           ⎫
            E   STA $A001   (PAD)     ⎬  Read out Table of Values
        $0351   INY                      ⎪
            2   BNE $034B   (DUMP)    ⎭
END     $0354   JMP $0343   (TRIG)      Refresh Display
```

AIM Printout - Successive Approximation

```
<K>*=0300
/38
 0300 A0 LDY #00
 0302 A9 LDA #FF
 0304 8D STA A003
 0307 A9 LDA #00
 0309 8D STA A000
 030C A9 LDA #80
 030E 85 STA 00
 0310 8D STA A001
 0313 AE LDX A000
 0316 30 BMI 031B
 0318 38 SEC
 0319 E5 SBC 00
 031B 46 LSR 00
 031D B0 BCS 0324
 031F 65 ADC 00
 0321 4C JMP 0310
 0324 AD LDA A001
 0327 99 STA 0200,Y
 032A C8 INY
 032B F0 BEQ 033C
 032D 20 JSR 0333
 0330 4C JMP 0309
 0333 A2 LDX #C8
 0335 20 JSR ED2C
 0338 CA DEX
 0339 D0 BNE 0335
 033B 60 RTS
 033C A9 LDA #01
 033E 8D STA A002
 0341 A0 LDY #00
 0343 AD LDA A000
 0346 49 EOR #01
 0348 8D STA A000
 034B B9 LDA 0200,Y
 034E 8D STA A001
 0351 C8 INY
 0352 D0 BNE 034B
 0354 4C JMP 0343
```

Exp. 35 - Interrupt-Driven A-> D Conversion (Success-
          ive Approximation) with Dynamic Readout on
          Laboratory Oscilloscope

GOAL: Timer T1 Interrupt-Driven A-> D Conversion and
      Storage of 256 Data Points into Page 2 of RAM with
      Dynamic Scope Readout. The number of 0.05 sec.
      intervals between data points is contained in loc-
      ation $0000 and the trigger value (in Hex) to start
      the conversion routine is contained in loc. $0001.

Note: Function key F1 is used to start a new conversion
      routine (after the present one is processed) while
      Keys F2 & F3 are used to enter the Display Routine.
      Hitting the <ESC> key exits the Display Routine and
      re-enters the Monitor. Zero Page locations $02, $03
      and $04 are used for temporary storage of variables.

START $0300   LDA #4C   Load F1, F2, F3 function
          2   STA $010C (F1)   locations with JMP
          5   STA $010F (F2)   instructions (i.e. $4C)
          8   STA $0112 (F3)
          B   LDA #37   (F1-L)   Level-triggered Start
          D   STA $010D   Conversion Routine-->
        $0310   LDA #03   (F1-H)   --> (LEVEL)
          2   STA $010E
          5   LDA #AA   (F2-L)   Display Routine (RDOUT)
          7   STA $0110
          A   LDA #03   (F2-H)
          C   STA $0111
          F   LDA #AA   (F3-L)   Display Routine (RDOUT)
        $0321   STA $0113
          4   LDA #03   (F3-H)
          6   STA $0114
          9   LDA #FF   Make Port A (ORA) Output
          B   STA $A003 (PADD)
          E   LDA #00   Initialize PB7 = 0 before
        $0330   STA $A000 (PBD)   starting Successive
                                       Approximation Routine
          3   STA $04   Initialize Table Index
          5   BRK   Return to Monitor
        $0336   NOP   No operation
LEVEL $0337   LDA $01   Load level-triggering
                                       value from loc. $0001
          9   STA $A001 (PAD)   and output to Port A

```
IDLE    $033C   LDX $A000 (PBD)     Test PBD. Stay in IDLE
        F       BPL $033C (IDLE)      routine if PB7 = 0
TIMER   $0341   SEI                 Set IRQ Disable Flag
        2       LDA $00             Load A with timing byte
        4       STA $02             Store A in temp. loc. $02
        6       LDA #76
        8       STA $A404 (IRQL)    Load IRQL
        B       LDA #03
        D       STA $A405 (IRQL)    Load IRQH
        $0350   LDA #40             Set Timer T1 in Free
        2       STA $A00B (ACR)       Running Mode with
                                      PB7 disabled
        5       LDA #C0             Set Interrupt Enable Reg-
        7       STA $A00E (IER)       ister (IER) to allow IRQ
                                      interrupt by T1 timeout
        A       LDA #4E             Load T1L-L with $4E
        C       STA $A004 (T1L-L)
        F       LDA #C3             Load T1L-H with $C3 and
        $0361   STA $A005 (T1L-H)     start Timer T1 --> cont-
                                      inuous 0.05sec. timeouts
        4       CLI                 Clear IRQ Disable Flag
        5       LDY #00             Initialize Y Index
        7       LDA #00             Initialize (to zero) the
INIT    $0369   STA $0200,Y           contents of Page 2
        C       INY
        D       BNE $0369 (INIT)
        F       LDA #00             Initialize Table Index
        $0371   STA $04
        3       JMP $03AA (RDOUT)   Go to Display Routine
IRQ     $0376   PHA                 Save Accumulator on Stack
        7       TYA                 Save Y Index on Stack
        8       PHA
        9       DEC $02             Is the prescribed number
                                      of timeouts completed?
        B       BEQ $0380 (CONVT)   If yes, go to conversion
                                      routine--> CONVT
        D       JMP $03CB (RESET1)  If no, go to RESET1
CONVT   $0380   LDA #00             Initialize PB7 = 0 before
        2       STA $A000 (PBD)       starting Successive
                                      Approximation Routine
        5       LDA #80             Load A with 1000 0000
        7       STA $03             Store in temp. loc. $03
TEST    $0389   STA $A001 (PAD)     Output value to Port A
        $038C   LDX $A000 (PBD)     Test PBD
        F       BMI $0394 (NEXT)    If PB7 = 1, branch to
                                      next significant bit
        $0391   SEC                 If PB7 = 0, subtract bit
        2       SBC $03               from current contents of
                                      Accumulator
```

```
NEXT     $0394   LSR $03                Shift to next sig. bit
           6    BCS $039D (TABLE)       Branch to TABLE is done
           8    ADC $03                 Add to A if not done
           A    JMP $0389 (TEST)        Test new approximation
TABLE    $039D   LDY $04                Load Y Register with
                                        current Table Index
           F    LDA $A001 (PAD)         Store Port A data in
         $03A2   STA $0200,Y             Page 2 of RAM
           5    INC $04                 Increment Table Index
           7    BNE $03D2 (RESET2)      Branch to RESET2 if
                                        Table is not complete
           9    SEI                     If Table is complete,
                                        set IRQ Disable Flag
RDOUT    $03AA   LDA #01                Enter Display Routine
           C    STA $A002 (PBDD)        Make PB0 output (Scope
                                        Trigger)
TRIG     $03AF   LDY #00                Initialize Y Index of
                                        Table
         $03B1   STY $A000 (PBD)        Initialize PB0 = 0
           4    LDA $A000 (PBD)         ⎫
           7    EOR #01                 ⎬ Toggle PB0 (Scope
                                        ⎭  Trigger)
           9    STA $A000 (PBD)
DUMP     $03BC   LDA $0200,Y            ⎫
           F    STA $A001 (PAD)         ⎬ Read out Table of Values
         $03C2   INY                    ⎭
           3    BNE $03BC (DUMP)
           5    JSR $E907 (RCHECK)      Escape to Monitor by
                                        hitting <ESC>
           8    JMP $03AF (TRIG)        Re-trigger scope and
                                        refresh display
RESET1   $03CB   LDA $A004 (T1L-L)      Clear T1 Flag in
                                        Interrupt Flag
                                        Register (IFR)
           E    PLA                     Restore Y Index
           F    TAY                      from Stack
         $03D0   PLA                    Restore A from Stack
           1    RTI                     Return from interrupt
                                        to Display Routine
RESET2   $0302   LDA $00                Reload A with timing byte
           4    STA $02                 Store A in temp. loc. $02
           6    LDA $A004 (T1L-L)       Clear T1 Flag in
                                        Interrupt Flag
                                        Register (IFR)
           9    PLA                     Restore Y Index
           A    TAY                      from Stack
           B    PLA                     Restore A from Stack
END      $03DC   RTI                    Return from interrupt
                                        to Display Routine
```

182

Note: A hex value of $01 written into location $0000 produces a total scan time of 256 x 0.05 x 1 = 12.8 secs. A value of $FF results in a total scan time of 256 x 0.05 x 255 = 54.4 mins. Scope sweep time for readout both <u>during</u> and after data acquisition is ca. 3.3 mS/Sweep.

<u>AIM Printout</u>

```
<K>*=0300
/33
 0300 A9 LDA #4C
 0302 8D STA 010C
 0305 8D STA 010F
 0308 8D STA 0112
 030B A9 LDA #37
 030D 8D STA 010D
 0310 A9 LDA #03
 0312 8D STA 010E
 0315 A9 LDA #AA
 0317 8D STA 0110
 031A A9 LDA #03
 031C 8D STA 0111
 031F A9 LDA #AA
 0321 8D STA 0113
 0324 A9 LDA #03
 0326 8D STA 0114
 0329 A9 LDA #FF
 032B 8D STA A003
 032E A9 LDA #00
 0330 8D STA A000
 0333 85 STA 04
 0335 00 BRK
 0336 EA NOP
 0337 A5 LDA 01
 0339 8D STA A001
 033C AE LDX A000
 033F 10 BPL 033C
 0341 78 SEI
 0342 A5 LDA 00
 0344 85 STA 02
 0346 A9 LDA #76
 0348 8D STA A404
 034B A9 LDA #03
```

```
<K>*=034D
/34
 034D 8D STA A405
 0350 A9 LDA #40
 0352 8D STA A00B
 0355 A9 LDA #C0
 0357 8D STA A00E
 035A A9 LDA #4E
 035C 8D STA A004
 035F A9 LDA #C3
 0361 8D STA A005
 0364 58 CLI
 0365 A0 LDY #00
 0367 A9 LDA #00
 0369 99 STA 0200,Y
 036C C8 INY
 036D D0 BNE 0369
 036F A9 LDA #00
 0371 85 STA 04
 0373 4C JMP 03AA
 0376 48 PHA
 0377 98 TYA
 0378 48 PHA
 0379 C6 DEC 02
 037B F0 BEQ 0380
 037D 4C JMP 03CB
 0380 A9 LDA #00
 0382 8D STA A000
 0385 A9 LDA #80
 0387 85 STA 03
 0389 8D STA A001
 038C AE LDX A000
 038F 30 BMI 0394
 0391 38 SEC
 0392 E5 SBC 03
 0394 46 LSR 03
```

```
<K>*=0396
/34
 0396 B0 BCS 039D
 0398 65 ADC 03
 039A 4C JMP 0389
 039D A4 LDY 04
 039F AD LDA A001
 03A2 99 STA 0200,Y
 03A5 E6 INC 04
 03A7 D0 BNE 03D2
 03A9 78 SEI
 03AA A9 LDA #01
 03AC 8D STA A002
 03AF A0 LDY #00
 03B1 8C STY A000
 03B4 AD LDA A000
 03B7 49 EOR #01
 03B9 8D STA A000
 03BC B9 LDA 0200,Y
 03BF 8D STA A001
 03C2 C8 INY
 03C3 D0 BNE 03BC
 03C5 20 JSR E907
 03C8 4C JMP 03AF
 03CB AD LDA A004
 03CE 68 PLA
 03CF A8 TAY
 03D0 68 PLA
 03D1 40 RTI
 03D2 A5 LDA 00
 03D4 85 STA 02
 03D6 AD LDA A004
 03D9 68 PLA
 03DA A8 TAY
 03DB 68 PLA
 03DC 40 RTI
```

7.4   HARDWARE A/D CONVERTERS

The preceding A->D conversion techniques can also be performed in hardware with a servo-type A/D converter.   These devices contain an on-board D/A converter, op-amp comparator, shift-register, clock and logic programmer.   By doing the conversion process in hardware instead of software, they permit the microprocessor/microcomputer to be available for other tasks during the conversion periods.   They are commercially available in IC form for interfacing to the I/O ports of a microcomputer or, in some cases, directly to the microprocessor busses (i.e. address, data and control).   These latter types are classified as MPU-compatible.   Depending upon the number of bits, conversion times for the common successive-approximation types are in the range of 1-30 microseconds.   A conversion cycle usually begins with a START or CONVERT (CNVT) pulse.   Upon completion of the conversion, an END OF CONVERSION (EOC), DATA READY (DR) or STATUS (STS) line will go low and the data will appear at the output in the form of n binary voltages or currents for an n-bit converter.   These two lines are employed in a handshake fashion with a microcomputer or VIA for the efficient transfer/storage of digitized information.   Fig. 7-10 demonstrates this concept for the Analog Devices´ AD570 8-bit A/D Converter interfaced to an output port (PAD) of a 6522 VIA.

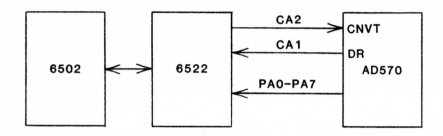

Fig. 7-10. Interfacing an 8-bit A/D Converter to a VIA.

Another type of A/D Converter called the tracking converter
is really based on the Ramp Approximation and employs a positive
or negative ramp through the use of up/down counters. It
continuously tracks the input voltage by monitoring a
comparator´s output to indicate which direction the ramp should
go to reach the unknown voltage.

In the dual-slope converter an unknown input voltage is
converted to a charge by applying a proportional current to an
integrating capacitor for an exact time. At the end of this
period, a START pulse is generated and a constant current source
of reverse polarity is applied to the capacitor. When the
capacitor is precisely discharged to zero volts, a STOP pulse is
generated. The measured time interval (a digital value) between
START and STOP pulses is proportional to the input voltage.
Conversion times for this type of A/D conversion are on the
order of 2^{n+1} clock cycles for an n-bit converter. So for a
12-bit converter óperating at 1MHz, a full scale conversion will

be completed in 8.192 milliseconds. Though too slow for fast data acquisition, dual-slope converters are adequate for such sensors as thermocouples and capacitance manometers where millisecond conversion times can be tolerated. One reason for the general acceptability of the dual-slope converter is its inherently good noise rejection. Noise pulses are reduced considerably by the integrating capacitor thereby allowing this converter's use in such commercial items as digital panel meters and digital voltmeters (DVM's).

7.5   OTHER ANALOG-> DIGITAL CONVERSION SCHEMES

Another technique for converting an analog input into a digital output involves the use of Voltage-to-Frequency (V/F) conversion. Although not as widely employed as the other analog-> digital conversion techniques, this method is useful in systems where slow conversion times can be tolerated and in those applications where a sensor is remotely situated with respect to the measurement/control system. Once an unknown input signal (from a sensor, for example) is converted to a frequency, it can be counted by a microcomputer using either software-timing loops and/or timer/counter routines. An example of this conversion process is demonstrated in Fig. 7-11 where a general-purpose 555 Timer IC is used to convert an unknown resistance into a digital frequency.

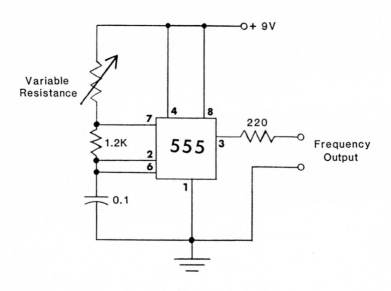

Fig. 7-11. Resistance-to-Frequency Converter.

For slowly changing analog signals (<100Hz), the
frequency-conversion technique can be modified to produce a
Pulse-Duration Converter. In this process, an analog signal
(usually a voltage, current or resistance) generates a pulse
whose duration or width is proportional to the magnitude of the
analog signal. A microcomputer is programmed to accurately
measure the length of the pulse by employing its
crystal-controlled index registers/counters or timers. An
overall analog--> digital conversion is thereby effected. If
16-bit external timers (such as Tl or T2 in the 6522 VIA) are
used to measure the pulse durations, 16-bit resolution or 0.002%
precision is possible. Although the corresponding conversion

times may be large (i.e. milliseconds), this may not be much of a problem in certain laboratory measurements (barometric pressure readings, for example).

Fig. 7-12 demonstrates one method of generating pulse-width modulated signals using an op amp comparator. Here, the output is a train of pulses whose frequency depends on the input sawtooth frequency and whose pulse width depends upon the _level_ of the DC input voltage.

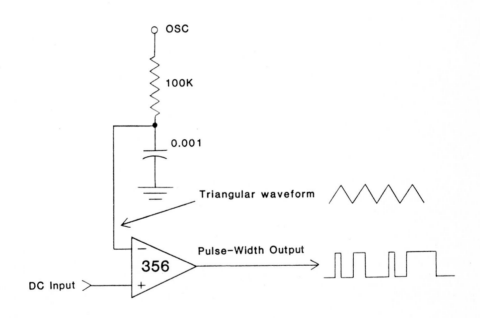

Fig. 7-12. Voltage-to-Pulse Width Converter.

For resistance measurements, a modification of the 555 Timer circuit is described in Fig. 7-13. It is configured in such a way that a trigger pulse (from a microcomputer) begins charging capacitor C_T to a fixed voltage through the unknown resistance R. The time required to charge C_T is directly proportional to the charging rate and hence the magnitude of the unknown resistance. Upon completion of this charging period, the 555 forces the output line, which is input to the microcomputer, to go high. Appropriate time-delays and range settings are selected by choosing different values for capacitor C_T. R can be either an externally variable resistance (potentiometer) or a resistance transducer such as a thermistor, photoresistor, or strain-gauge which is capable of transforming a physical variable (heat, light, stress) into a resistance value.

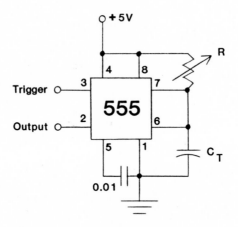

Fig. 7-13.   Resistance-to-Pulse Duration Converter.

One point worth noting in this circuit is the fact that the 555 IC begins discharging capacitor C_T <u>after</u> the output line is brought high. C_T will continue to discharge until the 555 is triggered again. Care should be taken to ensure that sufficient time is allowed for the capacitor to fully discharge between trigger pulses lest timing aberrations lead to erratic A->D conversions.

When extremely fast conversion times are required, the <u>flash</u> or <u>parallel</u> analog-to-digital converter is necessary. These devices are relatively new items and are finding increased application in such emerging fields as high-speed data analysis, speech recognition and flash spectroscopy among others. Their principle of operation relies on a comparison of an unknown input voltage with a series of prescribed reference potentials. A voltage/divider chain of resistors along with a bank of comparators and encoding circuitry perform the two basic functions of quantification and decoding. This is demonstrated in Fig. 7-14 for the simple 2-bit flash A/D converter. As the input voltage is increased from 0 to 8V, the comparators successively change states (at 2V intervals) to reflect the level of the incoming signal. An LED-bargraph indicator such as found on certain audio equipment is an example of this process. If this information is to be input to a microcomputer, appropriate encoding circuitry is needed to produce a normal binary code from the comparator output lines.

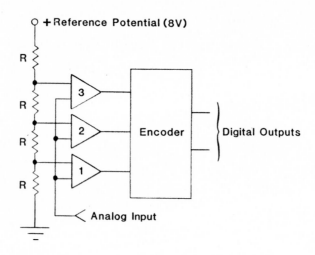

Fig. 7-14.   2-Bit Flash A/D Converter.

The encoding process, though it involves complex circuit design, does not significantly reduce the high speed of conversion which is a result of the simultaneous or parallel comparison of all output levels. Indeed, the singular drawback of the flash A/D converter is its circuit complexity. An n-bit converter requires 2^n-1 comparators. Consequently, an 8-bit A/D device of this type requires 255 comparators not to mention the encoding circuitry, latches, voltage reference and control lines. This is perhaps the chief reason why these converters have not been as rapidly developed as the more simpler types. Nevertheless, despite these complexities, TRW, Inc. manufactures an 8-bit flash A/D Converter, the TDC1007J which completes a conversion in 33 ns and RCA has recently developed a CMOS 8-bit

flash A/D, the CA3308 which completes a conversion in 70 ns.
Other manufacturers have also produced their versions of the
flash converter. As submicron lithographic techniques continue
to improve, there is no doubt that higher precision models of
this converter will evolve.

7.6   BEYOND 8-BITS

Interfacing 10, 12 and 16-bit A/D and D/A converters to an
8-bit microprocessor bus or I/O Port involves additional
hardware circuitry. For high precision A/D converters, the bit
pattern or total number of logical 0´s and 1´s which is output
from the converter must be presented to an 8-bit port in two
stages. The first process presents 8-bits for subsequent
capture and processing while the second involves the remaining
n-8 bits for an n-bit converter (16>n>8). Conversely, for a
high precision D/A converter to work properly the total n-bit
pattern must be presented simultaneously to its input pins.
Both of these processes involve circuitry which employ specific
hardware devices called digital data latches. One example of
this is the popular 74100 8-Bit Bistable Latch. This device
contains two sets of four synchronously-clocked D-type
flip-flops which are capable of snatching and holding 8-bits of
information for output at a later prescribed time. Data (i.e.
0´s and 1´s) applied to the input pins are output only when the
strobe terminals are brought high (_/‾). When the strobe

terminals are brought low (⌐), the output terminals maintain (latch) that data present at the last strobe-high transition.

An example demonstrating how two 74100′s can be used to interface a 12-bit D/A converter to two 8-bit output ports (Port A and Port B) of an I/O device (such as a 6522 VIA) is described in Fig. 7-15.

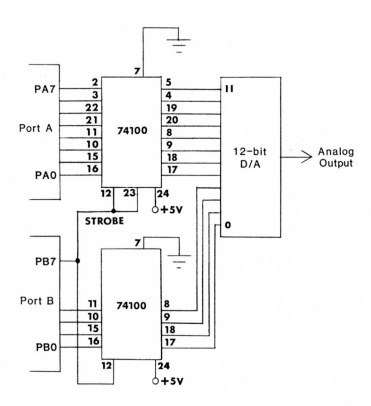

Fig. 7-15.   Interfacing a 12-bit D/A Converter.

The output ports (Port A, Port B) in the circuit are themselves latched ports. The strobe pins of one 74100 latch are tied together to enable 8-bit data transfer from Port A whereas a single strobe line is used in the second 74100 for 4-bit transfer from Port B. In one execution cycle, the highest 8 bits (nos. 4-15) of the 12-bit word are written to Port A. In the following (or later) cycle, the remaining 4 bits (nos. 0-3) are written to the output pins PB0-PB3 of Port B. Simultaneous with this last operation, both 74100 latches are strobed by writing a logical "1" to PB7 thereby enabling the entire 12-bit word to be presented to the D/A converter for output as an analog signal.

Interfacing high precision A/D converters to 8-bit microcomputers can be either simple or complex depending upon the type of A/D converter and the microcomputer port or bus. It is relatively simple for latched A/D converters and latched I/O Ports. Unlatched converters and I/O ports require the addition of external data latches thereby increasing the hardware (and timing) complexity. For the sake of simplicity, we will consider the former types. Fig. 7-16 illustrates this for the latched input ports of a 6522 VIA interfaced to the latched output pins of the Hybrid Systems´ HS574 12-Bit A/D Converter. Analog input voltages (from a sensor amplifier, for example) are restricted to the 0-10V range.

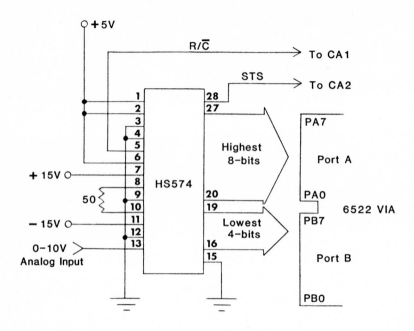

Fig. 7-16.   Interfacing a 12-bit A/D Converter.

In the configuration shown, a negative-going pulse (⌐⌐)
from CA1 applied to the R/C̄ (READ/CONVERT) line will initiate a
12-bit conversion.   Some 200 ns later, the STS (STATUS) line
will go high and remain that way until a conversion cycle is
completed (ca. 25 microseconds).   After that time, the STS line
will drop low and signal the 6522 via the CA2 line that a 12-bit
digitized version of an input analog voltage (0-10V) is
available on Ports A and B for readout and processing (i.e.
storage, addition, subtraction ---).   Moreover, since not all of
the Port B pins are used, control lines CA1 and CA2 can be
replaced by PB0 and PB1 for example.   In that event, PB0 would

have to be programmed for output (PBDD = 0000 0001 = $01) since
it is responsible for supplying the CONVERT pulse to initiate
the A->D conversion. Subsequently PB1, which is now connected
to the STS line, can be examined for a logical 1-->0 transition
(by an idling BIT loop, for example) which signals the end of
the conversion process.

7.7 SAMPLE AND HOLD CIRCUITS

When the rate of change of an analog signal approaches or
is greater than the speed of conversion of a sampling A/D
converter, the final digitized values are not representative of
the input signal waveform. This is a case where the measurement
system is slower than the system to be measured. In order to
overcome this difficulty, what is needed is some type of
"camera" which is capable of taking various snapshots of the
high speed analog signal at specified time intervals for later
processing by the A/D converter. This interface between the
signal and A/D converter is commonly referred to as a
sample-and-hold (S/H) circuit. As its name implies, the input
signal is sampled at a given instant in time and held for
subsequent processing. This is most often accomplished by
allowing the analog signal to charge/discharge a capacitor
during the sampling period and then isolating the capacitor in
the hold period using a fast analog switch for measurement of
its charge by a high input impedance amplifier. A typical 2-op

amp-based sample-and-hold circuit is depicted in Fig. 7-17.

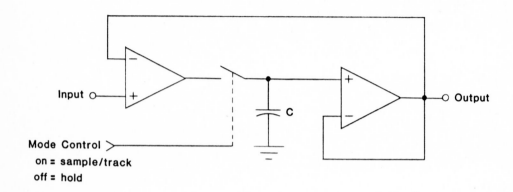

Fig. 7-17.   Sample and Hold Circuit.

The input buffer amplifier is usually a high gain op-amp with a current output that charges the capacitor via the logic controlled switch. The capacitor C is discharged by the unity gain buffer/follower. Since the output is tied to the inverting input of the op-amp follower, the charge on the capacitor is forced to follow the input in the sampling (or tracking) mode. In the hold mode, the capacitor retains its charge and is measured (slightly discharged) by the high impedance output amp.

The tracking capacitor C is commonly fabricated from a low loss dielectric such as teflon or polystyrene. Because of their low moisture retention and low dielectric absorption, these materials are capable of being repeatedly charged and discharged (i.e. polarized and depolarized) in a uniform and reproducible manner. The response time of the S/H circuit is limited by the

internal RC time constant which should be much less than the
rate of change of the input analog signal. This dictates a low
value for the internal resistance R. Acquisition time of the
S/H is defined as that minimum time necessary to acquire and
track the input voltage (within a specified error band) after
having been switched into the sample mode. Aperture time is
that total delay interval between the hold command and the
actual switching into the hold mode (ca. 10-50ns) during which
time the sampling process continues. Droop is the drift in the
output voltage per unit time (V/s) during the hold mode and slew
rate is the maximum rate of change in the output voltage (V/s)
of the S/H circuit.

Various monolithic IC versions of sample-and-hold circuits
are commercially available. They are finding increased
application in those high speed data acquisition systems where
high resolution (>12 bit) A/D-converters are employed. A fast
12-bit A/D-converter, for example, will digitize an input signal
in ca. 1 microsecond. For 12-bit resolution, this demands input
signal changes of less than 0.02% during the time necessary for
A-> D conversion. As a result of this restriction, input signal
waveforms must be confined to frequencies less than ca. 230Hz in
order to avoid substantial linearity errors. Extension to
higher speed signals dictates the use of a S/H circuit. The
digital counterpart to the sample-and-hold circuit is the data
latch.

CHAPTER 8

```
┌─────────────┐
│  CONTROL    │
└─────────────┘
```

* Solid-State Relays

* Stepper Motors

* Programmable-Gain Amplifiers

* Thyristors (SCR´s and Triacs)

* Power MOSFET´s

```
┌─────────────┐
│  CONTROL    │
└─────────────┘
```

A microcomputer can control an external device or process by way of its digital outputs. These digital outputs (0´s and 1´s) can be used directly in certain cases while in others they must first be converted to an analog value (i.e. D->A).

8.1   SOLID-STATE RELAYS

The simplest case of direct digital control is the binary on/off switch as exemplified in the Solid-State Relay (SSR). There are basically three common SSR´s, two of which have no moving parts. Although not truly solid-state, the reed-coupled triac is a hybrid-SSR (HSSR) which is comprised of a reed relay which controls a current-handling triac.

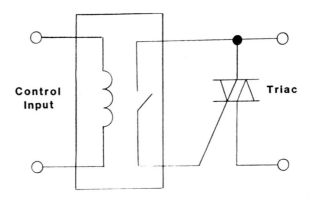

Fig. 8-1.   Reed-Coupled Triac.

The transformer-coupled SSR uses an oscillator which is excited by the input voltage and transformer-coupled to a Sense circuit that controls a high current triac.

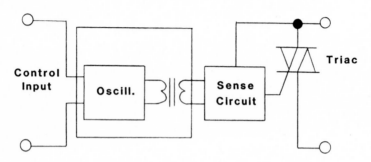

Fig. 8-2.   Transformer-Coupled Solid State Relay.

The opto-coupled SSR consists of a light-emitting diode (LED), which activates a phototransistor/sense circuit combination to energize a current-handling triac.   High voltage isolation between input/output circuitry and zero-voltage turn-on are the major advantages of this type of SSR.

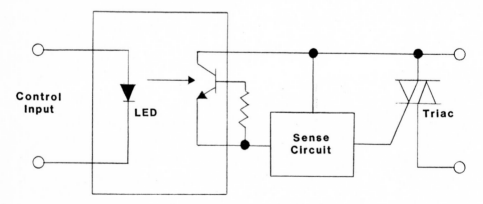

Fig. 8-3.   Opto-Coupled Solid State Relay.

These latter features are especially important considerations when interfacing static-prone digital circuits (i.e. microcomputers) to high voltage/current devices (viz. flash photolamps, large motors, lasers, RF transmitters ---).

8.2   STEPPER MOTORS

Quite often in a laboratory situation, it is necessary to precisely control the exact velocity or position of a specific device (a grating in a monochromator, for example). This can be accomplished under digital or computer control by a particular type of motor called a stepper motor.

As its name implies, a stepper motor's principle of operation relies on the response of a multipoled (usually 12 or 24) rotor to a precisely pulsed-voltage pattern applied to the surrounding stator windings (usually 2 or 4). The shaft of the stepper motor responds by rotating an exact fraction of a turn (usually given in step angles) for each sequential voltage pulse applied to the motor windings. A motor with a 12-pole rotor in a stator housing of 4 windings completes one revolution in exactly 48 steps. The step angle is therefore $360^{o}/48$ or 7.5^{o}. Between steps, the rotor is "frozen" in place by the magnetic field arrangement. Stepper motors are ideal positioning devices because their steps are precise, uniform and reproducible. Most applications are in the moderate speed range of 25-2000 steps/second with a torque range of 1-2000 oz./in.

They are used commercially in such products as printers, recorders, clocks, disk drives and metering-pumps and are finding increased application in the emerging field of Robotics.

One popular type of switching sequence is the two-phase unipolar drive in the 4-coil motor. In this type of motor, two coils comprise each half of the stator housing (bifilar winding). The winding flux is reversed by energizing one coil or the other from a single power supply in a 4-step sequence. Speed and direction of motor rotation is governed by the frequency and sequencing of the digital pulses applied to the stepper motor. Drive transistors are used to amplify the low level input pulses to appropriate voltage and current levels.

An illustration of a 4-coil stepper motor in the normal unipolar drive circuit is depicted in Fig. 8-4.

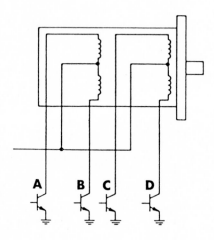

Fig. 8-4. Four-Coil Unipolar Drive Stepper Motor.

NORMAL 4-STEP SEQUENCE

Step No.	A	B	C	D	Binary	HEX
1	ON	OFF	ON	OFF	1010	$0A
2	ON	OFF	OFF	ON	1001	09
3	OFF	ON	OFF	ON	0101	05
4	OFF	ON	ON	OFF	0110	06
1	ON	OFF	ON	OFF	1010	0A

CW

CCW

In the 4-step sequence outlined above, a sequential voltage-pulse pattern (in HEX) of $0A, $09, $05, $06, $0A --- will rotate the motor shaft in the clockwise (CW) direction. The opposite sequence holds for the counter-clockwise (CCW) direction. Speed of rotation is approximated by the time-duration between pulses. For example, a series of 1-millisecond spaced pulses applied to a 48-step motor will cause the motor shaft to rotate at a speed of $(1/0.048)60 = 1250$ RPM (revolutions per minute).

Stepper motors can also be driven in a single phase fashion commonly referred to as wave drive . In this type of drive, only one coil is energized in each sequence. This makes for more efficient use since fewer windings are active per sequence although step accuracy is appreciably diminished.

WAVE DRIVE					

Step No.	A	B	C	D	Binary	HEX
1	ON	OFF	OFF	OFF	1000	$80
2	OFF	OFF	OFF	ON	0001	01
3	OFF	ON	OFF	OFF	0100	04
4	OFF	OFF	ON	OFF	0010	02
1	ON	OFF	OFF	OFF	1000	80

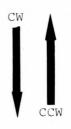

A third type of drive is the 1/2-Step 8-Step Sequence. This particular drive doubles the stepping resolution of a motor (i.e. 7.5°s.a. --> 3.75°). However, this is accomplished at the expense of stepping accuracy since the winding and flux conditions are not similar for each step as when full stepping.

1/2 STEP SEQUENCE					

Step No.	A	B	C	D	Binary	HEX
1	ON	OFF	ON	OFF	1010	$0A
2	ON	OFF	OFF	OFF	1000	08
3	ON	OFF	OFF	ON	1001	09
4	OFF	OFF	OFF	ON	0001	01
5	OFF	ON	OFF	ON	0101	05
6	OFF	ON	OFF	OFF	0100	04
7	OFF	ON	ON	OFF	0110	06
8	OFF	OFF	ON	OFF	0010	02
1	ON	OFF	ON	OFF	1010	0A

Other types of stepper motors such as mechanical steppers and variable-reluctance types are also available. Both have their drawbacks, however. The highest practical stepping rate for a mechanical stepper is ca. 15 steps/second while the variable-reluctance types have a tendency to overshoot at high stepping speeds. Hardware drive circuitry is either available or can be easily designed for the various motor types. Stepper motors (and their drive transistors) can also be software-controlled directly from the output ports of a microcomputer.

An example of how one may use the output ports of an interface device (such as a VIA) to ·control a 4-coil stepping motor via software programming is as follows;

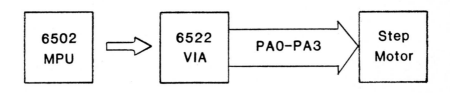

Fig. 8-5. Microprocessor Control of a Stepper Motor.

To step the motor in the clockwise (CW) direction, the following short assembly language program is used.

```
          INIT   LDA #0F      Initialize PADD for
                 STA PADD     outputs on PA0-PA3
          START  LDA #0A      Step 1
                 STA PAD
                 JSR DELAY    Delay between steps
                 LDA #09
                 STA PAD      Step 2
                 JSR DELAY
                 LDA #05
                 STA PAD      Step 3
                 JSR DELAY
                 LDA #06
                 STA PAD      Step 4
                 JSR DELAY
          END    JMP START    Repeat sequence
```

The DELAY (between pulses) routine can be implemented with index registers and/or timers, nested or otherwise. To operate the stepper-motor in the opposite (CCW) direction, the step sequence must be programmed in reverse order.

An illustration of hardware circuitry which can provide the normal 4-step switching sequence for a 4-coil stepper motor is shown in Fig. 8-6.

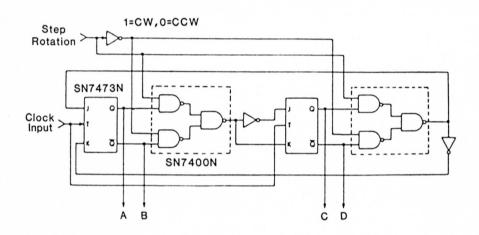

Fig. 8-6. Stepper Motor Interface.

Here, a dual J-K flip-flop (SN7473) is used with a quad-NAND gate (SN7400) to provide the correct stepping signals at the appropriate clock frequency. Clock signals and the sequence bit(s) are generated (via programming) by a microcomputer. In the simple program below, this is accomplished by using Bit#0 (PB0) of Port B (PBD) of a VIA to set the sequence (CW or CCW) bit while Bit#0 (PA0) of Port A (PAD) provides the clock signals as determined by the DELAY routine.

```
START   LDA #01      Initialize PBDD for
        STA PBDD     output to PB0
        STA PBD      Set PB0=1 for CW rotation
        LDA #01      Initialize PADD for
        STA PADD     output on PA0
        LDA #01
LOOP    STA PAD      Turn on PA0
        JSR DELAY    Delay between toggles
        EOR #01      Toggle PA0
END     JMP LOOP     Repeat sequence
```

One extension of this (or any other) motor-controller routine involves the use of interrupt-service routines which are called up after suitable delay intervals to provide the stepping signals. Such a modification has the singular advantage of allowing the microprocessor to be available (during the delay intervals) for other tasks such as monitoring the number of motor revolutions via shaft-encoders, for one.

Stepper motor interfaces and drivers are also available in IC form in standard 16-pin dual-in-line (DIP) packages. Examples include the Airpax/North American Philips SAA 1027 and the Sprague UCN-4202A, -4203A stepper-motor translator/drivers. Operating voltages can vary from 5V to 48V, although 12V and 24V are the most common.

The distinct advantages of stepper motors include: (1) brushless operation, (2) large speed ranges, (3) low cost, (4) ease of interfacing and (5) precise control.

8.3   PROGRAMMABLE-GAIN AMPLIFIERS

Besides controlling relays and stepper-motors, the digital outputs of a microcomputer can be used to control the gain of an amplifier. When this is accomplished under program control, a programmable-gain amplifier is the result.

Fig. 8-7 depicts a simple inverting amplifier built around a standard operational amplifier (op amp).

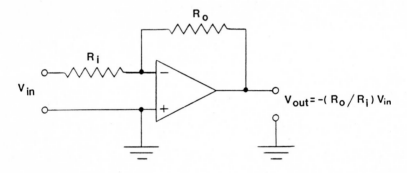

Fig. 8-7.   Op-Amp Inverter.

The voltage gain of the circuit is the ratio of the value of the feedback resistor (R_o) to the value of the input resistor (R_i). The polarity of the gain is negative since the amplifier operates in the inverting mode. If R_o or R_i were replaced by a potentiometer (or variable resistor), a variable-gain amplifier would result. Similarly, selectable fixed gain settings can be achieved by a parallel network of resistor/switch pairs as shown in Fig. 8-8.

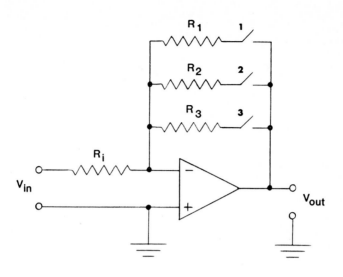

Fig. 8-8.   Selectable-Gain Amplifier.

The feedback resistor (R_o) is replaced by the parallel network combination in order to maintain a constant input impedance for the various gain settings.

Switch No.			
1	2	3	Voltage Gain
0	0	0	---
1	0	0	R_1/R_i
0	1	0	R_2/R_i
0	0	1	R_3/R_i
1	1	0	$R_1 R_2/R_i (R_1+R_2)$
1	0	1	$R_1 R_3/R_i (R_1+R_3)$
0	1	1	$R_2 R_3/R_i (R_2+R_3)$
1	1	1	$R_1 R_2 R_3/R_i (R_2 R_3+R_1 R_3+R_1 R_2)$

"1" = on

"0" = off

It is not too difficult to see that $2^N - 1$ gain settings are possible for N resistor/switch pairs. In practice however, this is limited by the maximum available (open-loop) gain of the op-amp and the tolerance ratings of the resistors.

If the manual switches are replaced with complementary metal oxide semiconductor (CMOS) analog switches, the gain of the op-amp can be digitally controlled via microcomputer. This is illustrated in Fig. 8-9 where an RCA CD4066 CMOS Quad Bilateral Switch is used in lieu of the three manual switches.

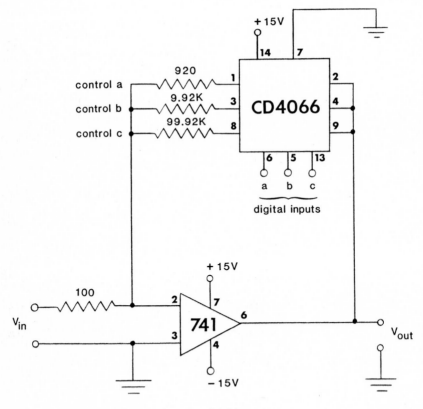

Fig. 8-9. Programmable-Gain Amplifier.

With the selected resistor values, which were chosen to offset the normal "on" resistance (80Ω) of the CD4066, gain settings of 10-1000 can be programmed by applying the proper digital code to the CMOS inputs (a-c).

a	b	c	GAIN
1	0	0	10
0	1	0	100
0	0	1	1000

The inverted output of this circuit can be re-inverted by the addition of another op-amp inverter configured for unity gain. Many available dual op-amp IC's (the 1458, for example) are useful in this regard. Although the gain range is large, one minor disadvantage of this design is its inability to provide uniform increments of gain throughout the range (i.e. 110, 101--> Gains of 9.09, 9.90). This can be somewhat obviated by the proper use of offset voltages.

Recently, several IC devices combining both functions of amplification and programmable gain have appeared on the market. One such example of this is the Analog Devices´ AD524 Programmable Instrumentation Amplifier. This particular 16-pin dual-in line-packaged (DIP) chip is pin-programmable for gains of 1, 10, 100, and 1000 with intermediate gains set by external resistors. It is shown in Fig. 8-10 for a gain setting of 100.

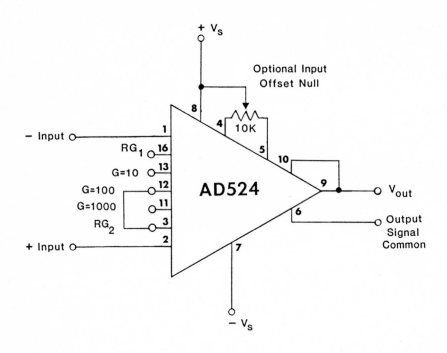

Fig. 8-10. Programmable Instrumentation Amplifier.

8.4 THYRISTORS (SCR's and Triacs)

Solid state semiconductor switches belong to the generic class of devices called thyristors. The name has functionally evolved as a consequence of their similarity to the earlier thyratron tubes. They are finding increased use in power switching/control applications at DC and AC voltages from 1-1000V and currents from 1-1000A. The two specific devices most often categorized as thyristors are the Silicon-Controlled Rectifier (SCR) and the Triac.

The SCR is basically a four-layer gated diode and is

represented symbolically in Fig. 8-11.

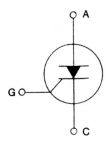

Fig. 8-11.   Circuit Symbol for a Silicon Controlled Rectifier.

A=Anode, C=Cathode and G=Gate.   In the normal course of events,
an SCR is triggered into conduction by the application of a
current pulse to the Gate(G) terminal.   In the absense of any
gate current, the applied voltage across A and C must reach the
breakover voltage of the SCR before switching occurs.   Normally,
SCR's are operated at voltages below this value and are turned
on by gate signals of sufficient amplitude to enable complete
turn-on independent of the applied voltage.   Once turned on, the
SCR will remain in the conducting state independent of gate
voltage or current until the primary current flow (between A and
C) is reduced to a value below what is known as the
characteristic holding current.   For SCR's, voltages are
considered to be in the forward direction when the anode(A) is
positive with respect to the cathode(C).   In this configuration,
there is only one mode of gate triggering capable of switching

the device into the conducting state, i.e. a positive gate signal for a positive anode(A). In situations where power control involves conversion of AC voltages and/or currents to DC and control of their values, SCR´s are employed because of their inherent rectifying properties.

Several of these restricting limitations of the SCR are lifted in the bidirectional thyristor more commonly known as the Triac. This device operates primarily as two SCR´s connected in a parallel head-to-tail fashion and is symbolically illustrated as such in Fig. 8-12.

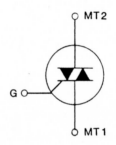

Fig. 8-12. Circuit Symbol for a Triac.

MT1, MT2 = Main Terminals 1 and 2 and G = Gate. An appropriate signal applied to the Gate(G) terminal in this device triggers conduction in both directions thereby effecting an AC Switch. Because of its structure, a triac can be triggered by either a positive or negative gate signal regardless of the voltage polarity across its main terminals MT1 and MT2. As with SCR´s, triacs are normally operated at voltages below their characteristic <u>breakover</u> voltages and are sustained in the conducting mode at currents above their characteristic <u>holding</u> <u>currents</u>. They can be triggered by both positive and negative DC currents as well as AC currents and pulses. Triacs were specifically developed for the control of AC power to a load.

A typical application of an SCR is the control of a DC motor from an AC source as depicted in Fig. 8-13.

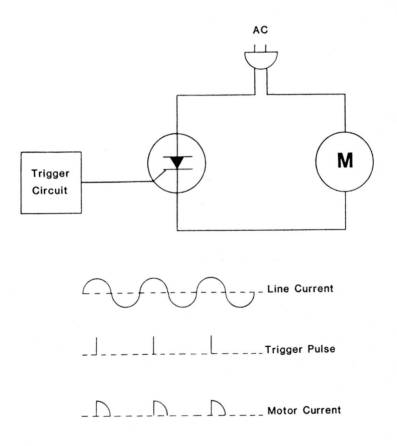

Fig. 8-13.   SCR Control of a DC Motor.

In this system, the trigger circuit turns the SCR on once during each AC cycle. When the AC line current approaches zero or drops below the holding current(usually milliamps) of the SCR, it ceases to conduct any current to the motor until it is triggered to do so again. By varying the timing of the trigger pulses, the average current supplied to the motor can be varied from zero to complete half-waves. This method of power regulation is called phase control and for the case of a single SCR is called half-wave phase control.

Full-wave phase control is achieved in the case of the triac whose analogous circuitry is depicted in Fig. 8-14 for the case of an AC motor. Here the triac is triggered into conduction during each half-cycle to produce an alternating current waveform. Suitable timing between trigger pulses can vary the average AC current supplied to the motor from zero to complete full-waves. This allows for total full-wave phase control of the AC current, a process which is inherently more efficient than resistive current control where the unused power(I^2R) is dissipated as heat. This particular feature of both SCR´s and triacs permits their use in commercial power control circuits where a limited amount of space is available(i.e. lamp-dimmers, variable-speed hand drills, electric blankets, cooking ranges....).

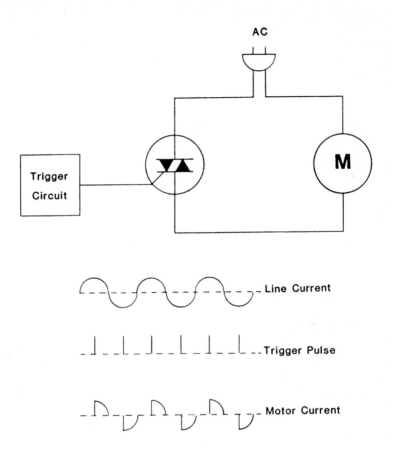

Fig. 8-14.   Triac Control of an AC Motor.

In most applications the trigger pulses for the SCR or

triac can be derived from the power line itself using

appropriate RC time constants.   In microprocessor and/or

microcomputer applications, they can be derived (usually via

opto-isolation) from the digital outputs of an appropriate I/O

chip interfaced to the system´s busses and control lines.   This allows for the complete digital control of DC and AC power circuits. An example of such an interface using a commercial opto-isolator in conjunction with a triac and AC load(i.e. heater, motor,...) is depicted in Fig. 8-15. Voltage dropping, current-limiting resistors are used to avoid burnout of the low voltage opto-isolator.

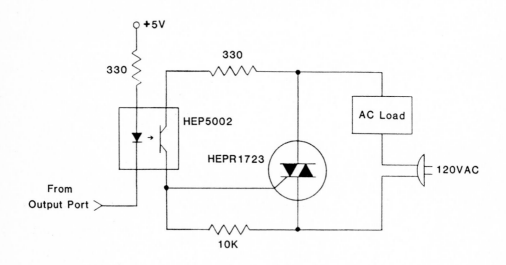

Fig. 8-15. Triac Control using Opto-Isolation.

The HEP5002 opto-isolator and HEPR1723 triac are devices manufactured by Motorola, Inc., Phoenix, AZ.

8.5 POWER MOSFET's

Power MOSFET's (Metal-Oxide Field Effect Transistors) represent a relatively new breed of device which is finding increasing application in power-control circuits. They were specifically designed to interface logic circuits with power devices. Depending upon their particular fabrication geometry and the manufacturer's penchant for abbreviation, they are also known as VMOS(V for Vertical), DMOS(D for Double-diffused), HEXFET(International Rectifier), TMOS(Motorola) and SIPMOS (Siemens) transistors.

Unlike SCR's and triacs which are phase-control devices and hard to switch off except when the power line voltage goes to zero, power MOSFET's can be rapidly turned on and off at will, operated as linear amplifiers, and are capable of being employed as voltage-variable resistors. They also possess the advantages of high input impedance and low "on" resistances (<1 ohm). In addition, their gates can be driven by low voltages(ca. 10V) thereby enabling sub-microsecond switching speeds for hundreds of volts and tens of amperes. Their two principal drawbacks are their processing expense (although this is diminishing almost continually) and their susceptibility to static discharge (a generic feature of FET's). This last problem can be circumvented to varying extents by special input protection circuitry.

An example of a power MOSFET used as a digitally programmable current regulator is depicted in Fig. 8-16. The current I_o flowing through the load resistance R_S is determined by the voltage V_R which, in turn, is generated via the

digital-to-analog converter (D/A). For example, if an 8-bit D/A
converter is employed in the circuit, the resultant current,
I_o, which is proportional to the voltage ratio V_R/V_S, can
be regulated in steps of 256 increments depending upon the byte
value(i.e. $00-->$FF) written to the D/A converter.

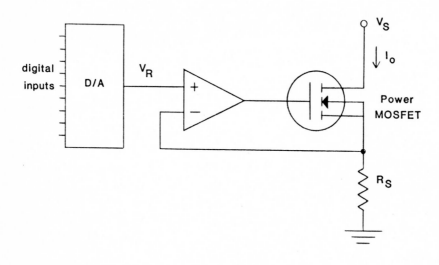

Fig. 8-16. Programmable Power MOSFET Current Regulator.

Alternatively, Fig. 8-17 demonstrates a pulsed-approach
which can be employed in power control circuits using these
devices. Here, the on-off switching characteristics of power
MOSFET´s can be employed to control the average power delivered
to a resistive(e.g. heater) or inductive(e.g. motor) load. The
heart of the system is the Pulse-Width Modulator(PWM) that

switches the MOSFET full-on and full-off for selected intervals of time. The ratio of "on" time to the total period(i.e. "on" time + "off" time) is commonly referred to as the <u>duty cycle</u>. It is controlled by the voltage output of the D/A converter which is fed to the noninverting(+) input of the op-amp comparator.

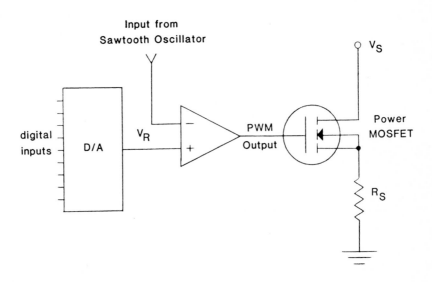

Fig. 8-17. Pulse-Width Modulated Power MOSFET.

The frequency of these variable-duty-cycle pulses is determined by the frequency of the sawtooth waveform fed to the inverting(-) input of the op-amp. By controlling the width of the voltage pulses, the average power supplied to the load(R_S) can be controlled. An n-bit D/A converter is capable of delivering 2^n different power levels to a load at a fixed input sawtooth frequency. If the sawtooth frequency is also varied, the number of power levels can be increased even further. This type of synchronous switching control is sometimes employed in heating systems and forms the heart of many temperature-proportional controllers where the power levels to a resistive heating element are controlled by the output from a temperature-sensing network. The overshoot/undershoot problems normally associated with a simple on/off system are minimized and better temperature regulation is achieved.

Finally, RCA Corporation has recently developed a power MOSFET which requires only 5V of gate drive and can be directly connected to logic circuits. These logic-level power MOSFET´s, or L^2FET´s as they are called, can be directly driven by TTL, NMOS or CMOS circuits to provide high current-handling capabilities at high speeds with very low "on" resistances(ca. 0.5 ohms).

CHAPTER 9

DATA COMMUNICATION INTERFACES

* Centronics Parallel Interface

* RS-232C Serial Interface

* IEEE-488 Parallel Interface

* Backplane Busses

A computer system´s busses (address, data, control) are made available to a peripheral I/O device by a data communication interface. Digital information is transmitted and received along the line(s) comprising the interface in a variety of different formats and protocols depending upon the particular application and/or peripheral device. Some of the more popular types are the Centronics® parallel, RS-232C serial, and the IEEE-488 parallel interfaces. Each is discussed in this section. A few points will be also made about other bus systems (S-100, STD, Multibus ---) which may be more appropriately regarded as "localized" interfaces and often referred to as backplane busses.

9.1 CENTRONICS PARALLEL INTERFACE

The parallel interface is sometimes called the Centronics interface after the company (Centronics Corp., Hudson, N.H.) that developed it for its low cost dot-matrix printers in the early 1970´s. Unlike the other types, the Centronics interface is not officially recognized as an industry standard. Nevertheless, because it was one of the first interfaces to be widely used in the industry, it became a de-facto standard.

The electrical and physical parameters specified for this interface call for eight unidirectional data lines, several control and signal lines and return and ground lines. It is a one-way interface in that it only transmits data (bytes) in one direction on the eight data lines. Its D-shaped 36-pin connector is standard and the Amphenol male/female versions are the (DDK)57-30360/(DDK)57-40360 connectors. Other connectors are available from other manufacturers in both ribbon and multiconductor cable versions. The complete pin-out diagram of a Centronics parallel connector is shown in Fig. 9-1. The voltage levels that represent the high/low (i.e. binary 1/0) control levels are TTL-compatible. Binary "1" is defined as a voltage between +2.5 and +5.0 volts and binary "0" is a voltage between 0 (ground) and +0.7 volts.

Besides the eight unidirectional data lines (labelled DATA 1-8) that transfer data (bytes) to a peripheral device, a BUSY line controlled by the peripheral is used to inform the computer that it is busy doing some operation. For example, a printer employs it to tell the computer that it is in the midst of printing a character, advancing the paper, etc. When the particular action is completed, the printer signals the computer via the ACK (Acknowledge) line which is active in its low state and represented as $\overline{ACK}$. Another active-low (or negative-true) line is the $\overline{STROBE}$ line which is used by the computer to inform the printer that a byte is ready on the data lines for processing. In the absence of this signal, the printer has no way of knowing if the proper arrangement of 8-bits (usually an ASCII Code) has been placed on the data lines.

CENTRONICS PARALLEL INTERFACE

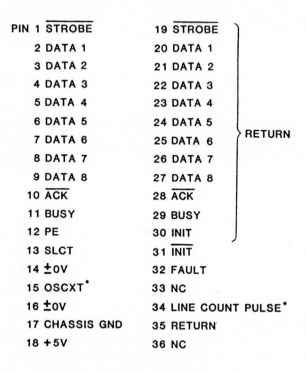

PIN 1 $\overline{\text{STROBE}}$		19 $\overline{\text{STROBE}}$	
2 DATA 1		20 DATA 1	
3 DATA 2		21 DATA 2	
4 DATA 3		22 DATA 3	
5 DATA 4		23 DATA 4	
6 DATA 5		24 DATA 5	
7 DATA 6		25 DATA 6	RETURN
8 DATA 7		26 DATA 7	
9 DATA 8		27 DATA 8	
10 $\overline{\text{ACK}}$		28 $\overline{\text{ACK}}$	
11 BUSY		29 BUSY	
12 PE		30 INIT	
13 SLCT		31 $\overline{\text{INIT}}$	
14 ±0V		32 FAULT	
15 OSCXT*		33 NC	
16 ±0V		34 LINE COUNT PULSE*	
17 CHASSIS GND		35 RETURN	
18 +5V		36 NC	

* Generally not used today

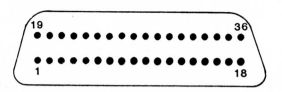

Fig. 9-1. Centronics Parallel Interface.

Several additional control signals are defined in this interface although few are used today. PE (Printer Error) indicates a printer malfunction (ribbon break, jammed mechanism...). SELECT is used by a printer to inform the computer of its on-line status. This simply means that the printer can accept data over the cable lines as opposed to other sources (keyboards, paper tape, disk...). FAULT is used to indicate an abnormal error condition such as paper run-out or an opened case. In more sophisticated printer/driver software routines, these error control signals are analyzed to inform the user of the exact nature of the error condition. In most applications, however, the BUSY signal is used to indicate all error conditions. In fact, the majority of 36-pin parallel interfaces on the market use only the $\overline{\text{STROBE}}$ and BUSY/$\overline{\text{ACK}}$ lines to control data transfer, a process commonly referred to as handshaking.

In a typical parallel-transmision scheme using the Centronics interface, the sequence of events is as follows: The computer puts 8-bits of data on the data lines (DATA 1-8) and approximately one microsecond later causes the $\overline{\text{STROBE}}$ line to go low. This signals the printer that valid data is ready for processing and it in turn makes the BUSY line go high (or the $\overline{\text{ACK}}$ line go low if so configured) until the data has been processed (i.e. printed). The computer usually sits idling in a software loop doing nothing but observing the BUSY line. When it goes low, the entire scheme is repeated with the computer placing valid data on the data lines and activating the $\overline{\text{STROBE}}$ line which is being continually watched by the printer. In this handshaking fashion, a slow peripheral device like a printer can accept and process data from a much faster computer.

9.2 RS-232C SERIAL INTERFACE

The most widely known and accepted interface is the EIA (Electronic Industries Association) RS-232C Interface. RS stands for Recommended Standard. The standard was introduced in 1962 as RS-232. The latest version (i.e. Version C) is the one presently in use, RS-232C.

Since the RS-232C interface was developed before the advent of TTL circuits and their associated voltages, logic "0" is represented as a positive voltage between +5 and +15V and logic "1" constitutes a negative voltage between -5 and -15V. The data lines (pins 2 and 3) are active low while all other signals are active high. Most RS-232C connectors use a 25-pin DB-25 connector which is available in many configurations including both multi-conductor and ribbon-cable adaptors. A pin diagram with signal names for the RS-232C Interface is depicted in Fig. 9-2.

As originally outlined, the RS-232C serial communications protocol was designed to connect Data Terminal Equipment (DTE) which was a terminal to Data Communucation Equipment (DCE) which was a modem. A modem (short for modulator/demodulator) is a device which converts serial data into standardized signals for transmission over dedicated lines. Frequently, though not always, these lines are standard telephone lines.

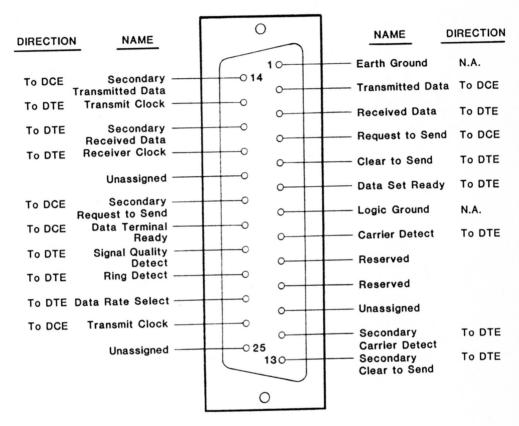

DIRECTION	NAME		NAME	DIRECTION
		1	Earth Ground	N.A.
To DCE	Secondary Transmitted Data — 14		Transmitted Data	To DCE
To DTE	Transmit Clock		Received Data	To DTE
To DTE	Secondary Received Data		Request to Send	To DCE
To DTE	Receiver Clock		Clear to Send	To DTE
	Unassigned		Data Set Ready	To DTE
To DCE	Secondary Request to Send		Logic Ground	N.A.
To DCE	Data Terminal Ready		Carrier Detect	To DTE
To DTE	Signal Quality Detect		Reserved	
To DTE	Ring Detect		Reserved	
To DTE	Data Rate Select		Unassigned	
To DCE	Transmit Clock		Secondary Carrier Detect	To DTE
	Unassigned — 25 / 13		Secondary Clear to Send	To DTE

Fig. 9-2. RS-232C Serial Interface.

In this case, the modulator section of the modem converts the 0
and 1 bits of the serial data into two different tones which are
transmitted over the telephone lines and re-converted to 0´s and
1´s by the demodulator section of the modem at the other end.
This type of modem is usually referred to as an <u>acoustic modem</u>.
In the early days before microprocessors or microcomputers, a

user terminal (DTE) was interfaced to a larger (and more
expensive) mainframe computer via the RS-232C interface to a
modem (DCE).

The RS-232C Interface is used for the serial transmission
of data. This simply means that each data bit is transmitted
(or received) one after the other in single-step fashion.
Signal timing is precise and the transmission speed is usually
given in bits per second (bps) sometimes called the baud rate.
Standard baud rates include 75, 110, 150, 300, 600, 1200, 2400,
9600 and 19,200. The nominal EIA-approved upper transmission
limit for RS-232C is 20K bps although this rate is often
exceeded by some computer manufacturers in some of their more
advanced products. Acoustic modems generally operate at 300
baud although some modems can operate as high as 1200 baud over
normal telephone lines. The RS-232C standard limits the cable
connection between devices to 50 feet although in practice
RS-232C signals can be run for 100-200 feet without serious
problem. The addition of a modem removes these limitations and
data transmission between devices is governed only by the
quality of the propagated signals (i.e. telephone tones, radio
waves, light pulses, etc.).

In normal ASCII Code transmission, as outlined in
Chapter 2, the DTE generates a start bit (active low) thereby
alerting the DCE of the beginning of a character transmission on
Pin No. 2. The next 7 (in some cases 8) bits are then

interpreted as an ASCII character. After the transmission of
all of the data bits, a parity bit and stop bit(s) are sent to
mark the end of the character. Parity is a form of error
checking for a loss of bits during transmission. Even parity
implies an even number of "on" bits and odd parity an odd number
of "on" bits. Stop bit(s) allow the receiver adequate time to
assemble and process the serial bits received. They can be 1,
1-1/2 or 2 bits long depending upon the transmission protocol.
As an example, the code for ASCII "R" is depicted in Fig. 9-3 in
odd-parity serial transmission.

The total number of characters transmitted per second can
be simply calculated by dividing the baud rate by the number of
total bits per character. For instance, a 1200 baud modem
transmits an 11-bit character (7 ASCII data bits + 1 start + 1

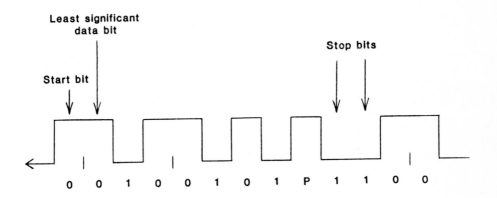

Fig. 9-3. Serial Transmission of ASCII "R".

parity + 2 stop bits) at the rate of 1200/11 or 109 characters
per second. Although we have chosen to focus on ASCII Code
transmission, other bit-oriented codes (BAUDOT, EBCDIC, etc.)
can be transmitted over the RS-232C interface as well.

Even though only two pins (i.e. Pins 2 and 3) are used for
the transmission and reception of data, they can be a major
source of error in some configurations. This arises when both
the DTE and the DCE are equipped with female DB-25 connectors
and it is not clear what is the DTE and what is the DCE. As a
rule, the DTE should have Pin 2 wired to transmit data and Pin 3
to receive data while a DCE should transmit on Pin 3 and receive
on Pin 2. If a computer is mistakenly wired as a DCE and it is
connected to a modem (also a DCE), they will not interact
properly. The solution to this problem (a not too uncommon
occurence) is a null modem adaptor which is a RS-232C connector
with Pins 2 and 3 cross-wired.

The remaining pins of the RS-232C connector comprise
several ground lines and a number of signal and handshaking
lines. In actual practice, however, a minimal number of these
lines are used. As illustrated in Fig. 9-4, the simplest
RS-232C connector uses just three lines.

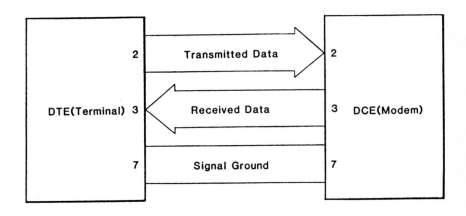

Fig. 9-4. RS-232C Signal Paths.

Two data lines enable full-duplex communication where data can
be simultaneously interchanged between devices. An extension of
full-duplex is echo-plex where a character entered at a terminal
is transmitted to a remote computer which returns or echoes the
character to the terminal´s screen. In this way, proper data
transmission is confirmed. Half-duplex is two-way communication
over one data line which is used to either transmit data or
receive data but not both simultaneously.

One final point worth noting is the use of the RS-232C
interface in the transfer of data (ASCII characters) to
printers. Unlike the parallel Centronics interface, there are
no standard handshake lines available for a printer to control
the rate of data transfer. Since this interface was originally
developed for use between a terminal and a modem, this was not a

problem at the time. In an effort to circumvent this
difficulty, several printer manufacturers have chosen to use
several pins which were not originally intended for data
handshaking. Because of this non-standard use of the RS-232C
interface, it is wise to consult the interface manuals of both
devices whenever a handshake mechanism in an RS-232C format is
implemented.

9.3   IEEE-488 PARALLEL INTERFACE

In comparison to the RS-232C serial interface, the IEEE-488
parallel interface is a more rigidly specified standard. It was
developed in the early 1970's by Hewlett-Packard and is also
known as the Hewlett-Packard Interface Bus (HPIB). In 1975 it
became adopted by the Institute of Electrical and Electronic
Engineers (IEEE) as approved Standard IEEE-488-1975, "Digital
Interface for Programmable Instrumentation". In mid-1978,
various editorial revisions were made in the standard to clear
up some potential ambiguities and it became known as
IEEE-488-1978, the "IEEE Standard Digital Interface for
Programmable Instrumentation". Today it is collectively known
as the IEEE-488, HPIB or the GPIB (General Purpose Interface
Bus) parallel interface.

The IEEE-488 differs from other parallel interfaces, which
are oftentimes used to connect a single device to a computer, by
allowing up to 15 external devices to be interconnected and

thereby rendered inter-communicative. In this aspect, the
IEEE-488 interface is also regarded as the IEEE-488 Bus.
Devices on the bus are categorized according to three types:
Controllers, Talkers, and Listeners. At any one time there is
exactly one controller on the bus. This controller allows a
specific talker to communicate with selected listeners. One
talker is active at any one time, but there may be several
listeners. Control is delegated from one controller to another
using specific sequences defined in the standard. Upon
power-up, one controller designated the System Controller is
active. Most often, this system controller is the main
computer. All remaining controllers become active only when
control is passed on to them. For example, an intelligent
plotter can become a controller and request data from other
system instruments (voltmeters, thermocouple amplifiers...).
After plotting out the data, control can be returned to the main
computer or another system device. The IEEE-488 interface
allows data rates of up to 1 Mbyte/second although most
instruments are limited to rates well below this maximum.
Typically, instrumental data rates are in the 1-10 Kbyte/second
range. In actual practice however, the rate of data transfer on
the IEEE-488 bus is governed by the slowest active listener.

Sixteen (16) signal lines make up the IEEE-488 interface.
They are divided as follows:

8 Data Lines (DIO1 through DIO8)

5 Control Lines (SRQ, IFC, ATN, EOI and REN)

3 Transfer Lines (DAV, NRFD, and NDAC)

All 16 signal lines in the IEEE-488 interface are active-low or negative-true which simply means that they become active when driven to low voltage levels. The common designation for a signal line with this negative-true logic is a bar placed over the specified line (i.e. DAV becomes $\overline{DAV}$). However, in order to avoid confusion (and repetition), we will eliminate the bar in the following discussions remembering all the while that the standard specifies negative-true logic.

The 8 Data Lines designated DIO1 through DIO8 are used to transfer all data to and from all instruments connected to the bus. This is accomplished by sending 8 bits of information in a parallel fashion (i.e. bit-parallel). These 8-bit groups (bytes) of information can represent any type of I/O, control, address or status information. Although all 8-bits are transmitted and received in parallel, bytes are sent in a byte-serial format where each byte is transmitted one after the other is serial fashion. In the case of a printer, each byte may represent an ASCII character. The printer interprets and processes each symbol and control character in a stepwise manner until the entire text is printed.

The 5 Control or Management Lines designated SRQ, IFC, ATN, EOI and REN are responsible for an orderly flow of information and control over the IEEE-488 bus. Their functional

descriptions are as follows:

SRQ - Service Request. This line is made active or driven low
    by a particular device on the bus requesting the
    attention of the controller and an interruption of the
    ongoing sequence of events. It may be either ignored or
    serviced by the controller. Except when IFC is active,
    the SRQ line can be activated at any time.

IFC - Interface Clear. When active, all devices assume an
    inactive status and control is returned to the system
    controler. When inactive, all bus operations proceed as
    normal. It is typically used in error/fault situations
    to override all bus activity.

ATN - Attention. When active, all devices are required to
    monitor the data lines (DIO1-DIO8) where the information
    is control/address information (messages to devices).
    When inactive, all information on the data lines is
    interpreted as data. ATN is asserted by the active
    controller.

EOI - End or Identify. Activated by a talker to identify a
    data byte as the last in a series of transmitted data
    bytes. It can also be used with the ATN line to effect
    a polling sequence.

REN - Remote Enable. Activated by the system controller and
    monitored by instruments capable of being remotely
    controlled. The status of the REN line informs active
    listeners on the data bus of the intent of an active
    controller to use information sent to it by an active
    talker. In this manner, the REN line is used to choose
    between two different sources of device program data.

The 3 Data Transfer Lines designated DAV, NRFD and NDAC

control the flow of information (bytes) over the data lines

DIO1-DIO8. They operate in a 3-wire interlocked handshake mode

which allows the asynchronous transfer of data-bytes between

devices on the bus. The speed of transfer is dictated by the

talker or the slowest active listener lest any data be lost by any of the listeners.

DAV - Data Valid. Activated by a talker (to potential
     listeners) when valid data is present on data lines DIO1-
     DIO8. When inactive, information on the data lines is
     regarded as invalid data.

NRFD- Not Ready for Data. Activated by a minimum of one
     listener on the bus to indicate (to the talker) its
     inability to receive data. When inactive, all potential
     listeners are ready to receive data (from the talker).

NDAC- Not Data Accepted. Activated by a minimum of one
     listener on the bus to indicate (to the talker) that it
     has not yet accepted the data. When this line is
     inactive, it indicates (to the talker) that all have
     accepted (or processed) the data.

The 16 signal lines of the IEEE-488 bus are depicted in the

interconnection diagram in Fig. 9-5.

Data transfer on the IEEE-488 bus is asynchronous and

controlled by the transfer lines, DAV, NRFD and NDAC. The DAV

signal is transmitted by an active talker for reception by

potential listeners. The opposite is true for the NRFD and NDAC

signals which are sent from the potential listeners to the

active talker. As each listener becomes available to accept

data, it releases its NRFD line. When all listeners are

available, the entire NRFD line is made high thereby signalling

the talker to place data on the data lines and assert its

validity by activating the DAV line. As each listener detects

DAV active, it in turn makes NRFD active to allow sufficient

time for accepting and processing the present data. The fastest

listener activates the NRFD line. As each listener on the bus

accepts the valid data, it releases its NDAC line.

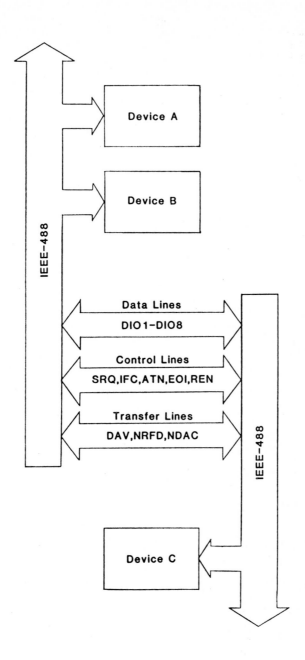

Fig. 9-5. IEEE-488 Parallel Interface.

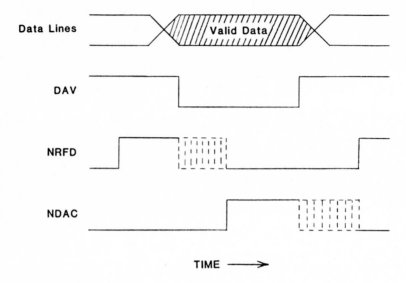

Fig. 9-6. Timing Diagram of IEEE-488 Transfer Lines.

When the last listener has finished accepting the data, the
entire NDAC line is released thereby indicating to the talker
that the data has been accepted (by all active listeners). This
informs the talker that it may release the DAV line to indicate
its intention of changing the information on the line.
Simultaneously with the release of the DAV line, each listener
pulls NDAC low to indicate unacceptable data. At this point the
contents on the data lines DIO1-DIO8 can be changed since they
are, in effect, disconnected from any listeners. When each
listener has finished processing the previously accepted data,
it releases its NRFD line. When all listeners have finished
their processing routines, the entire NRFD line is released and

a new data-transfer-cycle begins. The slowest listener is responsible for de-activating the NRFD line. This overall process is schematically depicted in the timing diagram of Fig. 9-6.

The primary attraction of the IEEE-488 interface is its limited number of signal lines with defined, standardized functions. Piggyback connection and daisy-chain configurations are possible. Although primarily used with laboratory instrumentation systems, the IEEE-488 interface is becoming increasingly available in commercial microcomputers and their peripherals. The applications of this bus will increase even further as microcomputers interact with increasingly complex laboratory devices.

9.4   BACKPLANE BUSSES

A backplane bus is so named on account of the backplane circuit board containing the electrical bus connectors. It differs from the preceding types by virtue of its "localized" nature. In its normal configuration, it is used to provide short-range communication paths between circuit boards via mating edge-card connectors in a supporting card cage. In this manner, physical and electrical paths with sockets attached are used for the addition of a number of peripheral circuit boards and external devices.

A variety of different backplane busses exist depending

upon the design needs of computer manufacturers. Some of the
more general types include the S-100, STD, and Multibus systems.
Other more specific types include the IBM PC Bus, Applebus and
the C-44 Bus. Each has its own merits and faults depending upon
the particular configuration.

The S-100 Bus was originally developed in the mid-1970´s
for use with the MITS Altair 8800 microcomputer manufactured by
Micro Instrumentation and Telemetry Systems (MITS) of
Albuquerque, NM. It was subsequently called the Altair Bus
after the 8080-based computer and used a 100-pin connector. It
soon became known as the Altair/IMSAI Bus after it found use in
the IMSAI 8080 microcomputer developed by IMS Associates, Inc.
In 1976, after other computer manufacturers adopted the same
architecture in their systems, it became generally known as
Standard-100 or S-100 for short. Upon final approval by the
Institute of Electrical and Electronic Engineers (IEEE) in late
1982, it became formally known as IEEE-696. Today it is
referred to by both names; S-100 or IEEE-696.

The 100 pins of the S-100 bus are generally organized into
eight (8) categories:

24 Address Lines

16 Data Lines

9 Status Lines

6 Control Input Lines

5 Control Output Lines

10 Interrupt Lines

8 DMA Control Lines

22 Utility Lines

Although a detailed description of each of the 100 pin functions is beyond the scope of this text, they can be organized into two general groups according to the type of device driving the board, i.e. Master and Slave devices.

Masters control the bus and comprise such devices as processor-cards and direct-memory access (DMA) boards. There are two types of Masters; permanent and temporary. Every S-100 system has a permanent Master but may (or may not) have up to 16 temporary bus Masters. Temporary control is delegated to the temporary bus Master from the permanent Master. Upon completion of its task, the temporary bus master returns control to the permanent master.

Slaves are devices or cards that are controlled by Masters (permanent or temporary). They receive data from or transmit data to the bus Master. Examples of Slaves are memory boards, I/O boards, serial/parallel I/O interfaces, terminals, etc.

The general acceptability of the S-100 bus today derives from its modularity, versatility and long-term cost effectiveness, particularly in a business-computing environment. Although a commercial S-100 system may be costly to implement initially, it becomes more cost-effective as the system is upgraded. A number of hardware/software developers prefer the S-100 bus because the latest technology seems to appear there first. For example, 16 S-100 data lines are ideal for 16-bit microprocessors while 24 address lines allow a total of 16 Megabytes (2^{24}) of directly-addressable semiconductor memory. In addition, the de facto industry standard operating system for microcomputers, CP/M,® was originally designed for an S-100 system thereby making that system accessible to a large variety of business-related software. Ease of upgrade, software availability and multi-user capabilities are important considerations in an office environment. These are compelling reasons to see continuing state-of-the-art developments on the S-100 bus, at least for the foreseeable future.

The STD-Bus is currently supported by a number of companies. Originally developed by several manufacturers for use in Z-80 based systems, it has since been adapted for use with many different 8-bit microprocessors. Standard size STD boards are approximately 4.5 in. wide and 6.5 in. long and terminate with a 56-pin edge connector. Sixteen address lines and eight data lines are present and are driven by 3-state bus drivers to allow their connection/disconnection to/from any system device. A variety of power, I/O, control, timing, interrupt and status lines comprise the remainder. The STD bus enjoys industry-wide popularity and will be made available for a number of peripheral devices for some time to come.

Other bus systems such as the Intel Multibus and IBM PC® Bus have their pros and cons. The Multibus has 20 address lines, 16 bidirectional data lines, 8 interrupt lines and a variety of power, status and control lines for a total of 86 lines. It is currently being standardized as IEEE-796. The IBM PC Bus also has 20 address lines although it specifies only 8 data lines since the 8-bit version of the Intel 8086 16-bit microprocessor was chosen for the IBM PC. Six interrupt lines and a number of control, handshaking and timing functions make up the remainder for a total of 62 lines. As the IBM PC bus was designed for compatability with the IBM PC, so too was the Applebus designed for expansion/peripheral devices for the Apple® II/IIe computers. Expansion memory cards and controller/peripheral boards currently exist and will continue to be manufactured for both of these popular personal computer systems.

A bus system which has been developed for low-power, battery-based systems is the C-44 Bus. Bus cards based on this system are available from two manufacturers at present (Onset Computer Corp., North Falmouth, MA and Quartic Systems, Salt Lake City, UT). C-44 bus cards are similiar in size to the STD bus cards. However, instead of 56 connecting pins, the C-44 cards are configured with 44-pin edge card connectors. They also differ physically from the STD bus card by being somewhat smaller in size and having larger pin-contact areas. Moreover, unlike the other backplane busses, the C-44 bus was not

developed for any one particular microprocessor thereby avoiding
many compatability-related problems.

The most prominent feature of the C-44 bus is its capacity
to control power dissipation in a system. This is an especially
important feature in portable, battery-based systems requiring
low-power dissipation. Two low power modes are specified for a
microprocessor on this bus to take advantage of the fact that an
MPU ordinarily spends a large amount of its time doing nothing
but waiting for an interruption or an external event. During
these waiting periods, the MPU can be programmed in a low-power
off-line mode then re-activated as the need arises. Two low
power modes (wait and stop) direct bus activity. In the wait
mode, all bus activity is halted with the system voltage
maintained at a nominal +5V. In the stop mode, this voltage is
reduced to +3V. This lower voltage is sufficient, in most
cases, to allow the system RAM and I/O chips to hold their
current values. Power dissipation in the stop mode is typically
50 microwatts for most peripheral C-44 bus cards, each of which
requires a single supply voltage of +8V to +18V. In small,
portable systems this particular bus design offers many
advantages.

CHAPTER 10

+-----------------------+
| |
| PROGRAM DEVELOPMENT |
| |
+-----------------------+

* Assemblers

* The FORTH Language

* Structured Programming

* Flowcharts

* Development Systems

10.1 ASSEMBLERS

All of the preceding experiments and programs developed thus far have been done so without the aid of any sophisticated hardware or software resources. The process of translating individual program instructions written in mnemonic or symbolic form (source code) into actual processor instructions (object code) is accomplished by a program called an Assembler. Up until now, we have been using a rather primitive version of an assembler to enter/alter/display programs. A more extended assembler, among its many features, allows both instructions and data addresses to be specified symbolically rather than requiring absolute addresses. Program relocation/alteration is simply and effectively accomplished. In this section, we will consider some of the more salient features of a typical 6502 Assembler and its use in machine language program development.

The program development process, briefly outlined in Chapter 1, is restated diagrammatically in Fig. 10-1. The programmer (human) normally uses a text editor (word processor) to create a text file of an assembly language program (source program). This is then input to an Assembler which produces an object program. This object program is then fed into a Loader which loads the executable machine language program into the memory of the target computer. The text editor and assembler can be run on another computer but the loader and machine language program must be run on the target computer.

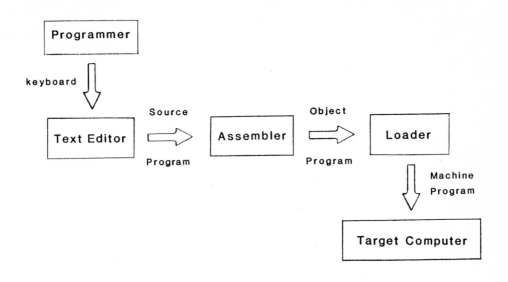

Fig. 10-1.   Assembly Language Program Development.

The Assembler (a type of program) reads each of the mnemonic instructions of the input program and translates it into the required bit pattern as specified by the encoding (i.e. TAX = 10101010).   It is designed to provide a convenient symbolic representation of the source program while at the same time providing a simple means of converting these mnemonics into their binary equivalents.   Assembler formats depend upon the particular microprocessor and, in some cases, upon the particular machine it is situated in.   There appears to be general agreement, however, on certain definitions and syntax conventions considered necessary in most 6502 Assemblers.

Several of these conventions are presented in the following
discussions.

Most assembly language programs can be categorized as being
line-oriented whereby each program statement is contained in a
single line according to a prescribed format. Each simple line
statement can be divided into as many as four fields arranged as
follows:

[LABEL] [OP-CODE]   [OPERAND] [;COMMENTS]

All of these fields are optional in an assembly language
statement although their relative order within a single line is
not. For example, if a Comment is chosen to be the first field
in a line statement, it must be the only field present in that
statement. At least one space must be present between fields on
the same line.

Labels

The LABEL field contains labels which are simply symbols of
1-6 characters beginning with a letter that designate the
address of the instruction that follows. When used, a label
must appear as the first field on a line, although in any
column. Op-code mnemonics and register names (A, X, Y, S and P)
are not permitted as symbols here.

Op-Codes

The OP-CODE field contains the standard mnemonics of either a machine instruction (1 of 56 for the 6502) or a symbolic assembler directive. Assembler directives are defined symbols that are not translated (i.e. pseudo-instructions) but rather direct the assembler to perform a specific task. Examples of these include the symbols,

```
        =
      .BYTE
      .WORD
      .DBYTE
      .PAGE
      .SKIP
      .OPT
      .FILE
      .END
```

where:

(1) the equate directive, "=", assigns a symbol to a constant or an expression containing no forward references. For example,

                    NAV = $3711

assigns the hex value $3711 to the NAV symbol. From that point on, wherever NAV is in a program, it will be replaced by the hex value $3711.

(2) the .BYTE directive loads specified bytes of data into one or more consecutive memory locations beginning with the labelled address. For example,

                  NAV .BYTE $32

loads the byte value $32 into the location specified by the

address symbol NAV.   In like manner, the expression

NAV .BYTE $32, $FF, $43

loads locations NAV, NAV+1, and NAV+2 with $32. $FF and $43
respectively.

(3) the .WORD directive is similar to .BYTE except that two
bytes of data are stored in memory, low-byte first.   Namely,

NAV .WORD $32FF

stores the hex values $FF and $32 into the symbolic address
locations NAV and NAV+1, respectively.

(4) the .DBYTE directive is equivalent to .WORD except that
the two bytes of data are stored in memory high-byte first.
Namely,

NAV .DBYTE $32FF

allocates memory as:

[NAV]   --> $32
[NAV+1] --> $FF

where the brackets denote "contents of".

(5) the .PAGE directive instructs the assembler to finish
the current output page listing, move on to the next page, and
print a title if so desired.

(6) the .SKIP directive inserts n blank lines into the
output listing according to the format .SKIP n.

(7) the .OPT directive allows the programmer to control
his/her output fields and expand ASCII strings in .BYTE
expressions.

```
.OPT LIST       generates a list file.
.OPT GENERATE   prints object code for ASCII strings in .BYTE.
.OPT ERROR      prints only the errors in an assembly listing.
.OPT SYMBOL     lists the symbol table.
```

(8) the .FILE directive allows the appending of files when the last statement in an existing file is .FILE NAME and NAME is the symbolic name of the next file.

(9) the .END directive is required as the last statement in the last file of the source program. It instructs the assembler to ignore the remaining information.

Operands

The OPERAND field specifies zero or more operands separated by commas. It may be an expression containing symbols, constants and operators. The 56 mnemonics of the 6502 and the reserved letters A, X, Y, S, and P may not be used as symbols here.

A location counter symbol, "*", is used by the assembler to:

(1) specify its location counter, i.e. * = $0400 means that the next executable instruction is stored at memory location $0400.

(2) reserve space in memory, i.e. * = * + 5 tells the assembler to jump over 5 addresses, leaving them for the programmer's use, and continue from that point forward.

(3) reference the current contents of its location counter,

i.e. NAV .WORD * stores the current value of the location counter at addresses NAV and NAV+1, low-byte first.

The symbolic expressions for the various addressing modes are defined as:

Addressing Mode	Example	
Immediate	LDA #NAV	where NAV = 1 byte
Absolute	LDA NAV	NAV = 2 bytes
Zero Page	LDA NAV	NAV = 1 byte
Implied	INX, etc.	
Accumulator	ASL, etc.	
Absolute Indexed, X	LDA NAV, X	NAV = 2 bytes
Absolute Indexed, Y	LDA NAV, Y	NAV = 2 bytes
Indexed Indirect	LDA (NAV, X)	NAV = 1 byte
Indirect Indexed	LDA (NAV), Y	NAV = 1 byte
Zero Page Indexed, X	LDA NAV, X	NAV = 1 byte
Zero Page Indexed, Y	LDA NAV, Y	NAV = 1 byte
Relative	BCC NAV	NAV = 1 byte
Indirect Absolute	JMP (NAV)	NAV = 2 bytes

Constants are usually expressed in either decimal, hexadecimal, octal or binary notation depending upon the particular prefix used;

```
none --> decimal number, 123
 $   --> hexadecimal number, $20FC
 @   --> octal number, @101
 %   --> binary number, %10101010
```

Care must be exercised when writing these numeric prefixes in the source program in order to avoid number-base errors. For example, the instruction LDA #15 will load the accumulator with the binary value 00001111 ($=15_{10}$) while LDA #$15 will load 00010101 ($=15_{16}$). This number-base distinction is not made in the primitive assembler used in the Instruction Mnemonic Entry

Mode <I> of the AIM 65 where all numerical values default to hexadecimal. It is available, however, in the 4K Assembler ROM Option. ASCII literal constants are enclosed by single quotes, i.e. LDA #´R´ and LDA #$52 are equivalent expressions.

Operators such as +, - and others further facilitate the generation of symbolic programs. They are evaluated in the usual left-to-right fashion. Special operators such as > and < truncate a two-byte value to its high (<) or low (>) byte value, respectively. More advanced assemblers also incorporate the multiply, divide, shift, logical and comparison operations. Unlike higher-level languages however, they usually don´t permit the use of parentheses or recognize operator precedence.

;Comments

The COMMENTS field is entirely optional and is intended for meaningful human-language descriptions of the program. It is ignored completely by the assembler. Comments are written to the right of the operand field or anywhere on a line if preceded by a semi-colon, ";". The liberal use of comments is always recommended as good programming practice.

Macros

A Macro is simply that name given to a group of assembly-language statements. It is a programming tool that is especially convenient in those cases where a given set of

instructions is called upon a number of times within a program.
A simple macro call inserts the particular sequence of
statements within the body of the calling program where it is
assembled along with the rest of the program. Unlike a
subroutine call which transfers program control from the main
program to the address of a defined subroutine and then back
again, macro calls occur only during the assembly process.
During program execution, the main program is not exited since
the assembly language statements that comprise the macro are
situated within the main program. The assembler simply replaces
the macro name with the appropriate sequence of instructions.
In this context, a macro can be regarded as an assembly-time
facility whereas a subroutine is an execution-time facility.
Like subroutine calls, macro calls may also be nested, i.e.
macros inside of macros.

Macro assemblers can also contain conditional assembly
operations that allow the assembly of subsequent statements only
if a specified condition is obeyed. A programmer can devise a
generalized program which can be conditionally assembled for
specific applications. This is particularly useful in
laboratory/industrial program development.

Two-Pass Assemblers

A Two-pass assembler is an assembler that passes through
the assembly language source program twice. During the first

pass, all symbols are collected and defined in a symbol table. As each line is scanned, the encountered symbols are used to build the symbol table. During the second pass, the lines are scanned again and actual machine language instructions and data values are generated via referencing the symbol table formed during the first pass and the op-code table contained within the assembler. Two-pass assemblers are usually employed in microprocessor-based systems.

10.2   THE FORTH LANGUAGE

In much of the preceding text attention was focused on the concepts and applications of assembly/machine language programming. Higher-level languages were not discussed in any great detail primarily because of their tendency to isolate the programmer further from the actual processes of the computer. An exception to this is the FORTH language.

FORTH is a relatively new computer language whose popularity is increasing rapidly. Unlike BASIC, it has the capability of providing a programmer with total control over the machine in a highly interactive environment. Also unlike most other computer languages, FORTH was developed by a single person, Charles H. Moore, formerly of the National Radio Astronomy Laboratory, over a span of time beginning from the early 1960's. It is a structured language whereby complicated programs can be fabricated from numerous simpler ones. It differs from most languages by the fact that it does not have a fixed vocabulary. Programming in FORTH is accomplished by defining new words out of the present ones available in the current FORTH dictionary. These new words may be executed or used in the definition of other new words which may be executed and so on... For each new application, a custom-built FORTH program can be designed simply by defining new words from old ones. The program is executed by executing the new word which, in turn, executes all of its composite words. All programs (words) are executed from a keyboard by simply typing in the word name and following it with a carriage return. Debugging is quick and easily accomplished by examining word definitions.

In contrast to most traditional computer languages (BASIC, FORTRAN...), FORTH uses Reverse Polish Notation (RPN). This is a form of post-fix notation which eliminates the need for parentheses and operator precedence. Some types of hand-held calculators (most notably certain Hewlett-Packard models) use RPN in their input command structures. A simple example of traditional (i.e. in-fix) and RPN (post-fix) notation is the following series of equivalent mathematical operations.

$$\text{Traditional} \quad (3-4)+9*78/26$$

$$\text{RPN} \quad 3 \ 4 \ - \ 9 \ 78 \ * \ + \ 26 \ /$$

Computer systems with FORTH use a data stack to pass arguments between operators. If a particular number is entered from the keyboard, it goes on the stack. Subsequent numbers, when entered, also go on the stack and push the preceding entries further down on the stack. Various mathematical operations (+, -, *,...) take the top two numbers off the stack, operate on them, then push the result on top of the stack. For example, if an 18 is typed and the carriage return hit, an 18 goes on the stack. If a 3 is similarly entered, it also goes on the stack leaving the stack containing 18 3 with the 3 on top. The contents of the stack are usually represented bottom-to-top in left-to-right fashion. If a "+" is then entered, the 18 and 3 are taken off the stack and replaced by a 21. If a 3 * is then executed, the 21 is removed and a 63 put in its place. In general, all words get (pull) their arguments from the stack and leave (push) their results on the stack.

Some examples of mathematical operations in FORTH are:

Operation	Function	Example	Results
+	PLUS	12 6 +	--> 18
-	MINUS	12 6 -	--> 6
*	TIMES	12 6 *	--> 72
/	DIVIDE	12 6 /	--> 2
1+	ONE PLUS	12 1+	--> 13
1-	ONE MINUS	12 1-	--> 11
2*	2 TIMES	12 2*	--> 24
2/	2 DIVIDE	12 2/	--> 6
*/	A*B/C	12 6 3 */	--> 24

Special stack-manipulating operations also exist in the FORTH language to effect additional flexibility and control. Some functional examples of these are:

	[Stack Contents, bottom -> top]	
Operation	Before --->	After
DUP	5 9 1 7	5 9 1 7 7
DROP	5 9 1 7	5 9 1
SWAP	5 9 1 7	5 9 7 1
ROT	5 9 1 7	5 1 7 9
OVER	5 9 1 7	5 9 1 7 1
2DROP	5 9 1 7	5 9
2DUP	5 9 1 7	5 9 1 7 1 7

The text interpreter in FORTH is extremely simple. All numbers and words are separated by one or more spaces. The number of operations is limited only by the number of characters allowed per line. Processing begins when a carriage return is pressed. The FORTH dictionary is searched for the first word. If it is present, the word is either executed or compiled depending upon the particular mode that FORTH is in (i.e. execute or compile mode). If the word is not found, FORTH will try to convert it to a number. Failing this, an error condition exists and FORTH will usually respond with a question mark (?). After the first word is processed, the remainder of the text is processed accordingly. When finished, FORTH responds with an "OK" and expects more input. Naturally, the input is not limited to the keyboard but may come from a tape, a disk or any device capable of storing text files. In this way, a FORTH program can be created by a simple word processor for later execution by FORTH.

In addition to mathematical and stack operations, FORTH also employs logic operators which use the stack in the same

way. For example, when the "=" operator is executed, it takes
the top two arguments (numbers, constants, variables) off the
stack and leaves a "1" if they are equal and a "0" if they are
unequal. In conditional structures, a "1" represents a TRUE
flag and a "0" a FALSE flag. Some of these conditional
structures are:

BEGIN....UNTIL

BEGIN....WHILE....REPEAT

1F....ELSE.....THEN

In the BEGIN-UNTIL structure, the operations (words)
between BEGIN and UNTIL are executed until the flag becomes
true. Similarly, in the BEGIN-WHILE-REPEAT structure, the
operations between BEGIN and REPEAT are executed until the flag
becomes false. In the IF-THEN-ELSE structure, both states (true
& false) of this flag are examined. Here, the operations
between IF and ELSE are executed if the flag is true, otherwise
the operations between ELSE and THEN are executed (i.e. flag =
false). Program execution continues after THEN.

An example of a non-conditional control structure in FORTH
is the DO-LOOP. In the DO...LOOP family of structures, the
operations between DO and LOOP are repeated a specific number of
times as determined by an index. When the DO operation is
executed, it takes two arguments from the stack; the top stack
number being the initial index value and the second argument the
final value + 1. At the completion of each LOOP, the index is

incremented by 1 and compared against the final value + 1. If
it is less than this number, another loop is performed and so
on... When the index equals the final value + 1, the DO-LOOP is
exited and control is passed on to the next word. For example,
in the structure

6 3 DO......LOOP

the operation(s) between DO and LOOP are performed exactly three
times. At the end of the third cycle, the index is incremented
(by 1) to yield a value of 6 whereby the loop is exited. Since
the increment-and-compare operation is not performed until LOOP
is encountered, a DO-LOOP will always be executed at least once.

Memory operations are also carried out by appropriate FORTH
words. The words represented by "!" and "@", for example,
represent a store (!) and a fetch (@) operation. The apostrophe
word, "!", stores a two-byte number (16 bits with sign) into a
specified location. The starting address of the location(s) and
the number are stored on the stack and followed by the ! word.
For example,

3711 400 !

stores the number 3711 at locations 400 and 401. The 8-bit
version of the ! word is represented by C!. Here a single byte
is written into a specific (16-bit) memory location;

37 400 C!

In the preceding operation, the number 37 is stored at memory
location 400.

The analogous memory-fetch operations are represented by
the words "@" and "C@", respectively. They fetch (copy) a two-
or one-byte number from a specified memory location and place it
on the top of the stack. For example,

$$400 \ @$$

places the contents of locations 400 and 401 on top of the stack
while

$$400 \ C@$$

places the contents of location 400 on top of the stack. Double
precision (i.e. 32-bit) store and fetch operations are
represented by the words "2!" and "2@" respectively. Other
memory operations enable moving blocks of memory, erasing and
filling memory, etc. For a more comprehensive treatment, the
reader is encouraged to consult the many available texts on the
FORTH language.

Up until now, FORTH appears to be a rather average
high-level language. Most of the preceding operations appear in
some form or another in other high-level languages. For
example, the FORTH words C! and C@ are functionally equivalent
to the POKE and PEEK structures in the BASIC language. FORTH,
however, is not simply just another computer language but
derives its real power from what is called its Colon
Definitions. These particular structures allow a programmer to
define his/her own words for addition to the FORTH dictionary.
In this manner, the vocabulary of FORTH words can grow

indefinitely, much like that of a natural language where new words are defined in terms of the old ones.

A colon definition begins with a ":" and ends with a ";". The colon (:) is really a FORTH word that creates a dictionary entry for the name after it. It also alerts the compiler and tells the text interpreter that the following words will not be executed but instead compiled. The semicolon word (;), which should always be preceded by a space, signals the end of the definition. The execution of a newly defined word is accomplished simply by typing in the word-name followed by a carriage-return. For example, suppose we want an operation that takes the top number on the stack, adds 3 to it and squares the result, i.e. $(x+3)^2$. If we choose the name ROOT for the operation, it can be defined as follows;

$$: \text{ROOT } 3 + \text{DUP} * ;$$

Thereafter, whenever a number (x) is entered from the keyboard and followed by the word ROOT and a carriage-return, the result $(x+3)^2$ is placed on top of the stack.

The overall process can be simply followed by examining the contents of the stack <u>after</u> each operation.

Operation -->	x	3	+	DUP	*
Stack Level 1	x	3	x+3	x+3	$(x+3)^2$
2	–	x	–	x+3	–
3	–	–	–	–	–
4	–	–	–	–	–

This entire process can also be verified by using the dot-word, ".", which removes the top number from the stack and prints it in the active number base (usually decimal upon power-up). The dot-word can also be used in colon definitions. So if we want to find and print the results of an algebraic multiplication such as $[(x+3)^2 -2]^2$, the following new word POLY can be defined in terms of the previously-defined word ROOT:

: POLY ROOT 2 - DUP * . ;

Subsequently, whenever a number (x) is entered from the keyboard and followed by the word POLY and a carriage-return, the value of $[(x+3)^2 -2]^2$ will be printed out.

x	POLY
0	49
1	196
2	529
.	.
.	.

When a colon definition is first executed, a program word is compiled or translated into a machine language program beginning at a specific starting address. Later, when the program word is typed in and executed, the FORTH operating system simply searches its dictionary for the name and, if found, jumps to the starting address of the machine language program. If the word doesn't exist in the dictionary, FORTH will usually respond with a question mark "?". In general, every word used inside of a colon definition compiles only two bytes--> the starting address of the machine language routine. This type of compact coding

(threaded code) makes for greatly reduced memory requirements.
Every address points to other addresses which eventually point
to executable machine language programs.

Other FORTH features include changing the number base of
the numeric input/output and controlling the print format. The
former is especially useful in number base conversions. If we
want to convert decimal 255 to its hexadecimal equivalent and
print the result, the following sequence can be used;

DECIMAL 255 HEX .

The resultant printout will read FF OK, the "OK" indicating a
valid operation. From that point on, FORTH will remain in the
hexadecimal number base until it is changed or re-initialized to
its default decimal base. Typical number base words include
DECIMAL, HEX, and OCTAL although in principle any number base,
N, can be selected with the N BASE ! word.

Finally, one of the most outstanding features of the FORTH
language is its speed, especially in those applications
requiring high-speed machine control. Although not as fast as
machine language (ML), FORTH is usually 20-100 times faster than
BASIC and uses one-half to one-third as much memory. A relative
speed comparison of each language can be demonstrated by
performing an "equivalent" operation in each of the languages
and comparing the execution times. With this in mind, the
following set of programs were used in conjunction with a 6522
Versatile Interface Adapter (VIA) in the AIM 65 computer.

Installation of the appropriate language ROM options enables the
generation of the FORTH and BASIC programs.

ML(Disassembled)			FORTH	BASIC(Interpreted)
START	$0300	LDA #$FF	HEX	10 POKE 40963, 255
	2	STA $A003	: WAVE FF A003	20 POKE 40961, 255
LOOP	$0305	LDA #$FF	C! BEGIN FF	30 POKE 40961, 0
	7	STA $A001	A001 C! 00	40 GOTO 20
	A	LDA #$00	A001 C! AGAIN ;	50 END
	C	STA $A001		
END	$030F	JMP $0305	(LOOP)	

Though written in three different languages (ML, FORTH and
Interpreted-BASIC), each program performs the functionally
equivalent task of writing an alternating 8-bit number ($FF or
$00) to a specific I/O location (Port A of the 6522 VIA). In
the machine language (ML) program (disassembled version), the
first two instructions initialize Port A for output by setting
all bits (=1) in PADD (location $A003). The remaining
instructions repeatedly set (=1) and clear (=0) all bits in the
Port A Register (location $A001) in an endless JMP-loop. In the
FORTH program, defined by the word WAVE, these operations are
carried out by the 8-bit store operation, C!, in an endless
BEGIN-AGAIN loop. The BASIC version uses the POKE command to
store the decimal equivalent of the 8-bit values $FF (= 255_{10})
and $00 (= 0_{10}) into locations $A003 (= 40963_{10}) and $A001
(= 40961_{10}). Here, an endless GOTO-loop alternately sets and
clears all bits in the Port A Register (location 40961_{10}).
The resultant square-wave patterns produced at the Port A pins

are contained in the oscilloscope traces of Fig. 10-2.

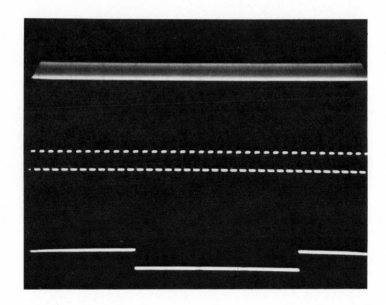

Fig. 10-2. Oscilloscope Traces of the Voltage Patterns
on the Port A Pins of the 6522 VIA.
ML(top), FORTH(middle), BASIC(bottom).

In this context, it is apparant from the resultant square-wave
frequencies that the FORTH program is ca. 30 times slower than
its ML version (ca. 67 kHz) although 30 times faster than its
BASIC (Interpreted) equivalent (ca. 67 Hz).

In its attributes, FORTH appears to present a unified
approach to computer programming. Total software development
time is greatly reduced as a consequence of its extreme
modularity and extensibility. Memory requirements are minimal
and execution times are fast.

10.3 STRUCTURED PROGRAMMING

Structured Programming is the name which has been given recently to a methodology of designing computer programs. Computer programming is the task of program development and must be done carefully. This task of developing a program can be subdivided into several steps which involve:

1. Defining the problem - Understand the problem, the input data and the desired results.

2. Producing an algorithm to solve the problem - Plan the overall job as a series of smaller jobs that the computer can do.

3. Coding the algorithm - Speak to the computer in a language that it understands.

4. Testing the program - Check/debug, check/debug .... until the desired results are output.

5. Iterating Steps 1 to 4 until the program is correct.

Each stage in this process is really an expansion of the previous step with a greater degree of detail. As it stands, this is really a top-down analysis whereby the problem is initially defined at a low level of complexity and gradually elaborated upon. The difficulty involved in each step will depend upon the problem and the solution constraints. Nevertheless, the structure should be kept as simple as possible to effect a complete understanding. The advantages of such an organized approach are:

1. Progress can be measured in stages.

2. Debugging is done in stages.

3. Errors are detected in a systematic manner.

4. The final structure is a logical consequence of the correctness of the algorithm.

10.4 FLOWCHARTS

A flowchart is a pictorial representation of what a piece of software does. It can be employed as a graphics aid before the writing process begins or as a description of the software after it has been written. The stepwise flow of the process is represented by lines and arrows while various tasks are depicted by boxes of different shapes.

Flowcharts are one possible way to conveniently develop and logically check segments of the program for correct operation. Using flowcharts it is possible to develop programs independent of any specific computer. When a flowchart is written and debugged, it can be coded into any computer language. It is also easier to discover logic errors in the flowchart representations than in the assembled program. In this respect, a picture is worth a thousand words.

The most commonly used standard flowchart symbols and their functions are described in the diagrams on the following pages.

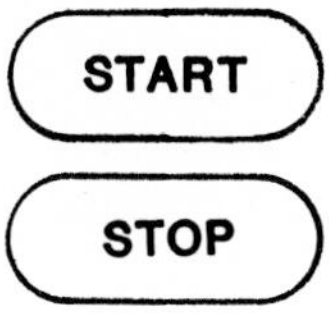

START

STOP

These symbols are used to designate the start and finish of a routine.

INPUT/ OUTPUT

Used when data is read from (ex. LDA or written to (STA) a device.

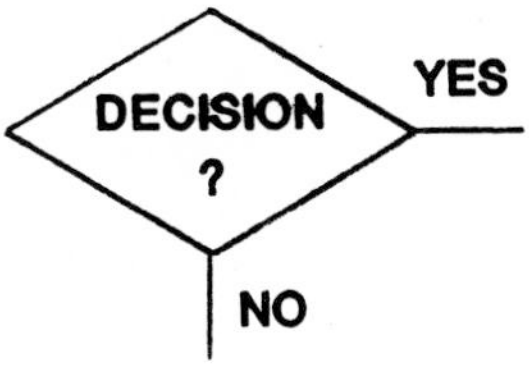

DECISION ? — **YES**

NO

Used when there are 2 possible routes for a program to take, depending upon a certain condition, i.e. is a>b?, is a=0?, is the I flag set?

PROCESS

Symbol used for mathematical or string calculations, i.e.--> Subtract b from a and store the result in a.

SUBROUTINE

Symbol used for subroutines.

A

Used to identify beginnings and ends of program segments.

Notes: 1. A process box can have any number of inputs but only one output.

2. A decision box can also have any number of inputs but only two outputs.

Fig. 10-3. Flowchart Symbols.

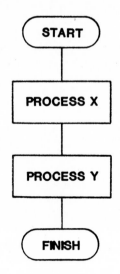

Fig. 10-4.   Sequential Routine.

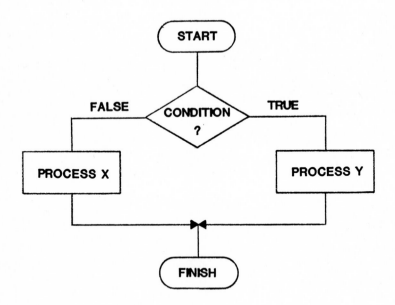

Fig. 10-5.   Branching Routine.

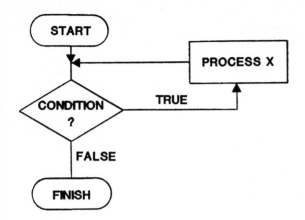

A specific process (X) is repeated over and over until the condition becomes false. The process (X) does not affect the condition.

Fig. 10-6.   Ummodified Loop.

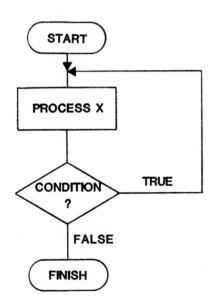

The process (X) is repeated over and over until the condition becomes false. Here, however, the process (X) does modify the condition.

Fig. 10-7.   Modified Loop.

274

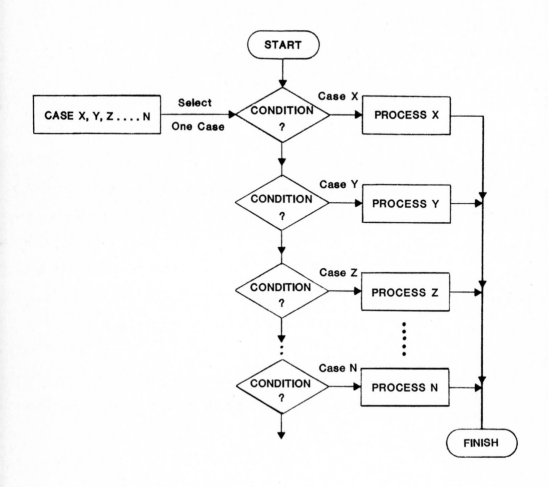

Fig. 10-8. Selective Branching Routine.

Depending upon the Case selected, there are several processes which may be chosen. If Case Y is selected, process Y is chosen to service it. Cases X, Y, Z, ...N may be devices which if selected require specific processes to service them. Ex., if an auto seatbelt is unfastened, an alarm will sound.

10.5   DEVELOPMENT SYSTEMS

The design and fabrication of a digital/analog data system involves three steps:

        (a)   debugging

        (b)   testing

        (c)   application

The overall process involves matching the performance of the system against the specifications/requirements and modifying the design parameters until satisfactory operation is achieved.

With microcomputer-based systems, this process is essential and often comprises what is usually called a 'development system'. The prime functions of such a development system are:

        (a)   categorizing symptoms

        (b)   diagnosing

        (c)   making corrections

Three approaches are considered here:

        (a)   Simulator

        (b)   Microcomputer with Monitor Program

        (c)   Microcomputer with Hardware Testing

Procedure

The transition from the first program to the final operational system can be broken down into steps:

1.   Select the peripheral hardware (A/D, D/A converters, relays, etc.) and connect to the development system.

2. Load the program from a permanent storage medium (viz. a printed listing) into the development system and test. Modify the program and peripheral hardware until satisfactory operation is achieved. Record each modification as you proceed.

3. Transfer the program to ROM or PROM (Programmable Read Only Memory) and test in the development system.

4. Replace development system with production system and test.

5. Apply that system in production configuration.

In the scheme just outlined, the peripherals are discrete units, separate from the microcomputer, but essential to the final system. Secondly, the hardware used in the development system may or may not be used in the final system. Finally, a good development system evolves into a production system with as simple a hardware change as possible.

The basic commands of a development system will include:

   (a) Run and stop program execution

   (b) Read and write memory locations, registers and
        I/O ports

   (c) Single step program

   (d) Trace program segments via breakpoints

Cosmetic features might include:

(a) Number conversion (i.e. hex --> decimal)

(b) Output to selected peripheral (i.e. scope, chart recorder, disk, printer, etc.)

(c) Data search (i.e. idling for an input)

(d) Output format/speed (a scope requires a fast repetitive refresh as opposed to a chart recorder where a single slow stream of data is processed

Simulator

A Simulator is usually a program which takes the machine code of the microprocessor as input and simulates the instruction execution sequence. It is usually run on a large computer where the error-checking aids and memory capabilities are more than adequate. The chief drawback is the slow execution time which, in some cases, may not reflect the true relationship between input and output. A simulator is primarily suited for checking the logical flow of events in a program.

Microcomputer with Monitor Program

A more realistic way of running the machine code of a microprocessor is to use the microprocessor itself or, more specifically, the Monitor Program. There are definite advantages in using the monitor as a communications link between the user and the development system.

In a single processor system, software is used to make the processor switch from the monitor to the user program and back again. In effect, one processor is made to look like two by switching from one program to the other. A wide range of debugging aids such as memory examination, trace operations, single-step execution, etc. becomes available to the user in this configuration. The primary drawback of a single-processor system is the inability to examine certain registers or operate trace routines at normal execution speed since the program must return to the monitor after every instruction. To a great extent, this drawback is overcome in multi-processor systems. Their discussion, however, is beyond the scope of this book.

Microcomputer with Hardware Testing

In the two approaches described thus far, the user may feel too remote from the hardware, a sensation many scientists and engineers dislike. With a hardware test setup, the user is more aware of what is happening because he/she is closer to the machine. A typical configuration is a development system including such components as the processor, Read/Write (RAM) memory, I/O modules, A/D, D/A converters, TTY, logic analyzers, debugging aids, oscilloscope, printers, recorders, etc. It can be either complicated or simple depending upon the eventual applications of the production system.

SELECTED REFERENCES

1. L. A. Leventhal, 6502 Assembly Language Programming, Osborne/McGraw-Hill, Berkeley, CA, 1979.

2. L. A. Leventhal and W. Saville, 6502 Assembly Language Subroutines, Osborne/McGraw-Hill, Berkeley, CA, 1982.

3. L. J. Scanlon, 6502 Software Design, Howard W. Sams and Co., Inc., Indianapolis, IN, 1980.

4. M. L. DeJong, Programming and Interfacing the 6502, Howard W. Sams and Co., Inc., Indianapolis, IN, 1980.

5. R. Zaks, Programming the 6502, Sybex, Inc., Berkeley, CA, 1982.

6. R. Zaks, 6502 Applications, Sybex, Inc., Berkeley, CA, 1979.

7. G. V. Rao, Microprocessors and Microcomputer Systems, Van Nostrand Reinhold Co., New York, NY, 1982.

8. J. H. Clark, Take AIM 65, Matrix Publishers Inc., Beaverton, OR, 1981.

9. R. C. Camp, T. A. Smay and C. J. Triska, Microprocessor Systems Engineering, Matrix Publishers, Inc., Beaverton, OR, 1979.

10. T. G. Windeknecht, 6502 Systems Programming, Little, Brown and Co., Boston, MA, 1983.

11. J. M. Holland, Advanced 6502 Interfacing, Howard W. Sams and Co., Inc., Indianapolis, IN, 1982.

12. C. C. Foster, Real Time Programming -Neglected Topics, Addison-Wesley Publ. Co., Reading, MA, 1981.

13. J. J. Carr, Microprocessor Interfacing, Tab Books, Inc., Blue Ridge Summit, PA, 1982.

14. J. J. Carr, Microcomputer Interfacing Handbook: A/D and D/A, Tab Books Inc., Blue Ridge Summit, PA, 1980.

15. J. J. Carr, Digital Interfacing With An Analog World, Tab Books, Inc., Blue Ridge Summit, PA, 1978.

16. S. Libes and M. Garetz, Interfacing to S-100/IEEE 696 Microcomputers, Osborne/McGraw-Hill, Berkeley, CA, 1981.

17. A. Colin, Programming for Microprocessors, Newnes-Butterworths Publishers Inc., Boston, MA, 1979.

18. D. Cassel, The Structured Alternative: Program Design, Style, and Debugging, Reston Publishing Co., Inc., Reston, VA, 1983.

19. M. H. Boillof, G. M. Gleason and L. W. Horn, Essentials of Flowcharting, W. C. Brown Co. Publishers, Dubuque, IA, 1975.

20. C. L. Hohenstein, Computer Peripherals For Minicomputers, Microprocessors and Personal Computers, McGraw-Hill, Inc., New York, NY, 1980.

21. J. T. Arnold, Simplified Digital Automation With Microprocessors, Academic Press, Inc., New York, NY, 1979.

22. J. A. Titus, C. A. Titus, P. R. Rony and D. G. Larsen, Microcomputer-Analog Converter Software and Hardware Interfacing, Howard W. Sams and Co., Inc., Indianapolis, IN, 1978.

23. D. L. Cannon and G. Luecke, Understanding Microprocessors, Texas Instruments, Inc., Dallas, TX, 1978.

24. D. Aspinall and E. L. Dagless, Introduction to Microprocessors, Pitnam Publishing Ltd., London, 1977.

25. L. Brodie, Starting FORTH, Prentice-Hall, Inc., Englewood Cliffs, NJ, 1981.

26. K. Knecht, Introduction to FORTH, Howard W. Sams and Co., Inc., Indianapolis, IN, 1982.

27. L. J. Scanlon, FORTH Programming, Howard W. Sams and Co., Inc., Indianapolis, IN, 1982.

28. A. H. Seidman, Integrated Circuits Applications Handbook, John Wiley and Sons, New York, NY, 1983.

29. H. V. Malmstadt, C. G. Enke and S. R. Crouch, Electronics
    and Instrumentation for Scientists, Benjamin/Cummings Publ.
    Co., Inc., Reading, MA, 1981.

30. F. F. Driscoll, Microprocessor-Microcomputer Technology,
    Breton Publishers, North Scituate, MA, 1983.

31. R. J. Tocci and L. P. Laskowski, Microprocessors and
    Microcomputers: Hardware and Software, Prentice-Hall, Inc.,
    Englewood Cliffs, NJ, 1982.

32. J. Markus, Modern Electronic Circuits Reference Manual,
    McGraw-Hill, Inc., New York, NY, 1980.

33. D. H. Sheingold, ed., Tranducer Interfacing Handbook,
    Analog Devices, Inc., Norwood, MA, 1980.

34. D. H. Sheingold, ed., Analog-Digital Conversion Notes,
    Analog Devices, Inc., Norwood, MA, 1977.

35. W. H. Buchsbaum, Buchsbaum´s Complete Handbook of Practical
    Electronic Reference Data, Prentice-Hall, Inc., Englewood
    Cliffs, NJ, 1978.

36. Linear Databook, National Semiconductor Corp., Santa Clara,
    CA, 1982.

37. Reference Data for Radio Engineers, Sixth Ed., Howard W.
    Sams and Co., Inc., Indianapolis, IN, 1977.

38. RCA COS/MOS Integrated Circuits, RCA Solid State Division,
    RCA Corporation, Somerville, NJ, 1977.

39. Solid State Devices Manual, RCA Solid State Division, RCA
    Corporation, Somerville, NJ, 1975.

40. Electro-Optics Handbook, RCA Electronic Component Division,
    RCA Corporation, Lancaster, PA, 1974.

41. R. E. Gasperini, Digital Troubleshooting , Movonics Co.,
    Los Altos, CA, 1975.

42. J. E. Bentley and K. M. Hess, A Programmed Review for
    Electrical Engineering, Van Nostrand Reinhold Co.,
    New York, NY, 1978.

APPENDIX A: REFERENCE INFORMATION
---

* R650X, R651X Microprocessors (CPU´s)

* R6522 Versatile Interface Adapter (VIA)

* AIM 65 Microcomputer

The following reprinted specification sheets are made available through the courtesy of the Semiconductor Products Division of Rockwell International Corporation, Newport Beach, CA. Copyright © 1983, 1983 and 1981 Rockwell International Corp. All rights reserved.

R650X and R651X MICROPROCESSORS (CPU)

DESCRIPTION

The 8-bit R6500 microprocessor devices are produced with N-Channel, Silicon Gate technology. Its performance speeds are enhanced by advanced system architecture. This innovative architecture results in smaller chips—the semiconductor threshold is cost-effectivity. System cost-effectivity is further enhanced by providing a family of 10 software-compatible microprocessor (CPU) devices, described in this document. Rockwell also provides memory and microcomputer system—as well as low-cost design aids and documentation.

Ten CPU devices are available. All are software-compatible. They provide options of addressable memory, interrupt input, on-chip clock oscillators and drivers. All are bus-compatible with earlier generation microprocessors like the M6800 devices.

The R650X and R651X family includes six microprocessors with on-board clock oscillators and drivers and four microprocessors driven by external clocks. The on-chip clock versions are aimed at high performance, low cost applications where single phase inputs, crystal or RC inputs provide the time base. The external clock versions are geared for multiprocessor system applications where maximum timing control is mandatory. All R6500 microprocessors are also available in a variety of packaging (ceramic and plastic), operating frequency (1 MHz, 2 MHz and 3 MHz) and temperature (commercial and industrial) versions.

ORDERING INFORMATION

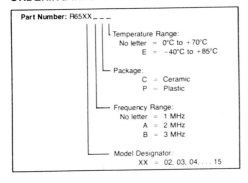

Part Number: R65XX _ _ _

Temperature Range:
No letter = 0°C to +70°C
E = −40°C to +85°C

Package:
C = Ceramic
P = Plastic

Frequency Range:
No letter = 1 MHz
A = 2 MHz
B = 3 MHz

Model Designator:
XX = 02, 03, 04, . . . 15

FEATURES

- N-channel, silicon gate, depletion load technology
- 8-bit parallel processing
- 56 Instructions
- Decimal and binary arithmetic
- Thirteen addressing modes
- True indexing capability
- Programmable stack pointer
- Variable length stack
- Interrupt request
- Non-maskable interrupt
- Use with any type of speed memory
- 8-bit bidirectional data bus
- Addressable memory range of up to 64K bytes
- "Ready" input
- Direct Memory Access capability
- Bus compatible with M6800
- 1 MHz, 2 MHz, and 3 MHz versions
- Choice of external or on-chip clocks
- On-chip clock options
  —External single clock input
  —Crystal time base input
- Commercial and industrial temperature versions
- Pipeline architecture
- Single +5V supply

R6500 CPU FAMILY MEMBERS

Microprocessors with Internal Two Phase Clock Generator

Model	No. Pins	Addressable Memory
R6502	40	64K Bytes
R6503	28	4K Bytes
R6504	28	8K Bytes
R6505	28	4K Bytes
R6506	28	4K Bytes
R6507	28	8K Bytes

Microprocessors with External Two Phase Clock Input

Model	No. Pins	Addressable Memory
R6512	40	64K Bytes
R6513	28	4K Bytes
R6514	28	8K Bytes
R6515	28	4K Bytes

Data Sheet Order No. D39
Rev. 5, August 1983

INTERFACE SIGNAL DESCRIPTIONS

CLOCKS (Ø1, Ø2)

The R651X requires a two phase non-overlapping clock that runs at the V_{CC} voltage level. The R650X clocks are supplied with an internal clock generator. The frequency of these clocks is externally controlled.

ADDRESS BUS (A0–A15, R6502)

The address line outputs access data in memory device locations or cells, access data in I/O device registers and/or effect logical operations in I/O or controller devices depending on system design. The addressing range is determined by the number of address lines available on the particular CPU device. The R6502 and R6512 can address 64K bytes with a 16-bit address bus (A0–A15); the R6504, R6507, and the R6514 can address 8K bytes with a 13-bit address bus (A0–A12); and the R6503, R6505, R6506, R6513, and R6515 can address 4K bytes with a 12-bit address bus (A0–A11). These outputs are TTL-compatible and are capable of driving one standard TTL load and 130 pF.

DATA BUS (D0–D7)

The data lines (D0–D7) form an 8-bit bidirectional data bus which transfers data between the CPU and memory or peripheral devices. The outputs are tri-state buffers capable of driving one standard TTL load and 130 pF.

DATA BUS ENABLE (DBE, R6512 ONLY)

The TTL-compatible DBE input allows external control of the tri-state data output buffers and will enable the microprocessor bus driver when in the high state. In normal operation DBE is driven by the phase two (Ø2) clock, thus allowing data output from microprocessor only during Ø2. During the read cycle, the data bus drivers are internally disabled, becoming essentially an open circuit. To disable data bus drivers externally, DBE should be held low.

READY (RDY)

The Ready input signal allows the user to halt or single cycle the microprocessor on all cycles except write cycles. A negative transition to the low state during or coincident with phase one (Ø1) will halt the microprocessor with the output address lines reflecting the current address being fetched. If Ready is low during a write cycle, it is ignored until the following read operation. This condition will remain through a subsequent phase two (Ø2) in which the Ready signal is low. This feature allows microprocessor interfacing with the low speed PROMs as well as Direct Memory Access (DMA).

INTERRUPT REQUEST (IRQ)

The TTL level active-low IRQ input requests that an interrupt sequence begin within the microprocessor. The microprocessor will complete the current instruction being executed before recognizing the request. At that time, the interrupt mask bit in the Processor Status Register will be examined. If the interrupt mask flag is not set, the microprocessor will begin an interrupt sequence. The Program Counter and Processor Status Register

are stored in the stack. The microprocessor will then set the interrupt mask flag high so that no further interrupts can occur. At the end of this cycle, the program counter low will be loaded from address FFFE, and program counter high from location FFFF, therefore transferring program control to the memory vector located at these addresses. The RDY signal must be in the high state for any interrupt to be recognized. A 3KΩ external resistor should be used for proper wire-OR operation.

NON-MASKABLE INTERRUPT (NMI)

A negative going edge on the NMI input requests that a non-maskable interrupt sequence be generated within the microprocessor.

NMI is an unconditional interrupt. Following completion of the current instruction, the sequence of operations defined for IRQ will be performed, regardless of the state interrupt mask flag. The vector address loaded into the program counter, low and high, are locations FFFA and FFFB respectively, thereby transferring program control to the memory vector located at these addresses. The instructions loaded at these locations cause the microprocessor to branch to a non-maskable interrupt routine in memory.

NMI also requires an external 3KΩ register to V_{CC} for proper wire-OR operations.

Inputs IRQ and NMI are hardware interrupts lines that are sampled during Ø2 (phase 2) and will begin the appropriate interrupt routine on the Ø1 (phase 1) following the completion of the current instruction.

SET OVERFLOW FLAG (S.O.)

A negative going edge on the S.O. input sets the overflow bit in the Status Code Register. This signal is sampled on the trailing edge of Ø1 and must be externally synchronized.

SYNC

The SYNC output line identifies those cycles in which the microprocessor is doing an OP CODE fetch. The SYNC line goes high during Ø1 of an OP CODE fetch and stays high for the remainder of that cycle. If the RDY line is pulled low during the Ø1 clock pulse in which SYNC went high, the processor will stop in its current state and will remain in the state until the RDY line goes high. In this manner, the SYNC signal can be used to control RDY to cause single instruction execution.

RESET (RES)

The active low RES resets, or starts, the microprocessor from a power down or restart condition. During the time that this line is held low, writing to or from the microprocessor is inhibited. When a positive edge is detected on the input, the microprocessor will immediately begin the reset sequence.

After a system initialization time of six clock cycles, the mask interrupt flag is set and the microprocessor loads the program counter from the memory vector locations FFFC and FFFD. This is the start location for program control.

After V_{CC} reaches 4.75 volts in a power up routine, reset must be held low for at least two clock cycles. At this time the R/W̄ and (SYNC) signal become valid.

R650X, R651X

R6500 Microprocessors (CPU)

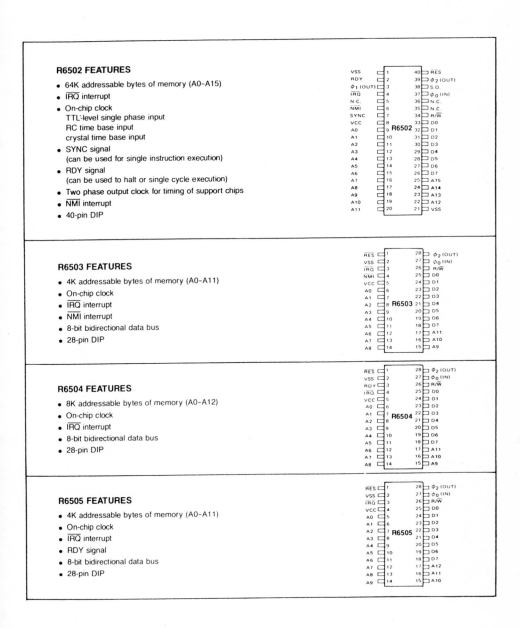

R6502 FEATURES

- 64K addressable bytes of memory (A0–A15)
- IRQ interrupt
- On-chip clock
  TTL-level single phase input
  RC time base input
  crystal time base input
- SYNC signal
  (can be used for single instruction execution)
- RDY signal
  (can be used to halt or single cycle execution)
- Two phase output clock for timing of support chips
- NMI interrupt
- 40-pin DIP

R6502 pin assignment:

Pin	Signal		Pin	Signal
1	VSS		40	RES
2	RDY		39	ϕ_2 (OUT)
3	ϕ_1 (OUT)		38	S.O.
4	IRQ		37	ϕ_0 (IN)
5	N.C.		36	N.C.
6	NMI		35	N.C.
7	SYNC		34	R/W
8	VCC		33	D0
9	A0		32	D1
10	A1		31	D2
11	A2		30	D3
12	A3		29	D4
13	A4		28	D5
14	A5		27	D6
15	A6		26	D7
16	A7		25	A15
17	A8		24	A14
18	A9		23	A13
19	A10		22	A12
20	A11		21	VSS

R6503 FEATURES

- 4K addressable bytes of memory (A0–A11)
- On-chip clock
- IRQ interrupt
- NMI interrupt
- 8-bit bidirectional data bus
- 28-pin DIP

R6503 pin assignment:

Pin	Signal		Pin	Signal
1	RES		28	ϕ_2 (OUT)
2	VSS		27	ϕ_0 (IN)
3	IRQ		26	R/W
4	NMI		25	D0
5	VCC		24	D1
6	A0		23	D2
7	A1		22	D3
8	A2		21	D4
9	A3		20	D5
10	A4		19	D6
11	A5		18	D7
12	A6		17	A11
13	A7		16	A10
14	A8		15	A9

R6504 FEATURES

- 8K addressable bytes of memory (A0–A12)
- On-chip clock
- IRQ interrupt
- 8-bit bidirectional data bus
- 28-pin DIP

R6504 pin assignment:

Pin	Signal		Pin	Signal
1	RES		28	ϕ_2 (OUT)
2	VSS		27	ϕ_0 (IN)
3	RDY		26	R/W
4	IRQ		25	D0
5	VCC		24	D1
6	A0		23	D2
7	A1		22	D3
8	A2		21	D4
9	A3		20	D5
10	A4		19	D6
11	A5		18	D7
12	A6		17	A11
13	A7		16	A10
14	A8		15	A9

R6505 FEATURES

- 4K addressable bytes of memory (A0–A11)
- On-chip clock
- IRQ interrupt
- RDY signal
- 8-bit bidirectional data bus
- 28-pin DIP

R6505 pin assignment:

Pin	Signal		Pin	Signal
1	RES		28	ϕ_2 (OUT)
2	VSS		27	ϕ_0 (IN)
3	IRQ		26	R/W
4	VCC		25	D0
5	A0		24	D1
6	A1		23	D2
7	A2		22	D3
8	A3		21	D4
9	A4		20	D5
10	A5		19	D6
11	A6		18	D7
12	A7		17	A12
13	A8		16	A11
14	A9		15	A10

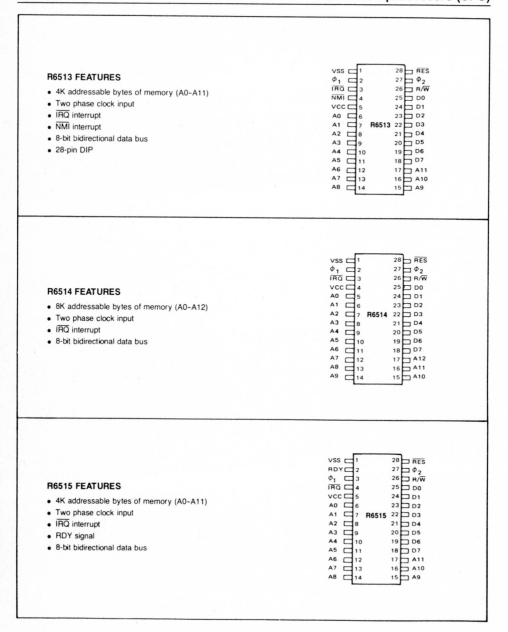

R6513 FEATURES

- 4K addressable bytes of memory (A0–A11)
- Two phase clock input
- $\overline{IRQ}$ interrupt
- $\overline{NMI}$ interrupt
- 8-bit bidirectional data bus
- 28-pin DIP

R6513 pin assignments:

Pin	Signal	Pin	Signal
1	VSS	28	$\overline{RES}$
2	ϕ_1	27	ϕ_2
3	$\overline{IRQ}$	26	R/$\overline{W}$
4	$\overline{NMI}$	25	D0
5	VCC	24	D1
6	A0	23	D2
7	A1	22	D3
8	A2	21	D4
9	A3	20	D5
10	A4	19	D6
11	A5	18	D7
12	A6	17	A11
13	A7	16	A10
14	A8	15	A9

R6514 FEATURES

- 8K addressable bytes of memory (A0–A12)
- Two phase clock input
- $\overline{IRQ}$ interrupt
- 8-bit bidirectional data bus

R6514 pin assignments:

Pin	Signal	Pin	Signal
1	VSS	28	$\overline{RES}$
2	ϕ_1	27	ϕ_2
3	$\overline{IRQ}$	26	R/$\overline{W}$
4	VCC	25	D0
5	A0	24	D1
6	A1	23	D2
7	A2	22	D3
8	A3	21	D4
9	A4	20	D5
10	A5	19	D6
11	A6	18	D7
12	A7	17	A12
13	A8	16	A11
14	A9	15	A10

R6515 FEATURES

- 4K addressable bytes of memory (A0–A11)
- Two phase clock input
- $\overline{IRQ}$ interrupt
- RDY signal
- 8-bit bidirectional data bus

R6515 pin assignments:

Pin	Signal	Pin	Signal
1	VSS	28	$\overline{RES}$
2	RDY	27	ϕ_2
3	ϕ_1	26	R/$\overline{W}$
4	$\overline{IRQ}$	25	D0
5	VCC	24	D1
6	A0	23	D2
7	A1	22	D3
8	A2	21	D4
9	A3	20	D5
10	A4	19	D6
11	A5	18	D7
12	A6	17	A11
13	A7	16	A10
14	A8	15	A9

R650X, R651X   **R6500 Microprocessors (CPU)**

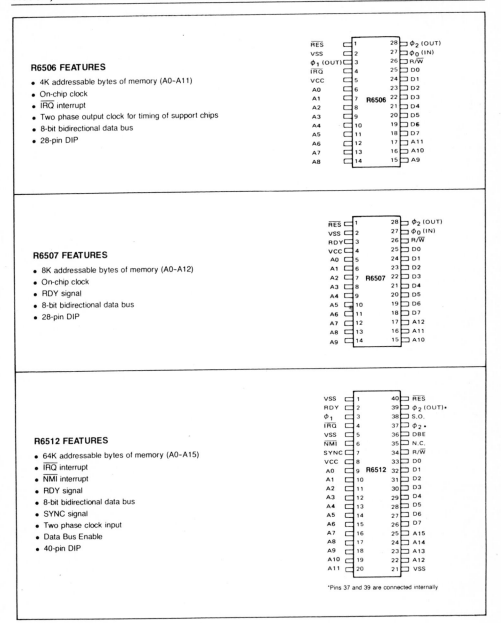

R6506 FEATURES

- 4K addressable bytes of memory (A0–A11)
- On-chip clock
- $\overline{IRQ}$ interrupt
- Two phase output clock for timing of support chips
- 8-bit bidirectional data bus
- 28-pin DIP

R6507 FEATURES

- 8K addressable bytes of memory (A0–A12)
- On-chip clock
- RDY signal
- 8-bit bidirectional data bus
- 28-pin DIP

R6512 FEATURES

- 64K addressable bytes of memory (A0–A15)
- $\overline{IRQ}$ interrupt
- $\overline{NMI}$ interrupt
- RDY signal
- 8-bit bidirectional data bus
- SYNC signal
- Two phase clock input
- Data Bus Enable
- 40-pin DIP

*Pins 37 and 39 are connected internally

FUNCTIONAL DESCRIPTION

The internal organization of all R6500 CPUs is identical except for some variations in clock interface, the number of address output lines, and some unique input/output lines between versions.

CLOCK GENERATOR

The clock generator develops all internal clock signals, and (where applicable) external clock signals, associated with the device. It is the clock generator that drives the timing control unit and the external timing for slave mode operations.

TIMING CONTROL

The timing control unit keeps track of the instruction cycle being monitored. The unit is set to zero each time an instruction fetch is executed and is advanced at the beginning of each phase one clock pulse for as many cycles as is required to complete the instruction. Each data transfer which takes place between the registers depends upon decoding the contents of both the instruction register and the timing control unit.

PROGRAM COUNTER

The 16-bit program counter provides the addresses which step the microprocessor through sequential instructions in a program.

Each time the microprocessor fetches an instruction from program memory, the lower byte of the program counter (PCL) is placed on the low-order bits of the address bus and the higher byte of the program counter (PCH) is placed on the high-order 8 bits. The counter is incremented each time an instruction or data is fetched from program memory.

INSTRUCTION REGISTER AND DECODE

Instructions fetched from memory are gated onto the internal data bus. These instructions are latched into the instuction register, then decoded, along with timing and interrupt signals, to generate control signals for the various registers.

ARITHMETIC AND LOGIC UNIT (ALU)

All arithmetic and logic operations take place in the ALU including incrementing and decrementing internal registers (except the program counter). The ALU has no internal memory and is used only to perform logical and transient numerical operations.

ACCUMULATOR

The accumulator is a general purpose 8-bit register that stores the results of most arithmetic and logic operations, and in addition, the accumulator usually contains one of the two data words used in these operations.

INDEX REGISTERS

There are two 8-bit index registers (X and Y), which may be used to count program steps or to provide an index value to be used in generating an effective address.

When executing an instruction which specifies indexed addressing, the CPU fetches the op code and the base address, and modifies the address by adding the index register to it prior to performing the desired operation. Pre- or post-indexing of indirect addresses is possible (see addressing modes).

STACK POINTER

The stack pointer is an 8-bit register used to control the addressing of the variable-length stack on page one. The stack pointer is automatically incremented and decremented under control of the microprocessor to perform stack manipulations under direction of either the program or interrupts ($\overline{\text{NMI}}$) and $\overline{\text{IRQ}}$). The stack allows simple implementation of nested subroutines and multiple level interrupts. The stack pointer should be initialized before any interrupts or stack operations occur.

PROCESSOR STATUS REGISTER

The 8-bit processor status register contains seven status flags. Some of the flags are controlled by the program, others may be controlled both by the program and the CPU.

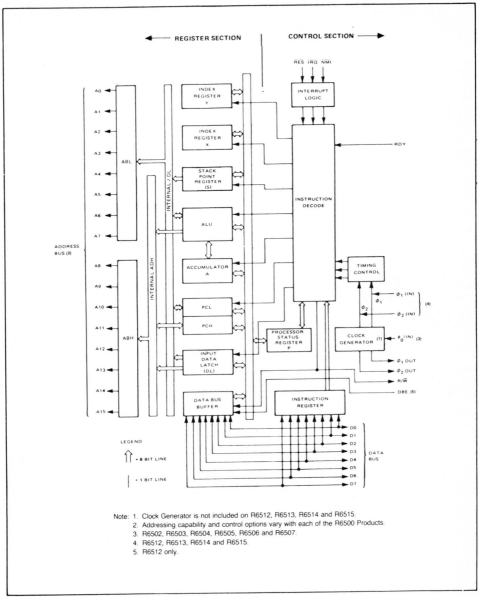

Note: 1. Clock Generator is not included on R6512, R6513, R6514 and R6515.
2. Addressing capability and control options vary with each of the R6500 Products.
3. R6502, R6503, R6504, R6505, R6506 and R6507.
4. R6512, R6513, R6514 and R6515.
5. R6512 only.

R650X and R651X Internal Architecture

R650X, R651X   R6500 Microprocessors (CPU)

INSTRUCTION SET

The R6500 CPU has 56 instruction types which are enhanced by up to 13 addressing modes for each instruction. The accumulator, index registers, Program Counter, Stack Pointer and Processor Status Register are illustrated below.

Alphabetic Listing of Instruction Set

Mnemonic	Function	Mnemonic	Function
ADC	Add Memory to Accumulator with Carry	JMP	Jump to New Location
AND	"AND" Memory with Accumulator	JSR	Jump to New Location Saving Return Address
ASL	Shift Left One Bit (Memory or Accumulator)		
		LDA	Load Accumulator with Memory
BCC	Branch on Carry Clear	LDX	Load Index X with Memory
BCS	Branch on Carry Set	LDY	Load Index Y with Memory
BEQ	Branch on Result Zero	LSR	Shift One Bit Right (Memory or Accumulator)
BIT	Test Bits in Memory with Accumulator		
BMI	Branch on Result Minus	NOP	No Operation
BNE	Branch on Result not Zero		
BPL	Branch on Result Plus	ORA	"OR" Memory with Accumulator
BRK	Force Break		
BVC	Branch on Overflow Clear	PHA	Push Accumulator on Stack
BVS	Branch on Overflow Set	PHP	Push Processor Status on Stack
		PLA	Pull Accumulator from Stack
CLC	Clear Carry Flag	PLP	Pull Processor Status from Stack
CLD	Clear Decimal Mode		
CLI	Clear Interrupt Disable Bit	ROL	Rotate One Bit Left (Memory or Accumulator)
CLV	Clear Overflow Flag	ROR	Rotate One Bit Right (Memory or Accumulator)
CMP	Compare Memory and Accumulator	RTI	Return from Interrupt
CPX	Compare Memory and Index X	RTS	Return from Subroutine
CPY	Compare Memory and Index Y		
		SBC	Subtract Memory from Accumulator with Borrow
DEC	Decrement Memory by One	SEC	Set Carry Flag
DEX	Decrement Index X by One	SED	Set Decimal Mode
DEY	Decrement Index Y by One	SEI	Set Interrupt Disable Status
		STA	Store Accumulator in Memory
EOR	"Exclusive-OR" Memory with Accumulator	STX	Store Index X in Memory
		STY	Store Index Y in Memory
INC	Increment Memory by One		
INX	Increment Index X by One	TAX	Transfer Accumulator to Index X
INY	Increment Index Y by One	TAY	Transfer Accumulator to Index Y
		TSX	Transfer Stack Pointer to Index X
		TXA	Transfer Index X to Accumulator
		TXS	Transfer Index X to Stack Register
		TYA	Transfer Index Y to Accumulator

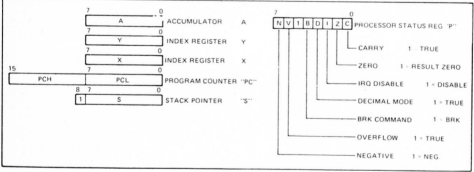

Programming Model

|

ADDRESSING MODES

The R6500 CPU family has 13 addressing modes. In the following discussion of these addressing modes, a bracketed expression follows the title of the mode. This expression is the term used in the Instruction Set Op Code Matrix table (later in this product description) to make it easier to identify the actual addressing mode used by the instruction.

ACCUMULATOR ADDRESSING |Accum|—This form of addressing is represented with a one byte instruction, implying an operation on the accumulator.

IMMEDIATE ADDRESSING |IMM|—In immediate addressing, the second byte of the instruction contains the operand, with no further memory addressing required.

ABSOLUTE ADDRESSING |Absolute|—In absolute addressing, the second byte of the instruction specifies the eight low order bits of the effective address while the third byte specifies the eight high order bits. Thus, the absolute addressing mode allows access to the entire 64K bytes of addressable memory.

ZERO PAGE ADDRESSING |ZP|—The zero page instructions allow for shorter code and execution times by fetching only the second byte of the instruction and assuming a zero high address byte. Careful use of the zero page can result in significant increase in code efficiency.

INDEXED ZERO PAGE ADDRESSING |ZP, X or Y|—(X, Y indexing)—This form of addressing is used with the index register and is referred to as "Zero Page, X" or "Zero Page, Y". The effective address is calculated by adding the second byte to the contents of the index register. Since this is a form of "Zero Page" addressing, the content of the second byte references a location in page zero. Additionally, due to the "Zero Page" addressing nature of this mode, no carry is added to the high order eight bits of memory and crossing of page boundaries does not occur.

INDEXED ABSOLUTE ADDRESSING |ABS, X or Y|—(X, Y indexing)—This form of addressing is used in conjunction with X and Y index register and is referred to as "Absolute, X" and "Absolute, Y". The effective address is formed by adding the contents of X or Y to the address contained in the second and third bytes of the instruction. This mode allows the index register to contain the index or count value and the instruction to contain the base address. This type of indexing allows any location referencing and the index to modify multiple fields, resulting in reduced coding and execution time.

IMPLIED ADDRESSING |Implied|—In the implied addressing mode, the address containing the operand is implicitly stated in the operation code of the instruction.

RELATIVE ADDRESSING |Relative|—Relative addressing is used only with branch instructions and establishes a destination for the conditional branch.

The second byte of the instruction becomes the operand which is an "Offset" added to the contents of the lower eight bits of the program counter when the counter is set at the next instruction. The range of the offset is -128 to +127 bytes from the next instruction.

INDEXED INDIRECT ADDRESSING |(IND, X)|—In indexed indirect addressing (referred to as (Indirect, X)), the second byte of the instruction is added to the contents of the X index register, discarding the carry. The result of this addition points to a memory location on page zero whose contents are the low order eight bits of the effective address. The next memory location in page zero contains the high order eight bits of the effective address. Both memory locations specifying the high and low order bytes of the effective address must be in page zero.

INDIRECT INDEXED ADDRESSING |(IND), Y|—In indirect indexed addressing (referred to as (Indirect), Y), the second byte of the instruction points to a memory location in page zero. The contents of this memory location are added to the contents of the Y index register, the result being the low order eight bits of the effective address. The carry from this addition is added to the contents of the next page zero memory location, the result being the high order eight bits of the effective address.

ABSOLUTE INDIRECT |Indirect|—The second byte of the instruction contains the low order eight bits of a memory location. The high order eight bits of that memory location are contained in the third byte of the instruction. The contents of the fully specified memory location are the low order byte of the effective address. The next memory location contains the high order byte of the effective address which is loaded into the sixteen bits of the program counter. (JMP (IND) only)

R650X, R651X   **R6500 Microprocessors (CPU)**

INSTRUCTION SET OP CODE MATRIX

The following matrix shows the Op Codes associated with the R6500 family of CPU devices. The matrix identifies the hexadecimal code, the mnemonic code, the addressing mode, the number of instruction bytes, and the number of machine cycles associated with each Op Code. Also, refer to the instruction set summary for additional information on these Op Codes.

MSD \ LSD	0	1	2	3	4	5	6	7	8	9	A	B	C	D	E	F	
0	BRK Implied 1 7	ORA (IND, X) 2 6				ORA ZP 2 3	ASL ZP 2 5	RMB0 ZP 2 5	PHP Implied 1 3	ORA IMM 2 2	ASL Accum 1 2			ORA ABS 3 4	ASL ABS 3 6	BBR0 ZP 3 5**	0
1	BPL Relative 2 2**	ORA (IND), Y 2 5*				ORA ZP, X 2 4	ASL ZP, X 2 6	RMB1 ZP 2 5	CLC Implied 1 2	ORA ABS, Y 3 4*				ORA ABS, X 3 4*	ASL ABS, X 3 7	BBR1 ZP 3 5**	1
2	JSR Absolute 3 6	AND (IND, X) 2 6			BIT ZP 2 3	AND ZP 2 3	ROL ZP 2 5	RMB2 ZP 2 5	PLP Implied 1 4	AND IMM 2 2	ROL Accum 1 2		BIT ABS 3 4	AND ABS 3 4	ROL ABS 3 6	BBR2 ZP 3 5**	2
3	BMI Relative 2 2**	AND (IND, Y) 2 5*				AND ZP, X 2 4	ROL ZP, X 2 6	RMB3 ZP 2 5	SEC Implied 1 2	AND ABS, Y 3 4*				AND ABS, X 3 4*	ROL ABS, X 3 7	BBR3 ZP 3 5**	3
4	RTI Implied 1 6	EOR (IND, X) 2 6				EOR ZP 2 3	LSR ZP 2 5	RMB4 ZP 2 5	PHA Implied 1 3	EOR IMM 2 2	LSR Accum 1 2		JMP ABS 3 3	EOR ABS 3 4	LSR ABS 3 6	BBR4 ZP 3 5**	4
5	BVC Relative 2 2**	EOR (IND), Y 2 5*				EOR ZP, X 2 4	LSR ZP, X 2 6	RMB5 ZP 2 5	CLI Implied 1 2	EOR ABS, Y 3 4*				EOR ABS, X 3 4*	LSR ABS, X 3 7	BBR5 ZP 3 5**	5
6	RTS Implied 1 6	ADC (IND, X) 2 6				ADC ZP 2 3	ROR ZP 2 5	RMB6 ZP 2 5	PLA Implied 1 4	ADC IMM 2 2	ROR Accum 1 2		JMP Indirect 3 5	ADC ABS 3 4	ROR ABS 3 6	BBR6 ZP 3 5**	6
7	BVS Relative 2 2**	ADC (IND), Y 2 5*				ADC ZP, X 2 4	ROR ZP, X 2 6	RMB7 ZP 2 5	SEI Implied 1 2	ADC ABS, Y 3 4*				ADC ABS, X 3 4*	ROR ABS, X 3 7	BBR7 ZP 3 5**	7
8		STA (IND, X) 2 6			STY ZP 2 3	STA ZP 2 3	STX ZP 2 3	SMB0 ZP 2 5	DEY Implied 1 2		TXA Implied 1 2		STY ABS 3 4	STA ABS 3 4	STX ABS 3 4	BBS0 ZP 3 5**	8
9	BCC Relative 2 2**	STA (IND), Y 2 6			STY ZP, X 2 4	STA ZP, X 2 4	STX ZP, Y 2 4	SMB1 ZP 2 5	TYA Implied 1 2	STA ABS, Y 3 5	TXS Implied 1 2			STA ABS, X 3 5		BBS1 ZP 3 5**	9
A	LDY IMM 2 2	LDA (IND, X) 2 6	LDX IMM 2 2		LDY ZP 2 3	LDA ZP 2 3	LDX ZP 2 3	SMB2 ZP 2 5	TAY Implied 1 2	LDA IMM 2 2	TAX Implied 1 2		LDY ABS 3 4	LDA ABS 3 4	LDX ABS 3 4	BBS2 ZP 3 5**	A
B	BCS Relative 2 2**	LDA (IND), Y 2 5*			LDY ZP, X 2 4	LDA ZP, X 2 4	LDX ZP, Y 2 4	SMB3 ZP 2 5	CLV Implied 1 2	LDA ABS, Y 3 4*	TSX Implied 1 2		LDY ABS, X 3 4*	LDA ABS, X 3 4*	LDX ABS, Y 3 4*	BBS3 ZP 3 5**	B
C	CPY IMM 2 2	CMP (IND, X) 2 6			CPY ZP 2 3	CMP ZP 2 3	DEC ZP 2 5	SMB4 ZP 2 5	INY Implied 1 2	CMP IMM 2 2	DEX Implied 1 2		CPY ABS 3 4	CMP ABS 3 4	DEC ABS 3 6	BBS4 ZP 3 5**	C
D	BNE Relative 2 2**	CMP (IND), Y 2 5*				CMP ZP, X 2 4	DEC ZP, X 2 6	SMB5 ZP 2 5	CLD Implied 1 2	CMP ABS, Y 3 4*				CMP ABS, X 3 4*	DEC ABS, X 3 7	BBS5 ZP 3 5**	D
E	CPX IMM 2 2	SBC (IND, X) 2 6			CPX ZP 2 3	SBC ZP 2 3	INC ZP 2 5	SMB6 ZP 2 5	INX Implied 1 2	SBC IMM 2 2	NOP Implied 1 2		CPX ABS 3 4	SBC ABS 3 4	INC ABS 3 6	BBS6 ZP 3 5**	F
F	BEQ Relative 2 2**	SBC (IND), Y 2 5*				SBC ZP, X 2 4	INC ZP, X 2 6	SMB7 ZP 2 5	SED Implied 1 2	SBC ABS, Y 3 4*				SBC ABS, X 3 4*	INC ABS, X 3 7	BBS7 ZP 3 5**	F
	0	1	2	3	4	5	6	7	8	9	A	B	C	D	E	F	

BRK	—OP Code
0 Implied	—Addressing Mode
1 7	—Instruction Bytes: Machine Cycles

*Add 1 to N if page boundary is crossed.
**Add 1 to N if branch occurs to same page.
add 2 to N if branch occurs to different page

R650X, R651X   **R6500 Microprocessors (CPU)**

INSTRUCTION SET SUMMARY

MNEMONIC	OPERATION	IMMEDIATE OP n #	ABSOLUTE OP n #	ZERO PAGE OP n #	ACCUM OP n #	IMPLIED OP n #	(IND, X) OP n #	(IND), Y OP n #	Z PAGE, X OP n #	ABS, X OP n #	ABS, Y OP n #	RELATIVE OP n #	INDIRECT OP n #	Z PAGE, Y OP n #	PROCESSOR STATUS CODES 7 6 5 4 3 2 1 0 / N V · B D I Z C	MNEMONIC
A D C	A + M + C → A (1)(4)	69 2 2	6D 4 3	65 3 2			61 6 2	71 5 2	75 4 2	7D 4 3	79 4 3				N V · · · · Z C	A D C
A N D	A ∧ M → A (1)	29 2 2	2D 4 3	25 3 2			21 6 2	31 5 2	35 4 2	3D 4 3	39 4 3				N · · · · · Z ·	A N D
A S L	C ← ☐ ← 0		0E 6 3	06 5 2	0A 2 1				16 6 2	1E 7 3					N · · · · · Z C	A S L
B C C	BRANCH ON C = 0 (2)											90 2 2			· · · · · · · ·	B C C
B C S	BRANCH ON C = 1 (2)											B0 2 2			· · · · · · · ·	B C S
B E Q	BRANCH ON Z = 1 (2)											F0 2 2			· · · · · · · ·	B E Q
B I T	A ∧ M		2C 4 3	24 3 2											M₇ M₆ · · · · Z ·	B I T
B M I	BRANCH ON N = 1 (2)											30 2 2			· · · · · · · ·	B M I
B N E	BRANCH ON Z = 0 (2)											D0 2 2			· · · · · · · ·	B N E
B P L	BRANCH ON N = 0 (2)											10 2 2			· · · · · · · ·	B P L
B R K	BREAK					00 7 1									· · · · 1 · 1 ·	B R K
B V C	BRANCH ON V = 0 (2)											50 2 2			· · · · · · · ·	B V C
B V S	BRANCH ON V = 1 (2)											70 2 2			· · · · · · · ·	B V S
C L C	0 → C					18 2 1									· · · · · · · 0	C L C
C L D	0 → D					D8 2 1									· · · · 0 · · ·	C L D
C L I	0 → I					58 2 1									· · · · · 0 · ·	C L I
C L V	0 → V					B8 2 1									· 0 · · · · · ·	C L V
C M P	A − M (1)	C9 2 2	CD 4 3	C5 3 2			C1 6 2	D1 5 2	D5 4 2	DD 4 3	D9 4 3				N · · · · · Z C	C M P
C P X	X − M	E0 2 2	EC 4 3	E4 3 2											N · · · · · Z C	C P X
C P Y	Y − M	C0 2 2	CC 4 3	C4 3 2											N · · · · · Z C	C P Y
D E C	M − 1 → M		CE 6 3	C6 5 2					D6 6 2	DE 7 3					N · · · · · Z ·	D E C
D E X	X − 1 → X					CA 2 1									N · · · · · Z ·	D E X
D E Y	Y − 1 → Y					88 2 1									N · · · · · Z ·	D E Y
E O R	A ∀ M → A (1)	49 2 2	4D 4 3	45 3 2			41 6 2	51 5 2	55 4 2	5D 4 3	59 4 3				N · · · · · Z ·	E O R
I N C	M + 1 → M		EE 6 3	E6 5 2					F6 6 2	FE 7 3					N · · · · · Z ·	I N C
I N X	X + 1 → X					E8 2 1									N · · · · · Z ·	I N X
I N Y	Y + 1 → Y					C8 2 1									N · · · · · Z ·	I N Y
J M P	JUMP TO NEW LOC		4C 3 3										6C 5 3		· · · · · · · ·	J M P
J S R	JUMP SUB		20 6 3												· · · · · · · ·	J S R
L D A	M → A (1)	A9 2 2	AD 4 3	A5 3 2			A1 6 2	B1 5 2	B5 4 2	BD 4 3	B9 4 3				N · · · · · Z ·	L D A
L D X	M → X (1)	A2 2 2	AE 4 3	A6 3 2							B4 4 2	BC 4 3		BE 4 2	B6 4 2	N · · · · · Z ·	L D X
L D Y	M → Y (1)	A0 2 2	AC 4 3	A4 3 2					B4 4 2	BC 4 3					N · · · · · Z ·	L D Y
L S R	0 → ☐ → C		4E 6 3	46 5 2	4A 2 1				56 6 2	5E 7 3					0 · · · · · Z C	L S R
N O P	NO OPERATION					EA 2 1									· · · · · · · ·	N O P
O R A	A ∨ M → A (1)	09 2 2	0D 4 3	05 3 2			01 6 2	11 5 2	15 4 2	1D 4 3	19 4 3				N · · · · · Z ·	O R A
P H A	A → Ms S − 1 → S					48 3 1									· · · · · · · ·	P H A
P H P	P → Ms S − 1 → S					08 3 1									· · · · · · · ·	P H P
P L A	S + 1 → S Ms → A					68 4 1									N · · · · · Z ·	P L A
P L P	S + 1 → S Ms → P					28 4 1									(RESTORED)	P L P
R O L	☐←☐←☐		2E 6 3	26 5 2	2A 2 1				36 6 2	3E 7 3					N · · · · · Z C	R O L
R O R	☐→☐→☐		6E 6 3	66 5 2	6A 2 1				76 6 2	7E 7 3					N · · · · · Z C	R O R
R T I	RTRN INT					40 6 1									(RESTORED)	R T I
R T S	RTRN SUB					60 6 1									· · · · · · · ·	R T S
S B C	A − M − C̄ → A (1)	E9 2 2	ED 4 3	E5 3 2			E1 6 2	F1 5 2	F5 4 2	FD 4 3	F9 4 3				N V · · · · Z C (3)	S B C
S E C	1 → C					38 2 1									· · · · · · · 1	S E C
S E D	1 → D					F8 2 1									· · · · 1 · · ·	S E D
S E I	1 → I					78 2 1									· · · · · 1 · ·	S E I
S T A	A → M		8D 4 3	85 3 2			81 6 2	91 6 2	95 4 2	9D 5 3	99 5 3				· · · · · · · ·	S T A
S T X	X → M		8E 4 3	86 3 2										96 4 2	· · · · · · · ·	S T X
S T Y	Y → M		8C 4 3	84 3 2					94 4 2						· · · · · · · ·	S T Y
T A X	A → X					AA 2 1									N · · · · · Z ·	T A X
T A Y	A → Y					A8 2 1									N · · · · · Z ·	T A Y
T S X	S → X					BA 2 1									N · · · · · Z ·	T S X
T X A	X → A					8A 2 1									N · · · · · Z ·	T X A
T X S	X → S					9A 2 1									· · · · · · · ·	T X S
T Y A	Y → A					98 2 1									N · · · · · Z ·	T Y A

(1) ADD 1 to N IF PAGE BOUNDARY IS CROSSED
(2) ADD 1 TO N IF BRANCH OCCURS TO SAME PAGE
    ADD 2 TO N IF BRANCH OCCURS TO DIFFERENT PAGE
(3) CARRY NOT = BORROW
(4) IF IN DECIMAL MODE Z FLAG IS INVALID
    ACCUMULATOR MUST BE CHECKED FOR ZERO RESULT

X	INDEX X	+	ADD
Y	INDEX Y	−	SUBTRACT
A	ACCUMULATOR	∧	AND
M	MEMORY PER EFFECTIVE ADDRESS	∨	OR
Ms	MEMORY PER STACK POINTER	∀	EXCLUSIVE OR
M₇	MEMORY BIT 7		
M₆	MEMORY BIT 6		
n	NO. CYCLES		
#	NO. BYTES		

R650X CLOCK TIMING

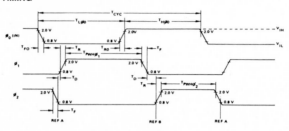

R651X CLOCK TIMING

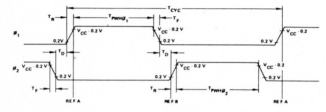

R65XX READ WRITE TIMING

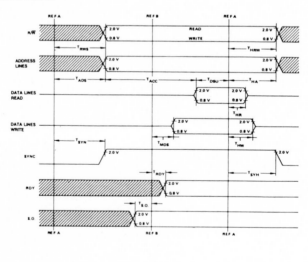

RECOMMENDED TIME BASE GENERATION

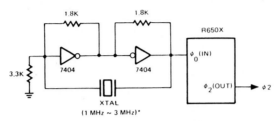

*CRYSTAL: CTS KNIGHTS MP SERIES, OR EQUIVALENT

R650X, R651X **R6500 Microprocessors (CPU)**

MAXIMUM RATINGS*

Rating	Symbol	Value	Unit
Supply Voltage	V_{CC}	−0.3 to +7.0	Vdc
Input Voltage	V_{IN}	−0.3 to +7.0	Vdc
Operating Temperature Range Commercial Industrial	T_A	 0 to +70 −40 to +85	°C
Storage Temperature	T_{STG}	−55 to +150	°C

*Note: This device contains input protection against damage to high static voltages or electric fields; however, precautions should be taken to avoid application of voltages higher than the maximum rating.

DC CHARACTERISTICS

(V_{CC} = 5.0V ± 5%, V_{SS} = 0, T_A = T_L to T_H, unless otherwise noted)

Characteristic	Symbol	Min.	Typ.	Max.	Unit[1]	Test Conditions
Input High Voltage Logic, $Ø0_{(IN)}$ $Ø1, Ø2$	V_{IH}	 2.0 −0.3		 V_{CC} V_{CC} + 0.25	V	
Input Low Voltage Logic, $Ø0_{(IN)}$ $Ø1, Ø2$	V_{IL}	 −0.3 −0.3		 0.8 0.4	V	
Input Leakage Current Logic (Excl. RDY, S.O.) $Ø1, Ø2$ $Ø0_{(IN)}$	I_{IN}	 — — —		 2.5 100 10	μA	V_{IN} = 0V to 5.25V V_{CC} = 0V
Input Current Input Leakage Current for Three-State Off Data Lines	I_{TSI}	 —	 —	 10	μA	V_{IN} = 0.4V to 2.4V V_{CC} = 5.25V
Output High Voltage SYNC, Data, A0-A15, R/W̄, Ø1, Ø2	V_{OH}	+2.4	—	—	V	I_{LOAD} = −100 μA V_{CC} = 4.75V
Output Low Voltage SYNC, Data Lines, A0-A15, R/W̄, Ø1, Ø2	V_{OL}			+0.4	V	I_{LOAD} = 1.6 mA V_{CC} = 4.75V
Power Dissipation 1 and 2 MHz 3 MHz	P_D	 — —	 450 500	 700 800	mW	
Input Capacitance Logic Data A0-A15, R/W̄, SYNC $Ø0_{(IN)}$ $Ø1$ $Ø2$	C C_{IN} C_{OUT} $CØ_{0(IN)}$ $CØ1$ $CØ2$	 — — — — — —	 — — — — 30 50	 10 15 12 15 50 80	pF	V_{CC} = 5.0V V_{IN} = 0V f = 1 MHz T_A = 25°C

Notes:
1. All units are direct current (DC).
2. Negative sign indicates outward current flow, positive indicates inward flow.
3. ĪRQ̄ and N̄M̄Ī require 3K pull-up resistor.
4. Ø1, Ø2 applies to R6512, 13, 14, and 15; $Ø0_{(IN)}$ applies to R6502, 03, 04, 05, 06 and 07.

R650X, R651X

R6500 Microprocessors (CPU)

AC CHARACTERISTICS

Characteristic	Symbol	R65XX (1 MHz)		R65XXA (2 MHz)		R65XX3 (3 MHz)		Unit
		Min	Max	Min	Max	Min	Max	
R650X CLOCK TIMING								
Clock Cycle Time	T_{CYC}	1.0	10	0.5	10	0.33	10	μS
Ø0$_{(IN)}$ Low Time	$T_{LØ0}$	480	—	240	—	160	—	ns
Ø0$_{(IN)}$ High Time	$T_{HØ0}$	470	—	240	—	160	—	ns
Ø0$_{(IN)}$ Rise and Fall Time[1,2]	T_{RO}, T_{FO}	—	10	—	10	—	10	ns
Ø1 Pulse Width	$T_{PWHØ1}$	460	—	235	—	155	—	ns
Ø2 Pulse Width	$T_{PWHØ2}$	470	—	240	—	160	—	ns
Delay Between Ø1 and Ø2	T_D	0	—	0	—	0	—	ns
Ø1, Ø2 Rise and Fall Time[1,2]	T_R, T_F	—	25	—	25	—	15	ns
R651X CLOCK TIMING								
Clock Cycle Time	T_{CYC}	1.0	10	0.5	10	0.33	10	μS
Ø1 Pulse Width	$T_{PWHØ1}$	430	—	215	—	150	—	ns
Ø2 Pulse Width	$T_{PWHØ2}$	470	—	235	—	160	—	ns
Delay Between Ø1 and Ø2	T_D	0	—	0	—	0	—	ns
Ø1, and Ø2 Rise and Fall Time[1,3]	T_R, T_F	—	25	—	20	—	15	ns
R65XX READ/WRITE TIMING								
R/W̄ Setup Time	T_{RWS}	—	225	—	140	—	110	ns
R/W̄ Hold Time	T_{HRW}	30	—	30	—	15	—	ns
Address Setup Time	T_{ADS}	—	225	—	140	—	110	ns
Address Hold Time	T_{HA}	30	—	30	—	15	—	ns
Read Access Time	T_{ACC}	—	650	—	310	—	170	ns
Read Data Setup Time	T_{DSU}	50	—	40	—	35	—	ns
Read Data Hold Time	T_{HR}	10	—	10	—	10	—	ns
Write Data Setup Time	T_{MDS}	—	175	—	100	—	85	ns
Write Data Hold Time	T_{HW}	30	—	30	—	30	—	ns
SYNC Hold Time	T_{SYH}	30	—	30	—	15	—	ns
RDY Setup Time	T_{RDY}	100	—	50	—	35	—	ns
S.O. Setup Time	T_{SO}	100	—	50	—	35	—	ns
SYNC Setup Time	T_{SYN}	—	225	—	175	—	100	ns

Notes:
1. Load = 130 pF + 1 TTL.
2. Measured between 0.8 and 2.0 points on waveform load.
3. Measured between 10% and 90% points on waveforms.
4. *RDY must never switch states within R_{RDY} to end of Ø2.

R650X, R651X   **R6500 Microprocessors (CPU)**

R6522
VERSATILE INTERFACE
ADAPTER (VIA)

DESCRIPTION

The R6522 Versatile Interface Adapter (VIA) is a very flexible I/O control device. In addition, this device contains a pair of very powerful 16-bit interval timers, a serial-to-parallel/parallel-to-serial shift register and input data latching on the peripheral ports. Expanded handshaking capability allows control of bidirectional data transfers between VIA's in multiple processor systems.

Control of peripheral devices is handled primarily through two 8-bit bidirectional ports. Each line can be programmed as either an input or an output. Several peripheral I/O lines can be controlled directly from the interval timers for generating programmable frequency square waves or for counting externally generated pulses. To facilitate control of the many powerful features of this chip, an interrupt flag register, an interrupt enable register and a pair of function control registers are provided.

FEATURES

- Two 8-bit bidirectional I/O ports
- Two 16-bit programmable timer/counters
- Serial data port
- TTL compatible
- CMOS compatible peripheral control lines
- Expanded "handshake" capability allows positive control of data transfers between processor and peripheral devices.
- Latched output and input registers
- 1 MHz and 2 MHz operation
- Single +5V power supply

ORDERING INFORMATION

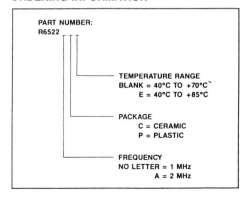

PART NUMBER:
R6522

TEMPERATURE RANGE
BLANK = 40°C TO +70°C
E = 40°C TO +85°C

PACKAGE
C = CERAMIC
P = PLASTIC

FREQUENCY
NO LETTER = 1 MHz
A = 2 MHz

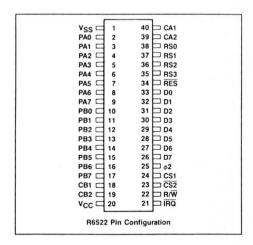

V$_{SS}$	1		40	CA1
PA0	2		39	CA2
PA1	3		38	RS0
PA2	4		37	RS1
PA3	5		36	RS2
PA4	6		35	RS3
PA5	7		34	$\overline{RES}$
PA6	8		33	D0
PA7	9		32	D1
PB0	10		31	D2
PB1	11		30	D3
PB2	12		29	D4
PB3	13		28	D5
PB4	14		27	D6
PB5	15		26	D7
PB6	16		25	$\phi2$
PB7	17		24	CS1
CB1	18		23	$\overline{CS2}$
CB2	19		22	R/$\overline{W}$
V$_{CC}$	20		21	$\overline{IRQ}$

R6522 Pin Configuration

R6522

Versatile Interface Adapter (VIA)

INTERFACE SIGNALS

RESET (RES)

A low reset (RES) input clears all R6522 internal registers to logic 0 (except T1 and T2 latches and counters and the Shift Register). This places all peripheral interface lines in the input state, disables the timers, shift register, etc. and disables interrupting from the chip.

INPUT CLOCK (PHASE 2)

The input clock is the system $\phi 2$ clock and triggers all data transfers between processor bus and the R6522.

READ/WRITE (R/W)

The direction of the data transfers between the R6522 and the system processor is controlled by the RW line in conjunction with the CS1 and CS2 inputs. When R/W is low, (write operation) and the R6522 is selected), data is transferred from the processor bus into the selected R6522 register. When R/W is high, (read operation) and the R6522 is selected, data is transferred from the selected R6522 register to the processor bus.

DATA BUS (D0–D7)

The eight bidirectional data bus lines transfer data between the R6522 and the system processor bus. During read cycles, the contents of the selected R6522 register are placed on the data bus lines. During write cycles, these lines are high-impedance inputs and data is transferred from the processor bus into the selected register. When the R6522 is not selected, the data bus lines are high-impedance.

CHIP SELECTS (CS1, CS2)

The two chip select inputs are normally connected to processor address lines either directly or through decoding. The selected R6522 register is accessed when CS1 is high and CS2 is low.

REGISTER SELECTS (RS0–RS3)

The coding of the four Register Select inputs select one of the 16 internal registers of the R6522, as shown in Table 1.

INTERRUPT REQUEST (IRQ)

The Interrupt Request output goes low whenever an internal interrupt flag is set and the corresponding interrupt enable bit is a logic 1. This output is open-drain to allow the interrupt request signal to be wire-OR'ed with other equivalent signals in the system.

PERIPHERAL PORT A (PA0–PA7)

Port A consists of eight lines which can be individuallly programmed to act as inputs or outputs under control of Data Direction Register A. The polarity of output pins is controlled by an Output Register and input data may be latched into an internal register under control of the CA1 line. All of these modes of operation are controlled by the system processor through the internal control registers. These lines represent one standard TTL load in the input mode and will drive one standard TTL load in the output mode. Figure 2 illustrates the output circuit.

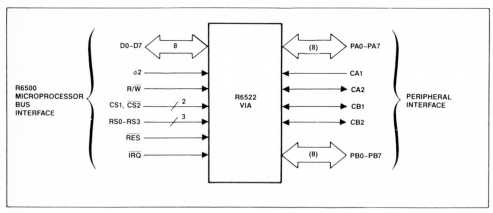

Figure 1. R6522 VIA Interface Signals

R6522

Versatile Interface Adapter (VIA)

PORT A CONTROL LINES (CA1, CA2)

The two Port A control lines act as interrupt inputs or as hand-shake outputs. Each line controls an internal interrupt flag with a corresponding interrupt enable bit. In addition, CA1 controls the latching of data on Port A input lines. CA1 is a high-impedance input only while CA2 represents one standard TTL load in the input mode. CA2 will drive one standard TTL load in the output mode.

PORT B (PB0–PB7)

Peripheral Port B consists of eight bidirectional lines which are controlled by an output register and a data direction register in much the same manner as the Port A. In addition, the polarity of the PB7 output signal can be controlled by one of the interval timers while the second timer can be programmed to count pulses on the PB6 pin. Port B lines represent one standard TTL load in the input mode and will drive one standard TTL load in the output mode. In addition, they are capable of sourcing 1.0 mA at 1.5 Vdc in the output mode to allow the outputs to directly drive Darlington transistor circuits. Figure 3 is the circuit schematic.

PORT B CONTROL LINES (CB1, CB2)

The Port B control lines act as interrupt inputs or as handshake outputs. As with CA1 and CA2, each line controls an interrupt flag with a corresponding interrupt enable bit. In addition, these lines act as a serial port under control of the Shift Register. These lines represent one standard TTL load in the input mode and will drive one standard TTL load in the output mode. Unlike PB0-PB7, CB1 and CB2 *cannot* drive Darlington transistor circuits.

Table 1. R6522 Register Addressing

Register Number	RS Coding				Register Desig.	Register/Description	
	RS3	RS2	RS1	RS0		Write (R/$\overline{W}$ = L)	Read (R/$\overline{W}$ = H)
0	0	0	0	0	ORB/IRB	Output Register B	Input Register B
1	0	0	0	1	ORA/IRA	Output Register A	Input Register A
2	0	0	1	0	DDRB	Data Direction Register B	
3	0	0	1	1	DDRA	Data Direction Register A	
4	0	1	0	0	T1C-L	T1 Low-Order Latches	T1 Low-Order Counter
5	0	1	0	1	T1C-H	T1 High-Order Counter	
6	0	1	1	0	T1L-L	T1 Low-Order Latches	
7	0	1	1	1	T1L-H	T1 High-Order Latches	
8	1	0	0	0	T2C-L	T2 Low-Order Latches	T2 Low-Order Counter
9	1	0	0	1	T2C-H	T2 High-Order Counter	
10	1	0	1	0	SR	Shift Register	
11	1	0	1	1	ACR	Auxiliary Control Register	
12	1	1	0	0	PCR	Peripheral Control Register	
13	1	1	0	1	IFR	Interrupt Flag Register	
14	1	1	1	0	IER	Interrupt Enable Register	
15	1	1	1	1	ORA/IRA	Output Register B*	Input Register B*

NOTE: *Same as Register 1 except no handshake.

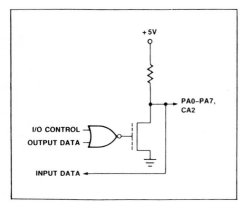

Figure 2. Port A Output Circuit

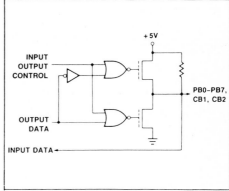

Figure 3. Port B Output Circuit

FUNCTIONAL DESCRIPTION

The internal organization of the R6522 VIA is illustrated in Figure 4.

PORT A AND PORT B OPERATION

The R6522 VIA has two 8-bit bidirectional I/O ports (Port A and Port B) and each port has two associated control lines.

Each 8-bit peripheral port has a Data Direction Register (DDRA, DDRB) for specifying whether the peripheral pins are to act as inputs or outputs. A 0 in a bit of the Data Direction Register causes the corresponding peripheral pin to act as an input. A 1 causes the pin to act as an output.

Each peripheral pin is also controlled by a bit in the Output Register (ORA, ORB) and the Input Register (IRA, IRB). When the pin is programmed as an output, the voltage on the pin is controlled by the corresponding bit of the Output Register. A 1 in the Output Register causes the output to go high, and a "0" causes the output to go low. Data may be written into Output Register bits corresponding to pins which are programmed as inputs. In this case, however, the output signal is unaffected.

Reading a peripheral port causes the contents of the Input Register (IRA, IRB) to be transferred onto the Data Bus. With input latching disabled, IRA will always reflect the levels on the PA pins. With input latching enabled, IRA will reflect the levels on the PA pins at the time the latching occurred (via CA1).

The IRB register operates similar to the IRA register. However, for pins programmed as outputs there is a difference. When reading IRA, the *level on the pin* determines whether a 0 or a 1 is sensed. When reading IRB, however, the bit stored in the *output register*, ORB, is the bit sensed. Thus, for outputs which have large loading effects and which pull an output "1" down or which pull an output "0" up, reading IRA may result in reading a "0" when a "1" was actually programmed, and reading a "1" when a "0" was programmed. Reading IRB, on the other hand, will read the "1" or "0" level actually programmed, no matter what the loading on the pin.

Figures 5 through 8 illustrate the formats of the port registers. In addition, the input latching modes are selected by the Auxiliary Control Register (Figure 14).

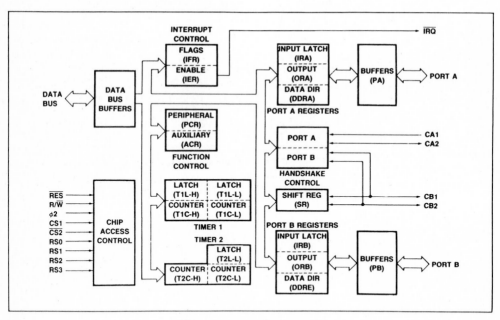

Figure 4. R6522 VIA Block Diagram

R6522   Versatile Interface Adapter (VIA)

HANDSHAKE CONTROL OF DATA TRANSFERS

The R6522 allows positive control of data transfers between the system processor and peripheral devices through the operation of "handshake" lines. Port A lines (CA1, CA2) handshake data on both a read and a write operation while the Port B lines (CB1, CB2) handshake on a write operation only.

Read Handshake

Positive control of data transfers from peripheral devices into the system processor can be accomplished very effectively using Read Handshaking. In this case, the peripheral device must generate the equivalent of a "Data Ready" signal to the processor signifying that valid data is present on the peripheral port. This signal normally interrupts the processor, which then reads the data, causing generation of a "Data Taken" signal. The peripheral device responds by making new data available. This process continues until the data transfer is complete.

In the R6522, automatic "Read" Handshaking is possible on the Peripheral A port only. The CA1 interrupt input pin accepts the "Data Ready" signal and CA2 generates the "Data Taken" signal. The "Data Ready" signal will set an internal flag which may interrupt the processor or which may be polled under program control. The "Data Taken" signal can either be a pulse or a level which is set low by the system processor and is cleared by the "Data Ready" signal. These options are shown in Figure 9 which illustrates the normal Read Handshake sequence.

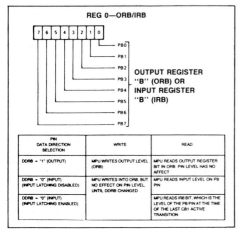

Figure 5. Output Register B (ORB), Input Register B (IRB)

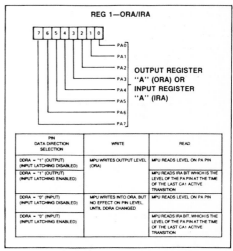

Figure 6. Output Register A (ORA), Input Register A (IRA)

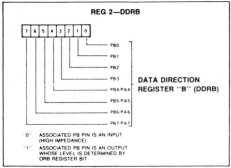

Figure 7. Data Direction Register B (DDRB)

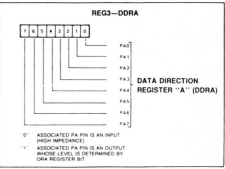

Figure 8. Data Direction Register A (DDRA0)

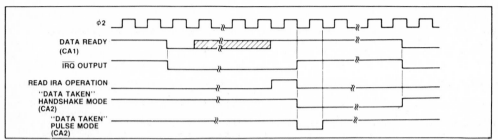

Figure 9. Read Handshake Timing (Port A, Only)

Write Handshake

The sequence of operations which allows handshaking data from the system processor to a peripheral device is very similar to that described for Read Handshaking. However, for Write Handshaking, the R6522 generates the "Data Ready" signal and the peripheral device must respond with the "Data Taken" signal. This can be accomplished on both the PA port and the PB port on the R6522. CA2 or CB2 act as a "Data Ready" output in either the handshake mode or pulse mode and CA1 or CB1 accept the "Data Taken" signal from the peripheral device, setting the interrupt flag and clearing the "Data Ready" output. This sequence is shown in Figure 10.

Selection of operating modes for CA1, CA2, CB1, and CB2 is accomplished by the Peripheral Control Register (Figure 11).

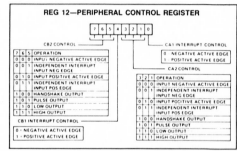

Figure 11. Peripheral Control Register (PCR)

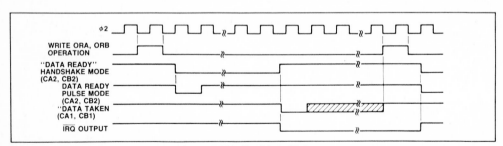

Figure 10. Write Handshake Timing

COUNTER/TIMERS

There are two independent 16-bit counter/timers (called Timer 1 and Timer 2) in the R6522. Each timer is controlled by writing bits into the Auxiliary Control Register (ACR) to select the mode of operation (Figure 14).

Timer 1 Operation

Interval Timer T1 consists of two 8-bit latches (Figure 12) and a 16-bit counter (Figure 13). The latches store data which is to be loaded into the counter. After loading, the counter decrements at Ø2 clock rate. Upon reaching zero, an interrupt flag is set, and IRQ goes low if the T1 interrupt is enabled. Timer 1 then disables any further interrupts, or automatically transfers the contents of the latches into the counter and continues to decrement. In addition, the timer may be programmed to invert the output signal on a peripheral pin (PB7) each time it "times-out". Each of these modes is discussed separately below.

Note that the processor does not write directly into the low-order counter (T1C-L). Instead, this half of the counter is loaded automatically from the low order latch (T1L-L) when the processor writes into the high order counter (T1C-H). In fact, it may not be necessary to write to the low order counter in some applications since the timing operation is triggered by writing to the high order latch.

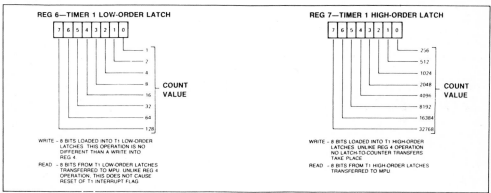

Figure 12. Timer 1 (T1) Latch Registers

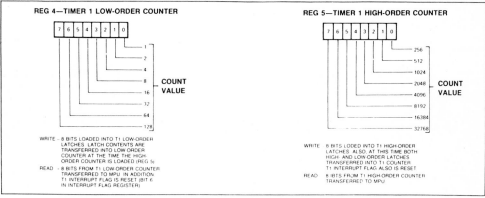

Figure 13. Timer 1 (T1) Counter Registers

R6522   Versatile Interface Adapter (VIA)

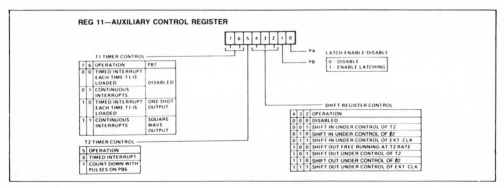

Figure 14. Auxiliary Control Register (ACR)

Timer 1 One-Shot Mode

The Timer 1 one-shot mode generates a single interrupt for each timer load operation. As with any interval timer, the delay between the "write T1C-H" operation and generation of the processor interrupt is a direct function of the data loaded into the timing counter. In addition to generating a single interrupt, Timer 1 can be programmed to produce a single negative pulse on the PB7 periphral pin. With the output enabled (ACR7=1) a "write T1C-H" operation will cause PB7 to go low. PB7 will return high when Timer 1 times out. The result is a single programmable width pulse.

T1 interrupt flag will be set, the $\overline{\text{IRQ}}$ pin will go low (interrupt enabled), and the signal on PB7 will go high. At this time the counter will continue to decrement at system clock rate. This allows the system processor to read the contents of the counter to determine the time since interrupt. However, the T1 interrupt flag cannot be set again unless it has been cleared as described in this specification.

Timing for the R6522 interval timer one-shot modes is shown in Figure 15.

In the one-shot mode, writing into the T1L-H has no effect on the operation of Timer 1. However, it will be necessary to assure that the low order latch contains the proper data before initiating the count-down with a "write T1C-H" operation. When the processor writes into the high order counter (T1C-H), the T1 interrupt flag will be cleared, the contents of the low order latch will be transferred into the low order counter, and the timer will begin to decrement at system clock rate. If the PB7 output is enabled, this signal will go low on the $\phi 2$ following the write operation. When the counter reaches zero, the T1 interrupt flag will be set, the IRQ pin will go low (interrupt enabled), and the signal on PB7 will go high. At this time the counter will continue to decrement at system clock rate. This allows the system processor to read the contents of the counter to determine the time since interrupt. However, the T1 interrupt flag cannot be set again unless it has been cleared as described in this specification.

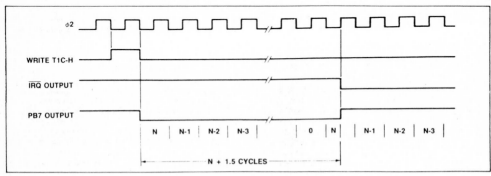

Figure 15. Timer 1 One-Shot Mode Timing

R6522

Versatile Interface Adapter (VIA)

Timer 1 Free-Run Mode

The most important advantage associated with the latches in T1 is the ability to produce a continuous series of evenly spaced interrupts and the ability to produce a square wave on PB7 whose frequency is not affected by variations in the processor interrupt response time. This is accomplished in the "free-running" mode.

In the free-running mode, the interrupt flag is set and the signal on PB7 is inverted each time the counter reaches zero. However, instead of continuing to decrement from zero after a time-out, the timer automatically transfers the contents of the latch into the counter (16 bits) and continues to decrement from there. The interrupt flag can be cleared by writing T1C-H, by reading T1C-L, or by writing directly into the flag as described later. However, it is not necessary to rewrite the timer to enable setting the interrupt flag on the next time-out.

All interval timers in the R6522 are "re-triggerable". Rewriting the

counter will always re-initialize the time-out period. In fact, the time-out can be prevented completely if the processor continues to rewrite the timer before it reaches zero. Timer 1 will operate in this manner if the processor writes into the high order counter (T1C-H). However, by loading the latches only, the processor can access the timer during each down-counting operation without affecting the time-out in process. Instead, the data loaded into the latches will determine the length of the next time-out period. This capability is particularly valuable in the free-running mode with the output enabled. In this mode, the signal on PB7 is inverted and the interrupt flag is set with each time-out. By responding to the interrupts with new data for the latches, the processor can determine the period of the next half cycle during each half cycle of the output signal on PB7. In this manner, very complex waveforms can be generated.

A precaution to take in the use of PB7 as the timer output concerns the Data Direction Register contents for PB7. *Both* DDRB bit 7 and ACR bit 7 must be 1 for PB7 to function as the timer output. If one is 1 and the other is 0, then PB7 functions as a normal output pin, controlled by ORB bit 7.

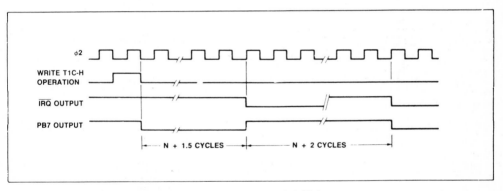

Figure 16. Timer 1 Free-Run Mode Timing

Timer 2 Operation

Timer 2 operates as an interval timer (in the "one-slot" mode only), or as a counter for counting negative pulses on the PB6 peripheral pin. A single control bit in the Auxiliary Control Register selects between these two modes. This timer is comprised of a "write-only" lower-order latch (T2L-L), a "read-only" low-order counter (T2C-L) and a read/write high order counter (T2C-H). The counter registers act as a 16-bit counter which decrements at $\phi2$ rate. Figure 17 illustrates the T2 Latch/Counter Registers.

Timer 2 One-Shot Mode

As an interval timer, T2 operates in the "one-shot" mode similar to Time 1. In this mode, T2 provides a single interrupt for each "write T2C-H" operation. After timing out, the counter will continue to decrement. However, setting of the interrupt flag is disabled after initial time-out so that it will not be set by the counter

decrementing again through zero. The processor must rewrite T2C-H to enable setting of the interrupt flag. The interrupt flag is cleared by reading T2C-L or by writing T2C-H. Timing for this operation is shown in Figure 18.

Timer 2 Pulse Counting Mode

In the pulse counting mode, T2 counts a predetermined number of negative-going pulses on PB6. This is accomplished by first loading a number into T2. Writing into T2C-H clears the interrupt flag and allows the counter to decrement each time a pulse is applied to PB6. The interrupt flag is set when T2 counts down past zero. The counter will then continue to decrement with each pulse on PB6. However, it is necessary to rewrite T2C-H to allow the interrupt flag to set on a subsequent time-out. Timing for this mode is shown in Figure 19. The pulse must be low on the leading edge of $\phi2$.

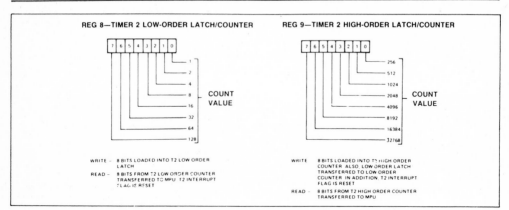

Figure 17. Timer 2 (T2) Latch/Counter Registers

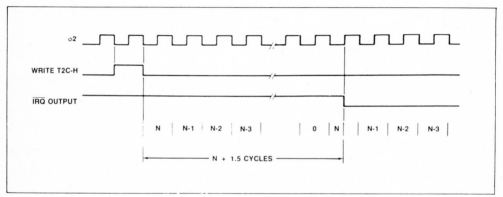

Figure 18. Timer 2 One-Shot Mode Timing

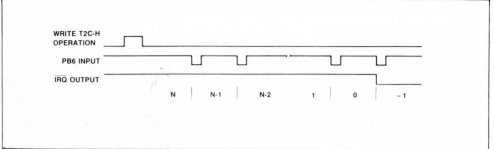

Figure 19. Timer 2 Pulse Counting Mode

R6522   Versatile interface Adapter (VIA)

SHIFT REGISTER OPERATION

The Shift Register (SR) performs serial data transfers into and out of the CB2 pin under control of an internal modulo-8 counter. Shift pulses can be applied to the CB1 pin from an external source or, with the proper mode selection, shift pulses generated internally will appear on the CB1 pin for controlling external devices.

The control bits which select the various shift register operating modes are located in the Auxiliary Control Register. Figure 20 illustrates the configuration of the SR data bits and Figure 21 shows the SR control bits of the ACR.

SR Mode 0 — Disabled

Mode 0 disables the Shift Register. In this mode the microprocessor can write or read the SR and the SR will shift on each CB1 positive edge shifting in the value on CB2. In this mode the SR interrupt Flag is disabled (held to a logic 0).

SR Mode 1 — Shift In Under Control of T2

In mode 1, the shifting rate is controlled by the low order 8 bits of T2 (Figure 22). Shift pulses are generated on the CB1 pin to control shifting in external devices. The time between transitions of this output clock is a function of the system clock period and the contents of the low order T2 latch (N).

The shifting operation is triggered by the read or write of the SR if the SR flag is set in the IFR. Otherwise the first shift will occur at the next time-out of T2 after a read or write of the SR. Data is shifted first into the low order bit of SR and is then shifted into the next higher order bit of the shift register on the negative-going edge of each clock pulse. The input data should change before the positive-going edge of the CB1 clock pulse. This data is shifted into the shift register during the Ø2 clock cycle following the positive-going edge of the CB1 clock pulse. After 8 CB1 clock pulses, the shift register interrupt flag will set and IRQ will go low.

SR Mode 2 — Shift In Under φ2 Control

In mode 2, the shift rate is a direct function of the system clock frequency (Figure 23). CB1 becomes an output which generates shift pulses for controlling external devices. Timer 2 operates as an independent interval timer and has no effect on SR. The shifting operation is triggered by reading or writing the Shift Register. Data is shifted, first into bit 0 and is then shifted into the next higher order bit of the shift register on the trailing edge of each φ2 clock pulse. After 8 clock pulses, the shift register interrupt flag will be set, and the output clock pulses on CB1 will stop.

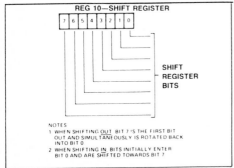

Figure 20. Shift Registers

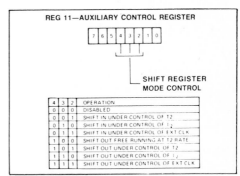

Figure 21. Shift Register Modes

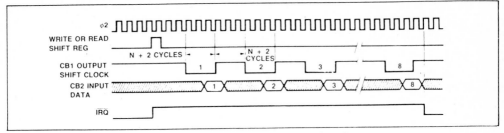

Figure 22. SR Mode 1 — Shift In Under T2 Control

R6522   Versatile Interface Adapter (VIA)

SR Mode 3 — Shift in Under CB1 Control

In mode 3, external pin CB1 becomes an input (Figure 24). This allows an external device to load the shift register at its own pace. The shift register counter will interrupt the processor each time 8 bits have been shifted in. However, the shift register counter does not stop the shifting operation; it acts simply as a pulse counter. Reading or writing the Shift Register resets the Interrupt Flag and initializes the SR counter to count another 8 pulses.

Note that the data is shifted during the first system clock cycle following the positive-going edge of the CB1 shift pulse. For this reason, data must be held stable during the first full cycle following CB1 going high.

SR Mode 4 — Shift Out Under T2 Control (Free-Run)

Mode 4 is very similar to mode 5 in which the shifting rate is set by

T2. However, in mode 4 the SR Counter does not stop the shifting operation (Figure 25). Since the Shift Register bit 7 (SR7) is recirculated back into bit 0, the 8 bits loaded into the shift register will be clocked onto CB2 repetitively. In this mode the shift register counter is disabled.

SR Mode 5 — Shift Out Under T2 Control

In mode 5, the shift rate is controlled by T2 (as in mode 4). The shifting operation is triggered by the read or write of the SR if the SR flag is set in the IFR (Figure 26). Otherwise the first shift will occur at the next time-out of T2 after a read or write of the SR. However, with each read or write of the shift register the SR Counter is reset and 8 bits are shifted onto CB2. At the same time, 8 shift pulses are generated on CB1 to control shifting in external devices. After the 8 shift pulses, the shifting is disabled, the SR Interrupt Flag is set and CB2 remains at the last data level.

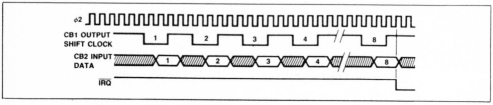

Figure 23. SR Mode 2 — Shift In Center φ2 Control

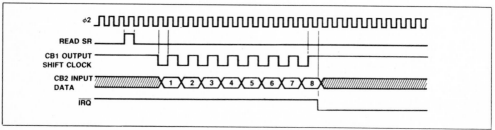

Figure 24. SR Mode 3 — Shift In Under CB1 Control

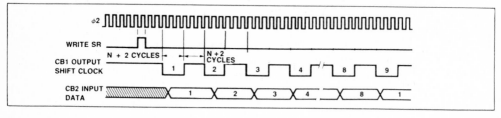

Figure 25. SR Mode 4 — Shift Out Under T2 Control (Free-Run)

SR Mode 6 — Shift Out Under $\phi2$ Control

In mode 6, the shift rate is controlled by the $\phi2$ system clock (Figure 27).

SR Mode 7 — Shift Out Under CB1 Control

In mode 7, shifting is controlled by pulses applied to the CB1 pin by an external device (Figure 28). The SR counter sets the SR

Interrupt Flag each time it counts 8 pulses but it does not disable the shifting function. Each time the microprocessor, writes or reads the shift register, the SR Interrupt Flag is reset and the SR counter is initialized to begin counting the next 8 shift pulses on pin CB1. After 8 shift pulses, the Interrupt Flag is set. The microprocessor can then load the shift register with the next byte of data.

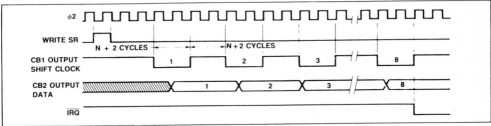

Figure 26. SR Mode 5 — Shift Out Under T2 Control

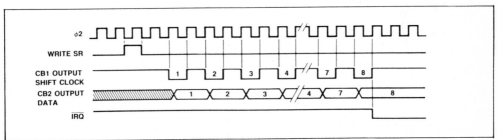

Figure 27. SR Mode 6 — Shift Out Under $\phi2$ Control

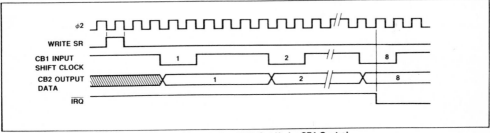

Figure 28. SR Mode 7 — Shift Out Under CB1 Control

R6522

Versatile Interface Adapter (VIA)

Interrupt Operation

Controlling interrupts within the R6522 involves three principal operations. These are flagging the interrupts, enabling interrupts and signaling to the processor that an active interrupt exists within the chip. Interrupt flags are set in the Interrupt Flag Register (IFR) by conditions detected within the R6522 or on inputs to the R6522. These flags normally remain set until the interrupt has been serviced. To determine the source of an interrupt, the microprocessor must examine these flags in order, from highest to lowest priority.

Associated with each interrupt flag is an interrupt enable bit in the Interrupt Enable Register (IER). This can be set or cleared by the processor to enable interrupting the processor from the corresponding interrupt flag. If an interrupt flag is set to a logic 1 by an interrupting condition, and the corresponding interrupt enable bit is set to a 1, the Interrupt Request Output ($\overline{IRQ}$) will go low. $\overline{IRQ}$ is an "open-collector" output which can be "wire-OR'ed" with other devices in the system to interrupt the processor.

Interrupt Flag Register (IFR)

In the R6522, all the interrupt flags are contained in one register, i.e., the IFR (Figure 29). In addition, bit 7 of this register will be read as a logic 1 when an interrupt exists within the chip. This allows very convenient polling of several devices within a system to locate the source of an interrupt.

The Interrupt Flag Register (IRF) may be read directly by the processor. In addition, individual flag bits may be cleared by writing a "1" into the appropriate bit of the IFR. When the proper chip select and register signals are appplied to the chip, the contents of this register are placed on the data bus. Bit 7 indicates the

status of the $\overline{IRQ}$ output. This bit corresponds to the logic function: $\overline{IRQ}$ = IFR6 × IER6 + IFR5 × IER5 + IFR4 × IER4 + IFR3 × IER3 + IFR2 × IER2 + IFR1 × IER1 + IFR0 × IER0.

Note:

× = logic AND, + = Logic OR.

The IFR bit 7 is not a flag. Therefore, this bit is not directly cleared by writing a logic 1 into it. It can only be cleared by clearing all the flags in the register or by disabling all the active interrupts as discussed in the next section.

Interrupt Enable Register (IER)

For each interrupt flag in IFR, there is a corresponding bit in the Interrupt Enable Register (IER) (Figure 30). Individual bits in the IER can be set or cleared to facilitate controlling individual interrupts without affecting others. This is accomplished by writing to the (IER) after bit 7 set or cleared to, in turn, set or clear selected enable bits. If bit 7 of the data placed on the system data bus during this write operation is a 0, each 1 in bits 6 through 0 clears the corresponding bit in the Interrupt Enable Register. For each zero in bits 6 through 0, the corresponding bit is unaffected.

Selected bits in the IER can be set by writing to the IER with bit 7 in the data word set to a 1. In this case, each 1 in bits 6 through 0 will set the corresponding bit. For each zero, the corresponding bit will be unaffected. This individual control of the setting and clearing operations allows very convenient control of the interrupts during system operation.

In addition to setting and clearing IER bits, the contents of this register can be read at any time. Bit 7 will be read as a logic 1, however.

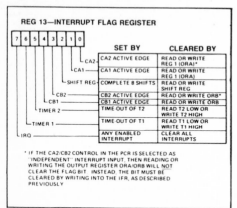

Figure 29. Interrupt Flag Register (IFR)

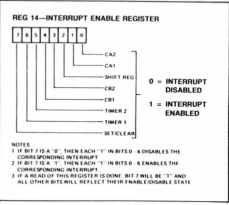

Figure 30. Interrupt Enable Register (IER)

R6522   # Versatile Interface Adapter (VIA)

PERIPHERAL INTERFACE CHARACTERISTICS

Symbol	Characteristic	Min.	Max.	Unit	Figure
t_r, t_f	Rise and Fall Time for CA1, CB1, CA2 and CB2 Input Signals	—	1.0	μS	—
t_{CA2}	Delay Time, Clock Negative Transition to CA2 Negative Transition (read handshake or pulse mode)	—	1.0	μS	31a, 31b
t_{RS1}	Delay Time, Clock Negative Transition to CA2 Positive Transition (pulse mode)	—	1.0	μS	31a
t_{RS2}	Delay Time, CA1 Active Transition to CA2 Positive Transition (handshake mode)	—	2.0	μS	31b
t_{WHS}	Delay Time, Clock Positive Transition to CA2 or CB2 Negative Transition (write handshake)	0.05	1.0	μS	31c, 31d
t_{DS}	Delay Time, Peripheral Data Valid to CB2 Negative Transition	0.20	1.5	μS	31c, 31d
t_{RS3}	Delay Time, Clock Positive Transition to CA2 or CB2 Positive Transition (pulse mode)	—	1.0	μS	31c
t_{RS4}	Delay Time, CA1 or CB1 Active Transition to CA2 or CB2 Positive Transition (handshake mode)	—	2.0	μS	31d
t_{21}	Delay Time Required from CA2 Output to CA1 Active Transition (handshake mode)	400	—	ns	31d
t_{IL}	Setup Time, Peripheral Data Valid to CA1 or CB1 Active Transition (input latching)	300	—	ns	31e
t_{AL}	CA1, CB1 Setup Prior to Transition to Arm Latch	300	—	ns	31e
t_{PDH}	Peripheral Data Hold After CA1, CB1 Transition	150	—	ns	31e
t_{SR1}	Shift-Out Delay Time — Time from ϕ_2 Falling Edge to CB2 Data Out	—	300	ns	31f
t_{SR2}	Shift-In Setup Time — Time from CB2 Data In to ϕ_2 Rising Edge	300	—	ns	31g
t_{SR3}	External Shift Clock (CB1) Setup Time Relative to ϕ_2 Trailing Edge	100	T_{CY}	ns	31g
t_{IPW}	Pulse Width — PB6 Input Pulse	$2 \times T_{CY}$	—		31i
t_{ICW}	Pulse Width — CB1 Input Clock	$2 \times T_{CY}$	—		31h
t_{IPS}	Pulse Spacing — PB6 Input Pulse	$2 \times T_{CY}$	—		31i
t_{ICS}	Pulse Spacing — CB1 Input Pulse	$2 \times T_{CY}$	—		31h

PERIPHERAL INTERFACE WAVEFORMS

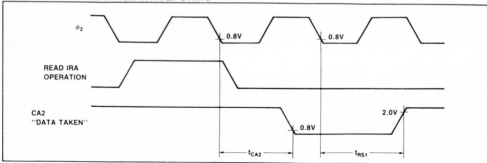

Figure 31a. CA2 Timing for Read Handshake, Pulse Mode

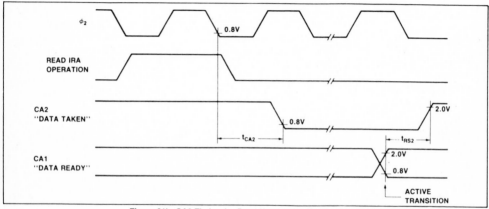

Figure 31b. CA2 Timing for Read Handshake, Handshake Mode

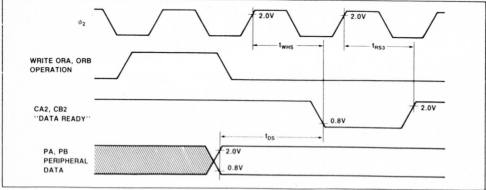

Figure 31c. CA2, CB2 Timing for Write Handshake, Pulse Mode

R6522   **Versatile Interface Adapter (VIA)**

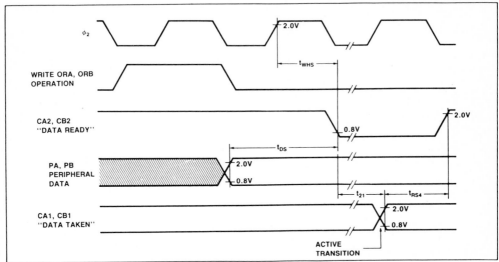

Figure 31d. CA2, CB2 Timing for Write Handshake, Handshake Mode

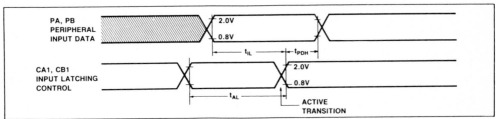

Figure 31e. Peripheral Data Input Latching Timing

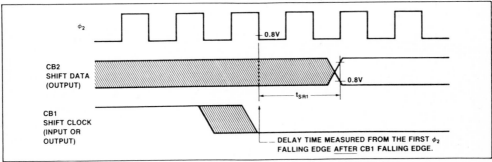

Figure 31f. Timing for Shift Out with Internal or External Shift Clocking

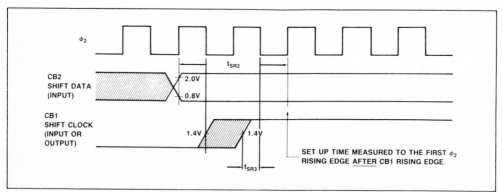

Figure 31g. Timing for Shift in with Internal or External Shift Clocking

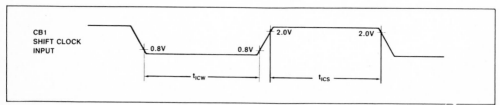

Figure 31h. External Shift Clock Timing

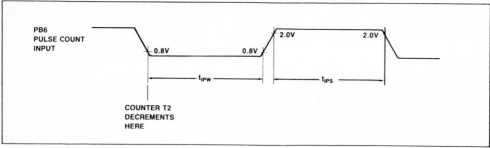

Figure 31i. Pulse Count Input Timing

R6522   Versatile Interface Adapter (VIA)

BUS TIMING CHARACTERISTICS

Read Timing

Symbol	Parameter	R6522 (1 MHz)		R6522A (2 MHz)		Unit
		Min.	Max.	Min.	Max.	
T_{CY}	Cycle Time	1	10	0.5	10	μs
T_{ACR}	Address Set-Up Time	180	–	90	–	ns
T_{CAR}	Address Hold Time	0	–	0	–	ns
T_{PCR}	Peripheral Data Set-Up Time	300	–	150	–	ns
T_{CDR}	Data Bus Delay Time	–	365	–	190	ns
T_{HR}	Data Bus Hold Time	10	–	10	–	ns

NOTE: tr, tf = 10 to 30ns.

Write Timing

Symbol	Parameter	R6522		R6522A		Unit
		Min.	Max.	Min.	Max.	
T_{CY}	Cycle Time	1	10	0.50	10	μs
T_C	φ2 Pulse Width	470	–	240	–	ns
T_{ACW}	Address Set-Up Time	180	–	90	–	ns
T_{CAW}	Address Hold Time	0	–	0	–	ns
T_{WCW}	R/$\overline{W}$ Set-Up Time	180	–	90	–	ns
T_{CWW}	R/$\overline{W}$ Hold Time	0	–	0	–	ns
T_{DCW}	Data Bus Set-Up Time	200	–	90	–	ns
T_{HW}	Data Bus Hold Time	10	–	10	–	ns
T_{CPW}	Peripheral Data Delay Time	–	1.0	–	0.5	μs
T_{CMOS}	Peripheral Data Delay Time to CMOS Levels	–	2.0	–	1.0	μs

NOTE: tr, tf = 10 to 30ns.

BUS TIMING WAVEFORMS

Read Timing Waveforms

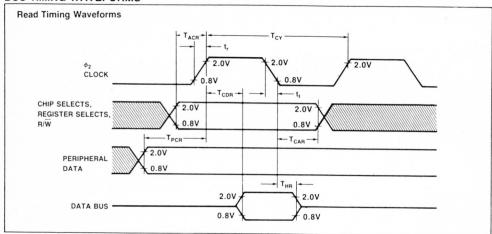

Write Timing Waveforms

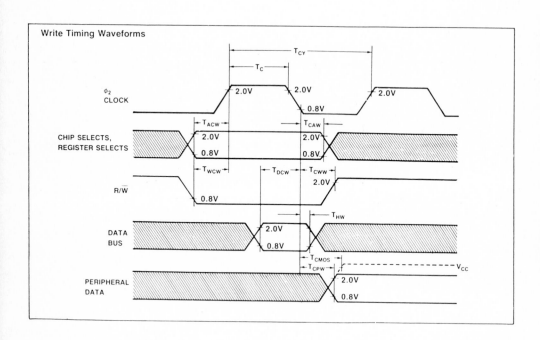

R6522   Versatile Interface Adapter (VIA)

MAXIMUM RATINGS*

*Note: This device contains circuitry to protect the inputs against damage due to high static voltages. However, normal precautions should be taken to avoid application of any voltage higher than maximum rated voltages.

Parameter	Symbol	Value	Unit
Supply Voltage	V_{CC}	-0.3 to -7.0	Vdc
Input Voltage	V_{IN}	-0.3 to $+7.0$	Vdc
Operating Temperature Commercial Industrial	T_A	0 to $+70$ -40 to $+85$	°C °C
Storage Temperature	T_{STG}	-55 to $+150$	°C

DC CHARACTERISTICS

(V_{CC} = 5.0 Vdc $\pm 5\%$, V_{SS} = 0 Vdc, T_A = T_L to T_H, unless otherwise noted)

Characteristic	Symbol	Min.	Max.	Unit	Test Conditions
Input High Voltage	V_{IH}	2.4	V_{CC}	V	
Input Low Voltage	V_{IL}	-0.3	0.4	V	
Input Leakage Current R/$\overline{W}$, $\overline{RES}$, RS0, RS1, RS2, RS3, CS1, $\overline{CS2}$, CA1, $\phi2$	I_{IN}	—	± 2.5	μA	V_{IN} = 0V to 5.0V V_{CC} = 0V
Input Leakage Current for Three-State Off D0-D7	I_{TSI}	—	± 10	μA	V_{IN} = 0.4V to 2.4V V_{CC} = 5.25V
Input High Current PA0-PA7, CA2, PB0-PB7, CB1, CB2	I_{IH}	-100	—	μA	V_{IN} = 2.4V
Input Low Current PA0-PA7, CA2, PB0-PB7, CB1, CB2	I_{IL}	—	-1.8	mA	V_{IL} = 0.4V
Output High Voltage PA0-PA7, CA2, PB0-PB7, CB1, CB2	V_{OH}	2.4	—	V	V_{CC} = 4.75V I_{LOAD} = -100 μA
Output Low Voltage PA0-PA7, CA2, PB0-PB7, CB1, CB2	V_{OL}	—	0.4	V	V_{CC} = 4.75V I_{LOAD} = 1.6 mA
Output High Current (Sourcing) PA0-PA7, PB0-PB7 (TTL drive), D0-D7 PB0-PB7 (other drive, e.g., Darlington)	I_{OH}	 -100 -1.0	 — —	 μA mA	V_{OH} = 2.4V V_{OH} = 1.5V
Output Low Current (Sinking)	I_{OL}	1.6	—	mA	V_{OL} = 0.4V
Output Leakage Current (Off State) $\overline{IRQ}$	I_{OFF}	—	10	μA	
Power Dissipation	P_D	—	700	mW	
Input Capacitance R/$\overline{W}$, $\overline{RES}$, RS0, RS1, RS2, RS3, CS1, $\overline{CS2}$, D0-D7, PA0-PA7, CA1, CA2, PB0-PB7 CB1, CB2 $\phi2$ Input	C_{IN}	— — —	7.0 10 20	pF pF pF	V_{CC} = 5.0V V_{IN} = 0V f = 1 MHz T_A = 25°C
Output Capacitance	C_{OUT}	—	10	pF	

NOTES:
1. All Units are direct current (DC).
2. Negative sign indicates outward current flow, positive indicates inward flow.

R6522

Versatile Interface Adapter (VIA)

PACKAGE DIMENSIONS

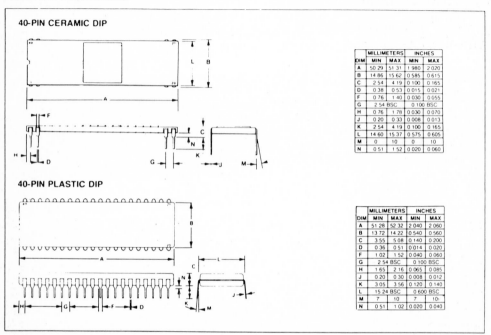

40-PIN CERAMIC DIP

DIM	MILLIMETERS		INCHES	
	MIN	MAX	MIN	MAX
A	50 29	51 31	1 980	2 020
B	14 86	15 62	0 585	0 615
C	2 54	4 19	0 100	0 165
D	0 38	0 53	0 015	0 021
F	0 76	1 40	0 030	0 055
G	2 54 BSC		0 100 BSC	
H	0 76	1 78	0 030	0 070
J	0 20	0 33	0 008	0 013
K	2 54	4 19	0 100	0 165
L	14 60	15 37	0 575	0 605
M	0	10	0	10
N	0 51	1 52	0 020	0 060

40-PIN PLASTIC DIP

DIM	MILLIMETERS		INCHES	
	MIN	MAX	MIN	MAX
A	51 28	52 32	2 040	2 060
B	13 72	14 22	0 540	0 560
C	3 55	5 08	0 140	0 200
D	0 36	0 51	0 014	0 020
F	1 02	1 52	0 040	0 060
G	2 54 BSC		0 100 BSC	
H	1 65	2 16	0 065	0 085
J	0 20	0 30	0 008	0 012
K	3 05	3 56	0 120	0 140
L	15 24 BSC		0 600 BSC	
M	7	10	7	10'
N	0 51	1 02	0 020	0 040

SEMICONDUCTOR PRODUCTS DIVISION REGIONAL ROCKWELL SALES OFFICES

HOME OFFICE
Semiconductor Products Division
Rockwell International
4311 Jamboree Road
Newport Beach, California 92660
(714) 833-4700
TWX 910 591-1698

Mailing Address:
P.O Box C, MS 501 300
Newport Beach, California 92660

UNITED STATES
Semiconductor Products Division
Rockwell International
1842 Reynolds
Irvine, California 92714
(714) 833-4655
TWX 910 595-2518

Semiconductor Products Division
Rockwell International
921 Bowser Road
Richardson, Texas 75080
(214) 996-6500
TLX 73 307

Semiconductor Products Division
Rockwell International
10700 West Higgins Rd , Suite 102
Rosemont, Illinois 60018
(312) 297-8862
TWX 910 233-0179 (RI MED ROSM)

Semiconductor Products Division
Rockwell International
5001B Greentree
Executive Campus, Rt 73
Marlton, New Jersey 08053
(609) 596-0090
TWX 710 940-1377

FAR EAST
Semiconductor Products Division
Rockwell International Overseas Corp
Itohpia Hirakawa-cho Bldg
7-6 2-chome Hirakawa-cho
Chiyoda-ku, Tokyo 102, Japan
(03) 265-8806
TLX J22198

Rockwell Collins International
Tai Sang Commercial Bldg   11th Floor
24-34 Hennessy Rd
Hong Kong
(5) 274-321
TLX 74071 HK

EUROPE
Semiconductor Products Division
Rockwell International GmbH
Fraunhoferstrasse 11
D-8033 Munchen-Martinsried
West Germany
(089) 857-6016
TLX 0521/2650 rimd d

Semiconductor Products Division
Rockwell International
Heathrow House, Bath Rd
Cranford, Hounslow
Middlesex, England
(01) 759-2366
TLX 851-25463

Semiconductor Products
Rockwell Collins Italiana S P A
Via Boccaccio, 23
20123 Milano, Italy
(02) 498 74 79
TLX 316562

YOUR LOCAL REPRESENTATIVE

11/83

PART NUMBER
A65-XXX

AIM 65
DATA SHEET

AIM 65 MICROCOMPUTER

PRODUCT OVERVIEW

The AIM 65 microcomputer is a complete, assembled microcomputer system featuring a 20-column thermal printer, a 20-character alphanumeric display, and a full-size terminal style keyboard. On-board memory sockets accept up to 20K bytes of PROM/ROM and 4K bytes of static RAM. A user R6522 Versatile Interface Adapter (VIA) dedicates 16 parallel I/O data lines and four handshaking control lines to application usage. The address, data, and control lines are also accessible for off-board memory, peripheral and I/O expansion. An 8K-byte ROM-resident debug monitor and text editor provides immediate interactive operation upon power turn-on.

With its self-contained printer and display, the AIM 65 microcomputer is ideal for educational and industrial desk-top applications. The on-board printer, unique to single-board microcomputers in its class, make the AIM 65 microcomputer a natural for any control and monitor application requiring hard copy output — such as equipment performance monitoring, data logging, test and evaluation, specialized data acquisition and reduction, laboratory measurements and analysis, and untold others.

The interactive monitor simplifies computer program checkout with single step functions which trace instruction execution and register contents as well as stop execution at specified breakpoint addresses. Memory and registers can be examined and altered to set up controlled execution conditions and to allow detailed analysis of program performance. The text editor allows computer program assembly and high level language instructions and data to be easily entered and edited at the source code level.

Optional ROM-based languages support computer program development in both R6500 assembly language and high level languages. BASIC (by Microsoft) is the most popular microcomputer language used for computation and low speed control applications. FORTH is a highly efficient language in terms of memory utilization and execution speed — and also greatly shortens program development time. PL/65 provides structured control statements and compiles to 6500 assembly language to serve as an efficient system implementation language. The AIM 65 Pascal is a unique implementation of a substantial subset of standard Pascal which features interactive statement entry and execution with debug features at the source statement level.

Standard documentation includes the comprehensive AIM 65 User's Guide, an assembly language listing of the Monitor/Editor computer program, the R6500 Programming Manual, the R6500 Hardware Manual, a handy pocket-size AIM 65 Summary Card and a wall-size schematic of the AIM 65 microcomputer.

FEATURES

- Single Board Computer with on-board RAM, ROM, and I/O
  - Powerful and Popular 6502 CPU
  - Up to 4K bytes of 2114 Static RAM
  - Up to 20K bytes of 2532 PROM or R2332 ROM
  - User-Dedicated Application Parallel I/O Interface
  - Low-Cost Audio Cassette Recorder Interface with 2 Recorder Remote Control Lines
  - 20 mA Current Loop Serial Interface
  - Expansion Bus Interface
- 20-Column Thermal Printer
  - 64 Character ASCII Format
  - 120 Lines per Minute
  - 5 x 7 Dot Matrix Character Font
- 20-Character Display
  - 64-Character ASCII Format
  - 16-Segment Font
  - High Contrast Monolithic Characters
- Full-Size 54-key Terminal Style Keyboard
  - 26 Alphabetic, 10 Numeric, and 22 Special Characters
  - 9 Control Functions and 3 User-Defined Functions
- ROM-Resident Interactive Debug Monitor
  - Monitor-Generated Prompts and Single Keystroke Commands
  - Single-Step Execution with Tracing and Breakpoints
  - Memory and Register Examine and Alter
  - Mnemonic Instruction Entry and Disassembly
- Text Editor
  - Line Oriented Commands (Read, Insert, Delete, List)
  - Character String Find and Change
- Parallel Application Interface
  - R6522 Versatile Interface Adapter (VIA)
  - Two 8-bit Parallel Bidirectional Data Ports
  - Two 2-bit Handshake Control Ports
  - Two Programmable 16-bit Counter/Timers
  - 8-bit Serial Interface
- Optional ROM-Based Languages
  - 4K Symbolic Assembler
  - 8K BASIC Interpreter
  - 8K PL/65 Compiler
  - 8K FORTH Compiler/Interpreter
  - 20K Pascal Compiler/Interpreter (16K Bytes Off-Board)

ORDERING INFORMATION

Part No.	Description
Systems	
A65-100	AIM 65 with 1K RAM and Monitor
A65-400	AIM 65 with 4K RAM and Monitor
A65-410	AIM 65 with 4K RAM, Monitor, & Assembler
A65-415	AIM 65 with 4K RAM, Monitor, & Basic
A65-420	AIM 65 with 4K RAM, Monitor, Basic & Assembler
A65-450	AIM 65 with 4K RAM, Monitor, & Forth
Firmware	
A65-010	Assembler for AIM 65
A65-020	Basic for AIM 65
A65-030	PL/65 for AIM 65
A65-040	Math Package for AIM 65
A65-050	Forth for AIM 65
A65-060	Instant Pascal for AIM 65
Accessories	
A65-002	AIM 65 Enclosure
A65-003	AIM 65 Service Test Board
A65-005	Lab Power Supply
A65-901	PROM Programmer & CO-ED

AIM 65 MICROCOMPUTER

Specifications subject to change without notice
Document No. 29000 D79
Order No. D79

FUNCTIONAL DESCRIPTION

The AIM 65 microcomputer consists of a Master Module (which includes the central processing and control circuitry, decoders, memory, I/O and printer control circuitry), an attached Display Module and a separate Keyboard Module. A thermal printer is mounted directly on the Master Module while the Display Module is mounted on angle brackets which are fastened to the Master Module.

Central Processing and Control

The R6502 8-bit microprocessor, the central processing unit (CPU) of the AIM 65 microcomputer, provides the overall control and monitoring of all AIM 65 operations. The R6502 communicates with other AIM 65 elements on three separate buses. A 16-bit address bus allows the CPU to directly address 65,536 memory locations. An 8-bit bidirectional data bus carries data from the CPU to/from memory and interface devices. The control bus carries various timing and control signals between the CPU and interfacing peripherals, devices, and off-board elements.

The CPU operates at 1 MHz, which is derived from a 4 MHz crystal-controlled oscillator. The Ø2 system clock and read/write control signals are generated by the CPU, and are buffered and routed to other devices on-board and to the expansion connector.

A decoder circuit provides chip select signals to the on-board PROM/ROM and RAM sockets and to the I/O devices. 4K-byte chip selects are sent to the PROM/ROM sockets ($BXXX–$FXXX) while 1K-byte select signals are routed to the RAM sockets ($00XX–$XCXX). On-board I/O is also decoded to 1K-byte selects ($A0XX–$ACXX).

A pushbutton switch initiates RESET to the on-board devices and to interfacing equipment through the expansion connector. Installed terminal posts allow connection to a remote RESET switch. The STEP/RUN switch selects program execution in either the single-step mode or the run mode. In single-step mode, execution of all instructions in the address range 0–$9FFF can be traced or can be stopped at any of four specified breakpoints. The KB/TTY switch selects operation using the AIM 65 keyboard and display or using a teletypewriter attached to the 20 mA current loop interface.

Memory

Two 1024 x 4 2114 static RAM devices are required for each 1K-byte of installed RAM. Both 1K and 4K versions are available. The 1K version may be expanded on-board in 1K increments up to 4K using the spare RAM sockets.

Five PROM/ROM sockets accept installation of the 4K-byte R2332 ROM, 2532 PROM, or smaller devices with compatible pinouts, e.g., 2K-byte 2516 PROM. The AIM 65 microcomputer comes with two R2332 ROMs containing the Debug Monitor/Text Editor installed at addresses $E000–$FFFF.

I/O

The 16 bidirectional data lines and 4 handshake control lines of the user-dedicated R6522 VIA are routed directly to the application connector. The high current capacity of the VIA's eight "B" port lines can directly drive many industry-standard devices, such as solid state relays. One of the lines can be used as either a serial input or output line.

The audio recorder interface connects to one or two low-cost audio cassette recorders. Two remote control lines can control two separate recorders independently during read and write operations using the AIM 65 blocked audio recording format.

Peripherals

The printer prints on heat-sensitive roll paper by means of ten thermal elements, mounted on a movable head, each of which can print two 5 x 7 matrix dot characters. The printed characters are formed by dot patterns stored in the AIM 65 Monitor/Editor ROMs. A motor-driven platen advances the paper after each row of horizontal dots is printed. The motor and thermal element driver voltages are derived from an external +24V power supply. The printing is controlled by subroutines resident in the Monitor/Editor ROMs.

The AIM 65 display consists of five four-digit 16-segment alphanumeric displays and an R6520 Peripheral Interface Adapter (PIA) mounted on the Display Module which connects to the Master Module through two short solid-conductor ribbon cables. Each display quad contains internal memory, decoder, and driver circuitry. The display quads interface with the Master Module through the PIA. Data may be sent to the display using Monitor ROM subroutines.

The Keyboard Module connects to the Master Module by a removable 16-conductor flat ribbon cable. The interface is through an R6532 RAM, i/O, and Timer (RIOT) device which supports the Monitor with the RAM and timer. The key matrix is strobed by eight lines output through the RIOT with the matrix returns routed back through eight R6532 input lines.

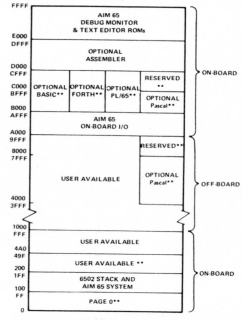

NOTES: *USER AVAILABLE IF MONITOR/EDITOR IS NOT USED.
**USER AVAILABLE IF OPTIONAL LANGUAGE IS NOT USED:

LANGUAGE	PAGE 0	PAGE 2-4
Assembler	0-DE-	NOT USED
BASIC	0-D6	200 - 211
FORTH	0-A4	200 - 30A
PL/65	0-04	200 - 49F
Pascal	06-B4, FC-FF	200 - 2FF
Monitor/Editor	DF-FF	NOT USED

AIM 65 Memory Map

Application Connector Pin Assignments

Top (Component Side)					Bottom (Solder Side)				
Signal Mnemonic	Signal Name	Type	I/O	Pin	Pin	Signal Mnemonic	Signal Name	Type	I/O
GND	Ground			1	A	+5V	+5V	Power	O
PA3	Port A Data Bit 3	NMOS	I/O	2	B		NC		
PA2	Port A Data Bit 2	NMOS	I/O	3	C	Ø2	CPU Phase 2 Clock	NMOS	O
PA1	Port A Data Bit 1	NMOS	I/O	4	D	R/W̄	CPU Read/Write	NMOS	
PA4	Port A Data Bit 4	NMOS	I/O	5	E	TAPE 1B RTN	Tape 1B Remote Control Return		I/O
PA5	Port A Data Bit 5	NMOS	I/O	6	F	TAPE 1B	Tape 1B Remote Control		I/O
PA6	Port A Data Bit 6	NMOS	I/O	7	H	TAPE 2B RTN	Tape 2B Remote Control Return		I/O
PA7	Port A Data Bit 7	NMOS	I/O	8	J	TAPE 2B	Tape 2B Remote Control		I/O
PB0	Port B Data Bit 0	NMOS	I/O	9	K		NC		
PB1	Port B Data Bit 1	NMOS	I/O	10	L	AUDIO IN	Audio Input Low		I
PB2	Port B Data Bit 2	NMOS	I/O	11	M	AUDIO OUT LO	Audio Output Low Level		O
PB3	Port B Data Bit 3	NMOS	I/O	12	N	+12V	+12 Vdc	Power	O
PB4	Port B Data Bit 4	NMOS	I/O	13	P	AUDIO OUT HIGH	Audio Output High Level		O
PA0	Port A Data Bit 0	NMOS	I/O	14	R	TTY KYBD RTN (+)	TTY Keyboard Return	20 mA (+)	
PB7	Port B Data Bit 7	NMOS	I/O	15	S	TTY PWR RTN (+)	TTY Power Return	20 mA (+)	
PB5	Port B Data Bit 5	NMOS	I/O	16	T	TTY KYBD	TTY Keyboard (Data In)	20 mA (-)	I
PB6	Port B Data Bit 6	NMOS	I/O	17	U	TTY PWR	TTY Power (Data Out)	20 mA (-)	O
CB1	Port B Control Bit 1	NMOS	I/O	18	V	TAPE 2A	Tape 2A Remote Control		I/O
CB2	Port B Control Bit 2	NMOS	I/O	19	W	TAPE 1A	Tape 1A Remote Control		I/O
CA1	Port A Control Bit 1	NMOS	I	20	X		NC		
CA2	Port A Control Bit 2	NMOS	I/O	21	Y	SERIAL IN	Serial Input		I
-12V	-12 Vdc*	Power	O	22	Z	+24V	+24 Vdc**	Power	O

NOTES

*Pin 22 jumpered to -12V through jumper.

**Pin Z jumpered to +24V through jumper.

Expansion Connector Pin Assignments

Top (Component Side)					Bottom (Solder Side)			
Signal Mnemonic	Signal Name	Input/ Output	Pin	Pin	Signal Mnemonic	Signal Name	Input/ Output	
SYNC	SYNC	O	1	A	A0	Address Bit 0	O	
RDY	Ready	I	2	B	A1	Address Bit 1	O	
Ø1	Phase 1 Clock	O	3	C	A2	Address Bit 2	O	
ĪRQ̄	Interrupt Request	I	4	D	A3	Address Bit 3	O	
S.O.	Set Overflow	I	5	E	A4	Address Bit 4	O	
N̄M̄Ī	Non-Maskable Interrupt	I	6	F	A5	Address Bit 5	O	
R̄ĒS	Reset	I	7	H	A6	Address Bit 6	O	
D7	Data Bit 7	I/O	8	J	A7	Address Bit 7	O	
D6	Data Bit 6	I/O	9	K	A8	Address Bit 8	O	
D5	Data Bit 5	I/O	10	L	A9	Address Bit 9	O	
D4	Data Bit 4	I/O	11	M	A10	Address Bit 10	O	
D3	Data Bit 3	I/O	12	N	A11	Address Bit 11	O	
D2	Data Bit 2	I/O	13	P	A12	Address Bit 12	O	
D1	Data Bit 1	I/O	14	R	A13	Address Bit 13	O	
D0	Data Bit 0	I/O	15	S	A14	Address Bit 14	O	
-12V	*-12 Vdc	O	16	T	A15	Address Bit 15	O	
+12V	*+12 Vdc	O	17	U	SYS Ø2	System Phase 2 Clock	O	
C̄S̄8̄	Chip Select 8	O	18	V	SYS R/W̄	System Read/Write	O	
C̄S̄9̄	Chip Select 9	O	19	W	R/W̄	Read/Write "Not"	O	
C̄S̄Ā	Chip Select A	O	20	X	TEST	Test	O	
+5V	+5 Vdc	O	21	Y	Ø̄2̄	Phase 2 Clock "Not"	O	
GND	Ground		22	Z	RAM R/W̄	RAM Read/Write	O	

NOTE

*Not used on AIM 65.

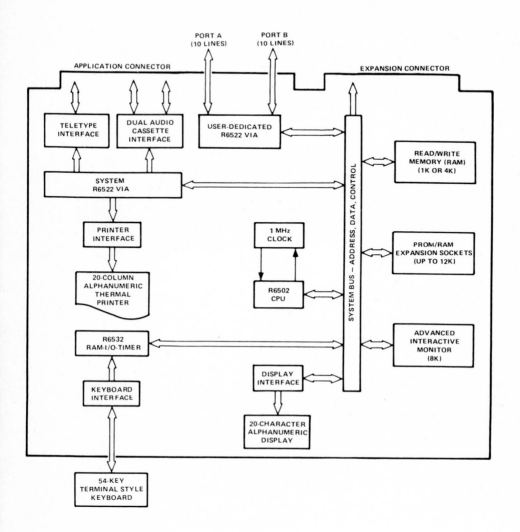

AIM 65 Block Diagram

ELECTRICAL CHARACTERISTICS

Power Requirements				
Voltage	Typ	Max	Peak	Units
+5V ±5% Regulated				
1K RAM + 2 ROMs*	1.1	1.8	1.8	A
4K RAM + 5 ROMs	1.8	2.8	2.8	A
+24V ± 15% Unregulated	0.5	1.5	2.5**	A

NOTES			
*For additional RAM and ROM, allow			
	Typ	Max	Units
1K 2114 RAM (2 devices)	0.160	0.200	A
4K 2332 ROM (1 device)	0.080	0.120	A
**+24V peak current specified as worst case with printer duty cycle of 75%. For most cases, a +24V 2A power supply is sufficient.			

NMOS Interface (Input Voltage = +5.0V, TA = 25°C)

Symbol	Parameter	Min	Max	Unit
V_{IH}	Input High Voltage	2.4	5.0	V
V_{IL}	Input Low Voltage	-0.3	+0.4	V
I_{IH}	Input High Current (V_{IH} = 2.4V)	-100	-300	μA
I_{IL}	Input Low Current (V_{IL} = 0.4A)	-1.0	-1.6	mA
V_{OH}	Output High Voltage ($I_{LOAD} \leqslant$ -100 A)	2.4	5.0	V
V_{OL}	Output Low Voltage ($I_{LOAD} \leqslant$ -3 mA)	—	0.4	V
I_{OH}	Output High Current (Sourcing) ($V_{OH} \geqslant$ 2.4V) ($V_{OH} \geqslant$ 1.5V, VIA PB0-PB7 only)	-100 / -1.0	— / —	μA / mA
I_{OL}	Output Low Current (Sinking) ($V_{OL} \leqslant$ 0.4V)	1.6	—	mA

TTL	—	Industry standard LS TTL.
OC TTL	—	Industry standard Open Collector LS TTL.
3S TTL	—	Industry standard Tri-State LS TTL.
TP TTL	—	Industry standard Totem Pole LS TTL.

PHYSICAL CHARACTERISTICS

Parameter	Value
Outside Dimensions*	
Master Module	
Width	11.5 in. (292 mm)
Depth	10.5 in. (267 mm)
Height**	2.35 in. (60 mm)
Weight	1 lb. 11 oz. (630 g)
Keyboard Module	
Width	11.5 in. (292 mm)
Depth	4.0 in. (102 mm)
Height	1.2 in. (30 mm)
Weight	1 lb. 3 oz. (443 g)
Environment	
Operating Temperature	0° to 50°C
Storage Temperature	0° to 70°C
Relative Humidity	0% to 85% (without condensation)
Power Connector	6-Post Terminal Block
Interface Connector	
J1 (Application) and	44-pin edge connector
J3 (Expansion)	(0.156 in. centers). Mates with Viking 2VH22/1AND5 or equivalent.
J2 (Printer)	17-pin flexible cable strip connector
J4 (Keyboard)	16-pin DIP connector
J5 (Display)	32-pin strip connector
Shipping Specifications	
Size (in box)	13 in. (330 mm) x 14 in. (355 mm) x 7.5 in. (190 mm)
Weight (in box)	8 lb. (3 kg)

NOTES

*Reference PA00-D010.
**To top of the display.

MONITOR COMMANDS

Major Function Entry
(RESET Button) — Enter and initialize Monitor
ESC — Reenter Monitor
E — Enter and initialize Text Editor
T — Reenter Text Editor
N — Jump to $B000
5 — Jump to $C000
6 — Jump to $C003
Instruction Entry and Disassembly
I — Enter mnemonic instruction entry mode
K — Disassemble memory
Display/Alter Registers and Memory
* — Alter Program Counter to (address)
A — Alter Accumulator to (byte)
X — Alter X Register to (byte)
Y — Alter Y Register to (byte)
P — Alter Processor Status to (byte)
S — Alter Stack Pointer to (byte)
R — Display all registers
M — Display four memory locations, starting at (address)
(SPACE) — Display next four memory locations
/ — Alter current memory location
Manipulate Breakpoints
— Clear all breakpoints
4 — Toggle breakpoint enable on/off
B — Set one to four breakpoint addresses
? — Display breakpoint addresses
Control Instruction/Trace
G — Execute user's program
Z — Toggle instruction trace mode on/off
V — Toggle register trace mode on/off
H — Trace Program Counter history

MONITOR COMMANDS (CON'T)

Control Peripheral Devices
L — Load object code into memory from peripheral I/O device
D — Dump object code to peripheral I/O device
1 — Toggle Tape 1 control on/off
2 — Toggle Tape 2 control on/off
3 — Verify tape checksum
CTRL PRINT — Toggle Printer on/off
LF — Line Feed
PRINT — Print Display contents
Call User-Defined Functions
F1 — Call User Function 1
F2 — Call User Function 2
F3 — Call User Function 3

TEXT EDITOR COMMANDS

R — Read lines into text buffer
I — Insert line into text buffer
K — Delete current line of text
(SPACE) — Display current line of text
L — List lines of text to peripheral I/O device
U — Move up one line
D — Move down one line
T — Go to top line of text
B — Go to bottom line of text
F — Find character string
C — Change character string
Q — Quit Text Editor, return to Monitor

APPENDIX B: 6502 INSTRUCTIONS

---

* Descriptions

* Addressing Modes

* Internal Registers

* Mnemonics/Op-Codes

* Execution Times

6502 INSTRUCTION SET

Mnemonic	Description
ADC	Add to Accumulator with Carry
AND	Logical AND
ASL	Arithmetic Shift Left
BCC	Branch if Carry Flag Clear (C = 0)
BCS	Branch if Carry Flag Set (C = 1)
BEQ	Branch if Zero Flag Set (Z = 1)
BIT	Test Bits in Memory with Accumulator
BMI	Branch if Negative Flag Set (N = 1)
BNE	Branch if Zero Flag Clear (Z = 0)
BPL	Branch if Negative Flag Clear (N = 0)
BRK	Break; Jump to Interrupt Routine
BVC	Branch if Overflow Flag Clear (V = 0)
BVS	Branch if Overflow Flag Set (V = 0)
CLC	Clear Carry Flag [C--> 0]
CLD	Clear Decimal Mode [D--> 0]
CLI	Clear Interrupt Disable Flag [I--> 0]
CLV	Clear Overflow Flag [V--> 0]
CMP	Compare Accumulator to Memory
CPX	Compare X Index Register to Memory
CPY	Compare Y Index Register to Memory
DEC	Decrement Contents of Memory by One
DEX	Decrement Contents of X Register by One
DEY	Decrement Contents of Y Register by One
EOR	Logical Exclusive-OR Accumulator with Memory
INC	Increment Contents of Memory by One
INX	Increment Contents of X Register by One
INY	Increment Contents of Y Register by One
JMP	Jump to New Memory Location
JSR	Jump to Subroutine Location
LDA	Load Accumulator
LDX	Load X Index Register
LDY	Load Y Index Register
LSR	Logical Shift Right
NOP	No Operation
ORA	Logical OR Accumulator with Memory
PHA	Push Accumulator on Stack
PHP	Push Processor Status Register on Stack
PLA	Pull Accumulator from Stack
PLP	Pull Processor Status Register from Stack

6502 INSTRUCTION SET

Mnemonic	Description
ROL	Rotate Left through Carry
ROR	Rotate Right through Carry
RTI	Return from Interrupt Routine
RTS	Return from Subroutine
SBC	Subtract from Accumulator with Borrow
SEC	Set Carry Flag [C--> 1]
SED	Set Decimal Mode [D--> 1]
SEI	Set Interrupt Disable Flag [I--> 1]
STA	Store Contents of Accumulator in Memory
STX	Store Contents of X Register in Memory
STY	Store Contents of Y Register in Memory
TAX	Transfer Contents of Accumulator to X Register
TAY	Transfer Contents of Accumulator to Y Register
TSX	Transfer Stack Pointer to X Register
TXA	Transfer Contents of X Register to Accumulator
TXS	Transfer Contents of X Register to Stack Pointer
TYA	Transfer Contents of Y Register to Accumulator

58 Instructions

6502 ADDRESSING MODES

No.	Mode	Abbreviation*
1	Immediate	#hh
2	Absolute (Non-Zero Page)	hhhh
3	Zero Page	hh
4	Implied	
5	Accumulator	A
6	Absolute Indexed, X	hhhh, X
7	Absolute Indexed, Y	hhhh, Y
8	Indexed Indirect or Pre-Indexed Indirect	(hh, X)
9	Indirect Indexed or Post-Indexed Indirect	(hh), Y
10	Zero Page Indexed, X	hh, X
11	Zero Page Indexed, Y	hh, Y
12	Relative	hh or hhhh
13	Indirect Absolute	(hhhh)

*h = hexadecimal address digit.

6502 INTERNAL REGISTERS

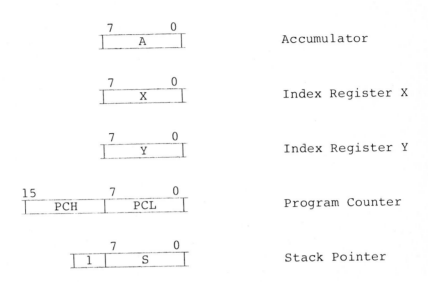

7	0	
	A	Accumulator

7	0	
	X	Index Register X

7	0	
	Y	Index Register Y

15	7	0	
PCH	PCL		Program Counter

	7	0	
1	S		Stack Pointer

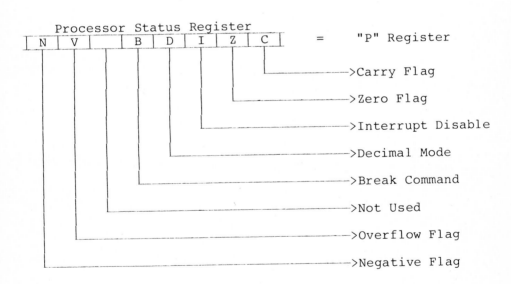

Processor Status Register

N	V		B	D	I	Z	C	= "P" Register

>Carry Flag

>Zero Flag

>Interrupt Disable

>Decimal Mode

>Break Command

>Not Used

>Overflow Flag

>Negative Flag

6502 Instruction Opcodes by Mnemonic and Addressing Mode

Instruction	Mnemonic	Addressing Mode	OP-CODE ★	Status Flags Affected
ADC	ADC #hh	Immediate	69 (2)	C,Z,V,N
	ADC hhhh	Absolute	6D (3)	
	ADC hh	Zero Page	65 (2)	
	ADC hhhh,X	Absolute,X	7D (3)	
	ADC hhhh,Y	Absolute,Y	79 (3)	
	ADC (hh,X)	Indirect,X	61 (2)	
	ADC (hh),Y	Indirect,Y	71 (2)	
	ADC hh,X	Zero Page,X	75 (2)	
AND	AND #hh	Immediate	29 (2)	Z,N
	AND hhhh	Absolute	2D (3)	
	AND hh	Zero Page	25 (2)	
	AND hhhh,X	Absolute,X	3D (3)	
	AND hhhh,Y	Absolute,Y	39 (3)	
	AND (hh,X)	Indirect,X	21 (2)	
	AND (hh),Y	Indirect,Y	31 (2)	
	AND hh,X	Zero Page,X	35 (2)	
ASL	ASL hhhh	Absolute	0E (3)	C,Z,N
	ASL hh	Zero Page	06 (2)	
	ASL A	Accumulator	0A (1)	
	ASL hhhh,X	Absolute,X	1E (3)	
	ASL hh,X	Zero Page,X	16 (2)	

★ Value in parenthesis is total no. of bytes/instruction.

Instruction	Mnemonic	Addressing Mode	OP-CODE ★	Status Flags Affected
BCC	BCC hh	Relative	90 (2)	NONE
BCS	BCS hh	Relative	B0 (2)	NONE
BEQ	BEQ hh	Relative	F0 (2)	NONE
BIT	BIT hhhh BIT hh	Absolute Zero Page	2C (3) 24 (2)	Z,N,V Z,N,V
BMI	BMI hh	Relative	30 (2)	NONE
BNE	BNE hh	Relative	D0 (2)	NONE
BPL	BPL hh	Relative	10 (2)	NONE
BRK	BRK	Implied	00 (1)	B,I
BVC	BVC hh	Relative	50 (2)	NONE
BVS	BVS hh	Relative	70 (2)	NONE

★Value in parenthesis is total no. of bytes/instruction.

Instruction	Mnemonic	Addressing Mode	OP-CODE ★	Status Flags Affected
CLC	CLC	Implied	18 (1)	C
CLD	CLD	Implied	D8 (1)	D
CLI	CLI	Implied	58 (1)	I
CLV	CLV	Implied	B8 (1)	V

CMP	CMP #hh
	CMP hhhh
	CMP hh
	CMP hhhh,X
	CMP hhhh,Y
	CMP (hh,X)
	CMP (hh),Y
	CMP hh,X
		Immediate
		Absolute
		Zero Page
		Absolute,X
		Absolute,Y
		Indirect,X
		Indirect,Y
		Zero Page,X
			C9 (2)
			CD (3)
			C5 (2)
			DD (3)
			D9 (3)
			C1 (2)
			D1 (2)
			D5 (2)
				C,Z,N ↓

CPX	CPX #hh CPX hhhh CPX hh	Immediate Absolute Zero Page	E0 (2) EC (3) E4 (2)	C,Z,N ↓
CPY	CPY #hh CPY hhhh CPY hh	Immediate Absolute Zero Page	C0 (2) CC (3) C4 (2)	C,Z,N ↓

★ Value in parenthesis is total no. of bytes/instruction.

Instruction	Mnemonic	Addressing Mode	OP-CODE ★	Status Flags Affected
DEC	DEC hhhh DEC hh DEC hhhh,X DEC hh,X	Absolute Zero Page Absolute,X Zero Page,X	CE (3) C6 (2) DE (3) D6 (2)	Z,N ↓
DEX	DEX	Implied	CA (1)	Z,N
DEY	DEY	Implied	88 (1)	Z,N
EOR	EOR #hh EOR hhhh EOR hh EOR hhhh,X EOR hhhh,Y EOR (hh,X) EOR (hh),Y EOR hh,X	Immediate Absolute Zero Page Absolute,X Absolute,Y Indirect,X Indirect,Y Zero Page,X	49 (2) 4D (3) 45 (2) 5D (3) 59 (3) 41 (2) 51 (2) 55 (2)	Z,N ↓
INC	INC hhhh INC hh INC hhhh,X INC hh,X	Absolute Zero Page Absolute,X Zero Page,X	EE (3) E6 (2) FE (3) F6 (2)	Z,N ↓
INX	INX	Implied	E8 (1)	Z,N
INY	INY	Implied	C8 (1)	Z,N

★ Value in parenthesis is total no. of bytes/instruction.

Instruction	Mnemonic	Addressing Mode	OP-CODE ★	Status Flags Affected
JMP	JMP hhhh JMP (hhhh)	Absolute Indirect	4C (3) 6C (3)	NONE NONE
JSR	JSR hhhh	Absolute	20 (3)	NONE

LDA	LDA #hh
	LDA hhhh
	LDA hh
	LDA hhhh,X
	LDA hhhh,Y
	LDA (hh,X)
	LDA (hh),Y
	LDA hh,X
		Immediate
		Absolute
		Zero Page
		Absolute,X
		Absolute,Y
		Indirect,X
		Indirect,Y
		Zero Page,X
			A9 (3)
			AD (3)
			A5 (2)
			BD (3)
			B9 (3)
			A1 (2)
			B1 (2)
			B5 (2)
				Z,N ↓

LDX	LDX #hh
	LDX hhhh
	LDX hh
	LDX hhhh,Y
	LDX hh,Y
		Immediate
		Absolute
		Zero Page
		Absolute,Y
		Zero Page,Y
			A2 (2)
			AE (3)
			A6 (2)
			BE (3)
			B6 (2)
				Z,N ↓

LDY	LDY #hh
	LDY hhhh
	LDY hh
	LDY hhhh,X
	LDY hh,X
		Immediate
		Absolute
		Zero Page
		Absolute,X
		Zero Page,X
			A0 (2)
			AC (3)
			A4 (2)
			BC (3)
			B4 (2)
				Z,N ↓

★Value in parenthesis is total no. of bytes/instruction.

Instruction	Mnemonic	Addressing Mode	OP-CODE ★	Status Flags Affected
LSR	LSR hhhh LSR hh LSR A LSR hhhh,X LSR hh,X	Absolute Zero Page Accumulator Absolute,X Zero Page,X	4E (3) 46 (2) 4A (1) 5E (3) 56 (2)	C,Z,N ↓
NOP	NOP	Implied	EA (1)	NONE
ORA	ORA #hh ORA hhhh ORA hh ORA hhhh,X ORA hhhh,Y ORA (hh,X) ORA (hh),Y ORA hh,X	Immediate Absolute Zero Page Absolute,X Absolute,Y Indirect,X Indirect,Y Zero Page,X	09 (2) 0D (3) 05 (2) 1D (3) 19 (3) 01 (2) 11 (2) 15 (2)	Z,N ↓
PHA	PHA	Implied	48 (1)	NONE
PHP	PHP	Implied	08 (1)	NONE
PLA	PLA	Implied	68 (1)	Z,N
PLP	PLP	Implied	28 (1)	ALL

★Value in parenthesis is total no. of bytes/instruction.

Instruction	Mnemonic	Addressing Mode	OP-CODE ★	Status Flags Affected
ROL	ROL hhhh ROL hh ROL A ROL hhhh,X ROL hh,X	Absolute Zero Page Accumulator Absolute,X Zero Page,X	2E (3) 26 (2) 2A (1) 3E (3) 36 (2)	C,Z,N ↓
ROR	ROR hhhh ROR hh ROR A ROR hhhh,X ROR hh,X	Absolute Zero Page Accumulator Absolute,X Zero Page,X	6E (3) 66 (2) 6A (1) 7E (3) 76 (2)	C,Z,N ↓
RTI	RTI	Implied	40 (1)	ALL
RTS	RTS	Implied	60 (1)	NONE
SBC	SBC #hh SBC hhhh SBC hh SBC hhhh,X SBC hhhh,Y SBC (hh,X) SBC (hh),Y SBC hh,X	Immediate Absolute Zero Page Absolute,X Absolute,Y Indirect,X Indirect,Y Zero Page,X	E9 (2) ED (3) E5 (2) FD (3) F9 (3) E1 (2) F1 (2) F5 (2)	C,Z,N,V ↓

★ Value in parenthesis is total no. of bytes/instruction.

Instruction	Mnemonic	Addressing Mode	OP-CODE ★	Status Flags Affected
SEC	SEC	Implied	38 (1)	C
SED	SED	Implied	F8 (1)	D
SEI	SEI	Implied	78 (1)	I
STA	STA hhhh STA hh STA hhhh,X STA hhhh,Y STA (hh,X) STA (hh),Y STA hh,X	Absolute Zero Page Absolute,X Absolute,Y Indirect,X Indirect,Y Zero Page,X	8D (3) 85 (2) 9D (3) 99 (3) 81 (2) 91 (2) 95 (2)	NONE ↓
STX	STX hhhh STX hh STX hh,Y	Absolute Zero Page Zero Page,Y	8E (3) 86 (2) 96 (2)	NONE ↓
STY	STY hhhh STY hh STY hh,X	Absolute Zero Page Zero Page,X	8C (3) 84 (2) 94 (2)	NONE ↓

★Value in parenthesis is total no. of bytes/instruction.

Instruction	Mnemonic	Addressing Mode	OP-CODE ★	Status Flags Affected
TAX	TAX	Implied	AA (1)	Z,N
TAY	TAY	Implied	A8 (1)	Z,N
TSX	TSX	Implied	BA (1)	Z,N
TXA	TXA	Implied	8A (1)	Z,N
TXS	TXS	Implied	9A (1)	NONE
TYA	TYA	Implied	98 (1)	Z,N

★Value in parenthesis is total no. of bytes/instruction.

6502 Instruction Execution Times (in Clock Cycles)

Addressing Mode	ADC	AND	ASL	BCC	BCS	BEQ	BIT	BMI	BNE	BPL
Immediate	2	2	–	–	–	–	–	–	–	–
Absolute	4	4	6	–	–	–	4	–	–	–
Zero Page	3	3	5	–	–	–	3	–	–	–
Implied	–	–	–	–	–	–	–	–	–	–
Accumulator	–	–	2	–	–	–	–	–	–	–
Absolute,X	4*	4*	7	–	–	–	–	–	–	–
Absolute,Y	4*	4*	–	–	–	–	–	–	–	–
Indirect,X	6	6	–	–	–	–	–	–	–	–
Indirect,Y	5*	5*	–	–	–	–	–	–	–	–
Zero Page,X	4	4	6	–	–	–	–	–	–	–
Zero Page,Y	–	–	–	–	–	–	–	–	–	–
Relative	–	–	–	2**	2**	2**	–	2**	2**	2**
Indirect	–	–	–	–	–	–	–	–	–	–

Addressing Mode	BRK	BVC	BVS	CLC	CLD	CLI	CLV	CMP	CPX	CPY
Immediate	–	–	–	–	–	–	–	2	2	2
Absolute	–	–	–	–	–	–	–	4	4	4
Zero Page	–	–	–	–	–	–	–	3	3	3
Implied	7	–	–	2	2	2	2	–	–	–
Accumulator	–	–	–	–	–	–	–	–	–	–
Absolute,X	–	–	–	–	–	–	–	4*	–	–
Absolute,Y	–	–	–	–	–	–	–	4*	–	–
Indirect,X	–	–	–	–	–	–	–	6	–	–
Indirect,Y	–	–	–	–	–	–	–	5*	–	–
Zero Page,X	–	–	–	–	–	–	–	4	–	–
Zero Page,Y	–	–	–	–	–	–	–	–	–	–
Relative	–	2**	2**	–	–	–	–	–	–	–
Indirect	–	–	–	–	–	–	–	–	–	–

 * Add 1 cycle if indexing crosses page boundary.
** Add 1 cycle if branch occurs; Add 2 cycles if branching
   crosses page boundary.

6502 Instruction Execution Times (in Clock Cycles)

Addressing Mode	DEC	DEX	DEY	EOR	INC	INX	INY	JMP	JSR	LDA
Immediate	–	–	–	2	–	–	–	–	–	2
Absolute	6	–	–	4	6	–	–	3	6	4
Zero Page	5	–	–	3	5	–	–	–	–	3
Implied	–	2	2	–	–	2	2	–	–	–
Accumulator	–	–	–	–	–	–	–	–	–	–
Absolute,X	7	–	–	4*	7	–	–	–	–	4*
Absolute,Y	–	–	–	4*	–	–	–	–	–	4*
Indirect,X	–	–	–	6	–	–	–	–	–	4*
Indirect,Y	–	–	–	5	–	–	–	–	–	6
Zero Page,X	6	–	–	4	6	–	–	–	–	5*
Zero Page,Y	–	–	–	–	–	–	–	–	–	4
Relative	–	–	–	–	–	–	–	–	–	–
Indirect	–	–	–	–	–	–	–	5	–	–

Addressing Mode	LDX	LDY	LSR	NOP	ORA	PHA	PHP	PLA	PLP	ROL
Immediate	2	2	–	–	2	–	–	–	–	–
Absolute	4	4	6	–	4	–	–	–	–	6
Zero Page	3	3	5	–	3	–	–	–	–	5
Implied	–	–	–	2	–	3	3	4	4	–
Accumulator	–	–	2	–	–	–	–	–	–	2
Absolute,X	–	4*	7	–	4*	–	–	–	–	7
Absolute,Y	4*	–	–	–	4*	–	–	–	–	–
Indirect,X	–	–	–	–	6	–	–	–	–	–
Indirect,Y	–	–	–	–	5*	–	–	–	–	–
Zero Page,X	–	4	6	–	4	–	–	–	–	6
Zero Page,Y	4	–	–	–	–	–	–	–	–	–
Relative	–	–	–	–	–	–	–	–	–	–
Indirect	–	–	–	–	–	–	–	–	–	–

* Add 1 cycle if indexing crosses page boundary.

6502 Instruction Execution Times (in Clock Cycles)

Addressing Mode	Instruction									
	ROR	RTI	RTS	SBC	SEC	SED	SEI	STA	STX	STY
Immediate	–	–	–	2	–	–	–	–	–	–
Absolute	6	–	–	4	–	–	–	4	4	4
Zero Page	5	–	–	3	–	–	–	3	3	3
Implied	–	6	6	–	2	2	2	–	–	–
Accumulator	2	–	–	–	–	–	–	–	–	–
Absolute,X	7	–	–	4*	–	–	–	5	–	–
Absolute,Y	–	–	–	4*	–	–	–	5	–	–
Indirect,X	–	–	–	6	–	–	–	6	–	–
Indirect,Y	–	–	–	5*	–	–	–	6	–	–
Zero Page,X	6	–	–	4	–	–	–	4	–	4
Zero Page,Y	–	–	–	–	–	–	–	–	4	–
Relative	–	–	–	–	–	–	–	–	–	–
Indirect	–	–	–	–	–	–	–	–	–	–

Addressing Mode	TAX	TAY	TSX	TXA	TXS	TYA
Immediate	–	–	–	–	–	–
Absolute	–	–	–	–	–	–
Zero Page	–	–	–	–	–	–
Implied	2	2	2	2	2	2
Accumulator	–	–	–	–	–	–
Absolute,X	–	–	–	–	–	–
Absolute,Y	–	–	–	–	–	–
Indirect,X	–	–	–	–	–	–
Indirect,Y	–	–	–	–	–	–
Zero Page,X	–	–	–	–	–	–
Zero Page,Y	–	–	–	–	–	–
Relative	–	–	–	–	–	–
Indirect	–	–	–	–	–	–

* Add 1 cycle if indexing crosses page boundary.

INDEX

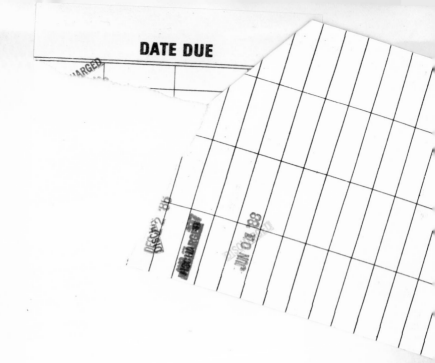